W0114770

SAGE was founded in 1965 by Sara Miller McCune to support the dissemination of usable knowledge by publishing innovative and high-quality research and teaching content. Today, we publish over 900 journals, including those of more than 400 learned societies, more than 800 new books per year, and a growing range of library products including archives, data, case studies, reports, and video. SAGE remains majority-owned by our founder, and after Sara's lifetime will become owned by a charitable trust that secures our continued independence.

Los Angeles | London | New Delhi | Singapore | Washington DC | Melbourne

UNEQUAL
LIFE
CHANCES

Thank you for choosing a SAGE product!
If you have any comment, observation or feedback,
I would like to personally hear from you.

Please write to me at **contactceo@sagepub.in**

Vivek Mehra, Managing Director and CEO, SAGE India.

Bulk Sales

SAGE India offers special discounts
for purchase of books in bulk.
We also make available special imprints
and excerpts from our books on demand.

For orders and enquiries, write to us at

Marketing Department
SAGE Publications India Pvt Ltd
B1/I-1, Mohan Cooperative Industrial Area
Mathura Road, Post Bag 7
New Delhi 110044, India

E-mail us at **marketing@sagepub.in**

Subscribe to our mailing list
Write to **marketing@sagepub.in**

This book is also available as an e-book.

UNEQUAL LIFE CHANCES

Equity and the Demographic Transition in India

HARSH MANDER, ANIRBAN BHATTACHARYA,
ASTHA SINGLA, VIVEK MISHRA
and
USMAN JAWED SIDDIQI

Los Angeles | London | New Delhi
Singapore | Washington DC | Melbourne

Copyright © Centre for Equity Studies, 2019

All rights reserved. No part of this book may be reproduced or utilized in any form or by any means, electronic or mechanical, including photocopying, recording, or by any information storage or retrieval system, without permission in writing from the publisher.

First published in 2019 by

SAGE Publications India Pvt Ltd
B1/I-1 Mohan Cooperative Industrial Area
Mathura Road, New Delhi 110 044, India
www.sagepub.in

YODA Press
79 Gulmohar Enclave
New Delhi 110049
www.yodapress.co.in

SAGE Publications Inc
2455 Teller Road
Thousand Oaks, California 91320, USA

SAGE Publications Ltd
1 Oliver's Yard, 55 City Road
London EC1Y 1SP, United Kingdom

SAGE Publications Asia-Pacific Pte Ltd
18 Cross Street #10-10/11/12
China Square Central
Singapore 048423

Published by Vivek Mehra for SAGE Publications India Pvt Ltd. Typeset in 10.5/13pt Adobe Caslon Pro by Fidus Design Pvt. Ltd, Chandigarh.

Library of Congress Cataloging-in-Publication Data Available

ISBN: 978-93-5328-802-0 (HB)

SAGE Yoda Team: Aruna Ramachandran, Arpita Das, Amrita Dutta and Guneet Kaur Gulati

Contents

List of Figures

List of Tables

List of Abbreviations

BE	budget estimate
BJP	Bharatiya Janata Party
BRICS	Brazil, Russia, India, China and South Africa
CEO	chief executive officer
CSS	centrally sponsored schemes
GBS	Gender Budget Statement
GDP	gross domestic product
GST	Goods and Services Tax
ICDS	Integrated Child Development Services
ILO	International Labour Organization
IMF	International Monetary Fund
IMR	infant mortality rate
MDM	Mid-Day Meal (Scheme)s
NREGA	National Rural Employment Guarantee Act
MMR	maternal mortality rate
MoMA	Ministry of Minority Affairs
MSDP	Multi-Sectoral Development Programme
NDP	net domestic product
NFHS	National Family Health Survey
NGO	non-governmental organisation
NSS	National Sample Survey
OBC	Other Backward Classes
PDS	Public Distribution System
RE	revised estimate
RSoC	Rapid Survey on Children
SC	Scheduled Caste
SCP	Special Component Plan
SCSP	Scheduled Caste Sub Plan
SECC	Socio-Economic Caste Census
SSA	Sarva Shiksha Abhiyan

ST	Scheduled Tribe
TFR	total fertility rate
TSP	Tribal Sub Plan
U5MR	under-5 mortality rate
UN	United Nations

Prologue
Surging Tides of Inequality

In India, as in much of the world, the accident of where a person is born continues to determine her life chances, education and wealth. According to a 2018 report by Oxfam titled *Reward Work, Not Wealth*, 82 per cent of the wealth generated in 2017 globally went to the richest 1 per cent of the global population, while the 3.7 billion people who make up the poorest half of the world saw no increase in their wealth (Oxfam 2018a). It takes just four days for a CEO (chief executive officer) from one of the top five global fashion brands to earn what a Bangladeshi female garment worker earns in her lifetime (ibid.). It would take around 17.5 days for the best-paid executive at a top Indian garment company to earn what a minimum wage worker in rural India earns in a lifetime (presuming 50 years at work) (Oxfam 2018b). If Bill Gates were to cash all his wealth and spend a million dollars each day, it would take him 218 years to exhaust all his wealth (Oxfam 2014).

Beyond all the layers of complexities that there may be, at the end of the day, the manifestation of this surging inequality is as stark as daylight. According to the *Global Wealth Databook 2017*, 42 people own as much wealth as the bottom half of humanity (Credit Suisse 2017). Oxfam (2018a) notes that during 2017, the wealth of India's richest 1 per cent increased by over ₹20.9 lakh crore (1 lakh crore = 1 trillion)—an amount equivalent to the total budget of the central government in 2017–18 (see also *Wire* 2018a).

The unfairness of this unequal world is enhanced because the majority of the richest persons are born into their wealth. Children and grandchildren of the rich will largely replace their parents and grandparents on the steep economic ladder, as much as children and grandchildren of the poor will remain impoverished, regardless of their potential and hard work. As Oxfam International Executive Director Winnie Byanyima observes,

> A child born to a rich family, even in the poorest countries, will go to the best school and will receive the highest quality care if they are sick. At the same time, poor families will see their children taken away from them, struck down by easily preventable diseases because they do not have the money to pay for treatment. (Oxfam 2014: 4)

Many people believe that inequality is an inevitable part of the surge of economic growth and globalised technological progress. Is it? Or is this 'there is no alternative' syndrome being thrust upon us by the few but powerful lot who benefit from the absence of an alternative? There is plenty to indicate that there is no 'inevitability' to inequality, and that the latter is the product of deliberate economic and political policies, of which the two biggest drivers are market fundamentalism and the capture of power by economic elites. Both of these are in abundant evidence in the India of today. Market fundamentalism—much in favour with successive governments in India, but pursued with particular fervour by the government led by Narendra Modi—is the insistence that economic growth requires reduced government interventions and further freeing up markets. It opposes public investments in education, nutrition and health, and progressive taxation, and demands dilutions of labour protections and acquisition of people's lands and forests, all of which further fuels inequality. Accordingly, the decades since liberalisation have witnessed dramatic reductions in public investments in the social sector and weakening of labour protections and the land acquisition law, processes that have seen a ruthless acceleration in the tenure of the Modi government.

The other feature of elite capture of the levers of power is the unreported story of India's public life. Economic elites buy political clout, which in turn purchases tax exemptions, land concessions, cheap credit and subsidies on electricity and water. In India, the tax exemptions to corporate India of around ₹5 lakh crore in every recent budget could substantially finance India's education, nutrition and healthcare gaps. Oxfam (2016) calculates that if a tax of even 1.5 per cent were imposed on the wealth of all the world's billionaires, it could get every child into school and deliver health services in all the poorest countries of the world, saving an estimated 23 million lives. According to Oxfam, if India just stopped inequality from rising, it could have ended extreme poverty for 90 million people by 2019 (ibid.). If it reduced inequality by 36 per cent, it could completely eliminate extreme poverty.

Contrary to the widely propagated belief that fighting inequality would damage the pace of economic growth, the report by Oxfam (2018a) points instead to evidence that extremes of poverty are bad for growth. Robust and lasting growth requires reducing inequalities, which otherwise undermine the productivity and morale of working people, and limit the number of people who could participate in the market. Indeed, public investments like the Mahatma Gandhi National Rural Employment Guarantee Scheme (NREGA) not only extend social protection to India's impoverished populations, they also place more disposable income in millions of more hands, which spurs growth, but equitably, from below.

India today has the third largest number of dollar billionaires in the world, but at the same time, within its borders live a third of the world's poor and hungry. India added 17 new billionaires in 2017, taking the total number to 101 (Oxfam 2018b). There are only four women billionaires, and three of them inherited family wealth. The Indian billionaires' wealth increased to over ₹20.7 lakh crore—increasing during a year by ₹4.89 lakh crore, an amount sufficient to finance 85 per cent of all the states' budgets for health and education. By contrast, if judged by the median developing-country poverty line of 2 dollars a day based on purchasing power parity, more than 80 per cent of rural and just below 70 per cent of urban inhabitants in India continue to be poor. The burdens of birth weigh even more heavily on those born into disadvantaged castes, genders, religions and tribes. In the countryside, poverty rates are 14 per cent higher for Adivasis and 9 per cent for Dalits compared to non-scheduled groups. In urban areas, likewise, the poverty of Dalits and Muslims is 14 per cent higher than among other groups.

Oxfam observes that income concentration at the top fell in the first three decades after independence, but since then, for the top 0.01 per cent, real wages have grown annually at 11 per cent. By contrast, real household expenditure for the rest of the population has risen by only 1.5 per cent. In agriculture, growth in real wages was 5 per cent in the 1980s, but fell to 2 per cent in the 1990s, and was virtually 0 per cent in the 2000s. No wonder that farmers across large tracts of rural India continue to despair enough to take their own lives.

Oxfam India CEO Nisha Agrawal says,

> it is alarming that the benefits of economic growth in India continue to concentrate in fewer hands. The billionaire boom is not a sign of a thriving economy, but a symptom of a failing economic system. Those working hard, growing food for the country, building infrastructure, working in factories are struggling to fund their child's education, buy medicines for family members and manage two meals a day. The growing divide undermines democracy and promotes corruption and cronyism. (*Economic Times* 2018)

Rajan Gurukkal (2018) echoes the same view as regards the fact that corporate cronyism thrives at the cost of democracy. 'The impairment of democracy, an inevitable consequence of capitalist development, has been progressing in India for the last two decades', he says, 'and is slowly turning the democratic state into a functional autocracy.' In effect, 'corporate houses create state power, which efficiently mobilises people's consent for functional autocracy.' This process, he adds, is facilitated by 'uncritical masses, moved by sentiments of divisiveness, rooted in caste and communalism' (ibid.). Crony capital is also obfuscated by degenerate nationalism sold in jingoist packages.

This brings us to the question of demographic transition. India is passing through a phase where a major share of its population is in its prime and of working age. Many have spoken of the 'dividend' that we could reap from what is being called the 'youth bulge'. Even Prime Minister Narendra Modi has referred to the same (failing miserably however to generate enough jobs for them). With the gaping inequalities in our society, the youth in this country encounter gross disparities in their life chances and in their opportunities to realise their potential. In this book, we attempt to look closely at India's demographic transition, specifically from the perspective of social, economic and gender equity. We will make the following five main arguments in the pages of this study on India's demographic transition:

1. Demographic transition does not automatically yield a demographic dividend. The 'youthful bulge' is created by lags in the decline of fertility vis-à-vis declines in mortality rates. But for this to actually translate into high economic growth, the requirement on the one hand is that the young people who are entering the workforce should be equipped with the nutrition, health, education, training and morale to be able to contribute to their full potential to the economy and society (and to their own sense of well-being and worth). On the other hand, it requires that sufficient employment opportunities of decent work are available for all these young people.

2. In India, the evidence is that both these conditions are being very imperfectly met. The state continues to make very low public investments in nutrition, healthcare, education and social protection, relative to most comparable countries in the world. At the same time, markets are entirely unable to compensate for these failures in state provisioning for the access of large populations to these essential public goods. Equally damaging to India's capacity to harness its demographic dividend is that high economic growth has yielded almost jobless growth, with the few jobs being created being low-end, low-paid, insecure and unprotected. The situation is aggravated by the continuing agrarian crisis, deepened by abysmally low public investments in agriculture, a sector which still employs more than half the workforce. A vast majority of the young are therefore being excluded from decent economic opportunities, and are being condemned instead to distress migration and low-end exploitative employment.

3. Life chances, in terms of nutrition, health, child and maternal survival, life expectancy and economic well-being have improved in India. But the improvement has been slower relative to comparable countries, and significantly unequal for socially disadvantaged

groups by class, gender, caste, religious identity and disability. Life chances, understood as opportunities to improve one's social and economic situation, are equally stymied for these same historically disadvantaged and dispossessed groups.

4. These are not insolvable problems, if we recognise first that this situation of unequal life chances is not inevitable, but is the direct consequence of public policy in neoliberal times. The state can reverse these trends only with high public investment in its greatest wealth, human beings, by extending universal quality nutrition, healthcare, education and social protection to all its people, and by ensuring significantly higher investments in agriculture, especially to protect the incomes of farm workers and small and marginal rain-fed farmers, fish workers, forest workers and artisans.

5. The argument does not hold that we lack sufficient funds for such public investments. How much we tax, and whom we tax, are also public choices, and India's low tax–GDP (gross domestic product) ratio and high burdens of indirect taxation are the causes of the country's inability to invest in its people, squandering a great part of its demographic dividend, jeopardising growth, and causing both lost potential and avoidable human suffering among millions of people. This can and must change with more just and compassionate public policies.

The strongest finding of our study of demographic trends in India in the 21st century is one of great and persisting if not growing inequality. It is a story of highly unequal life chances for persons on the lower rungs of the social and economic order, of growing gender gaps in life chances even with growing wealth and education, of growing gaps between the cities and their margins, of agriculture turning into a wasteland of despair, of jobless growth, and of a growing army of young workers desperate for any work on any terms in any corner of the country.

It has been more than a quarter of a century today since economic liberalisation became the central focus of macroeconomic policy for the Indian state. Seeking greater integration with the global economy, India's markets were sought to be opened up and the role of the public sector reduced as India was to be set on a 'high growth' path, led by private capitalist enterprise. In 1991, the then finance minister Dr Manmohan Singh had presented a budget speech which was to alter the destinies of India and its people in fundamental ways. Quoting Victor Hugo—'no power on earth can stop an idea whose time has come'—he declared that 'the emergence of India as a major economic power in the world happens to be one such idea. Let the whole world hear it loud and clear. India is now wide awake. We shall prevail. We shall overcome' (M. Singh 1991: 31).

Every successive government since then, and every shade in the political spectrum, beyond rhetorical differences, has in effect accepted this shift and advanced it with varying degrees of urgency and priority. Over recent decades, policies of economic liberalisation have made way for global private enterprise to enter and increasingly occupy the commanding heights of the Indian economy, which had earlier been dominated by the state. The reform package opened the economy to global competition. It stressed fiscal consolidation and discipline for macroeconomic stability; it liberalised trade and capital markets; it dismantled the notorious licence permit raj that had stymied local enterprise by rent seeking; and it facilitated and expanded competitive private provisioning of public goods like health, education, public transport and infrastructure.

Reforms came with three main promises. The first was that these reforms would unfetter the economy and spur economic growth and development. The second was that growth would crank up manifold the creation of wealth and jobs, and thus erase poverty, hunger and want. And the third was that reforms would significantly reduce corruption and rent seeking by ending the practices of licensing and bureaucratic regulation of private enterprise.

Where do we stand on each of these promises? It is high time that we assess, with the hindsight of a quarter-century, what indeed was accomplished and what has been the fallout, intended or not. This would mean evaluating the continuing trend of growing inequity in the domains of health, education, economic well-being, agriculture and employment opportunities; and analysing how government spending in education, health, social protection and agriculture/employment has not improved in relative terms, and in fact may have plummeted. It goes without saying that with such trends in government spending, the possibility of reaping a potential demographic dividend is far-fetched.

Reforms did bring about faster economic growth; growth rates soared two to three times higher than what the country had settled into until then. India today is one of the fastest-growing economies in the world. It has created unprecedented levels of wealth (however unequally distributed), so that today India is home to the third largest population of dollar billionaires in the world. 'The ranks of middle-class Indians have grown, as they have transitioned from lives of customary austerity to substantial improvements in their material well-being, from habitual thrift to unrestrained consumption' (Mander 2018). However, because of official reluctance to expand India's direct tax base significantly, public spending as a share of GDP remains one of the lowest in India relative to comparable countries.

'This is where we feel that the good news of economic reforms ends. Reforms did stimulate high economic growth and yield greater wealth creation. But this wealth was very unequally distributed, raising sharply levels of economic inequality in a country that was already historically profoundly unequal' (Mander 2018). Levels of absolute poverty have no doubt declined, as has the incidence of malnourishment or hunger. But they haven't declined fast enough, or commensurate to the rate of growth of the economy. Even neighbouring Bangladesh with half India's per capita income has been able to eliminate want and malnourishment far more successfully than India.

It is not just the widening gorge of inequality that we ought to worry about, however, but also that it is blind. Amartya Sen in his new book of essays, *The Country of First Boys* (2016), writes of the 'overarching division between the privileged and the rest', and 'the silence with which it is tolerated, not to mention the smugness with which it is sometimes dismissed', which should keep us awake at night. Even more worrying than the facts of inequality is the indifference, the absence of outrage among people of privilege about the monumental levels of preventable suffering that surrounds them. As Mander argues in *Looking Away: Inequality, Prejudice and Indifference in New India* (2015), historical ideas of caste and class that justify inequality have been topped up in neoliberal times with the belief that greed is good. 'This has resulted in a particularly uncaring middle-class, and the exile of the poor from their conscience and their consciousness' (Mander 2018).

Amongst the promises made by reforms, the one that has been belied the most is that galloping growth will unleash millions of jobs. However, as we will see in this study, what was witnessed in reality was an accelerated but unequal expansion of wealth, but not the expansion of decent work for India's poor. On the contrary, the shrinking of decent work in the sunshine years of high growth has been coupled with the burgeoning of informal/casualised work. As Coen Kompier (2014) establishes in the *India Exclusion Report 2013–14* prepared by the Centre for Equity Studies, 'very few jobs have been added, mostly of low quality, whereas employment opportunities in public enterprises, the formal private sector, and agriculture actually declined.' In the decade of 1999–2000 to 2009–10,

> while GDP growth accelerated to 7.52 per cent per annum, employment growth during this period was just 1.5 per cent, below the long-term employment growth of 2 per cent per annum, over the four decades since 1972–73. Only 2.7 million jobs were added in the period from 2004–10, compared to over 60 million during the previous five-year period. (Ibid.)

The fate of the third big promise was no different. It was claimed that reforms would dismantle the proverbial licence permit raj and would help greatly reduce corruption and rent seeking. But far from reducing corruption, official malfeasance has risen incrementally. In the 1980s, the Bofors scandal, alleging a kickback of around ₹80 crore (1 crore = 10 million) for the purchase of Swedish weapons, fatally shook the union government of the time. Today we routinely observe crony capitalism involving losses to the public exchequer of sums that are often beyond comprehension.

The culture of public life has changed dramatically. For the first half-century after Independence, accepted norms for probity in public life required that public officials kept a careful public distance from private business. Today they are so closely bound together by the hip that it is routine for people in high office to benefit from and share the opulent life-styles of the super-rich, and they pass this off as contributions to nation-building. (Mander 2018: 8)

Among the worst sufferers at the receiving end of this definition of 'development' or 'nation building' are the tribals, who are faced with rampant dispossession, often actively and ruthlessly facilitated by state authorities at the behest of big industry.

The 'ease of doing business' model has also meant loan waivers for big corporates to the tune of lakhs of crores, while healthcare, education, water, sanitation, social protection and the farm sector are starved of public funds. This has led development economist Jean Drèze (2014) to describe India as a world champion of social under-spending! For instance, out-of-pocket expenditure on healthcare in India is twice the level of public spending on the sector, a disgraceful record unmatched by most countries. Our public schools are shamefully under-resourced, lacking trained and motivated teachers and basic infrastructure, and only 7 per cent of people are able to complete their college graduation. Nine in 10 persons are engaged in informal employment, and they are deprived of any or adequate pensions in their old age.

Many believe that the retreat of the Indian state from the principle of primary public responsibility for health, education and social protection for its disadvantaged populations, and from redistributive taxation since the 1990s, was dictated by the 'Washington Consensus' of the World Bank and the International Monetary Fund (IMF). But of late, particularly since the recession of 2008, even these institutions have begun to acknowledge that they may have been drastically wrong. In 2014, the president of the World Bank, Jim Yong Kim, admitted that the assumption that people in poor countries should pay for healthcare was wrong. 'There's now just overwhelming evidence that those user fees actually worsened health outcomes. So did the bank get it wrong before? Yeah. I think the bank was ideological' (Elliott 2014). At a time when free-market fundamentalists have been fiercely declaring the end of ideology, such an admission comes as a revelation.

In a similar self-critical tone, Christine Lagarde, managing director of the IMF, has said, 'In far too many countries the benefits of growth are being enjoyed by far too few people. This is not a recipe for stability and sustainability' (*Hindu Business Line* 2014). She goes on:

Let me be frank: in the past, economists have underestimated the importance of inequality. They have focused on economic growth, on the size of the pie rather than its distribution. Today, we are more keenly aware of the damage done by inequality. Put simply, a severely skewed income distribution harms the pace and sustainability of growth over the longer term. It leads to an economy of exclusion, and a wasteland of discarded potential. (Ibid.)

Comparing the rising inequality in the US and India, Lagarde observes:

In the US, inequality is back to where it was before the Great Depression, and the richest 1 per cent captured 95 per cent of all income gains since 2009, while the bottom 90 per cent got poorer. In India, the net worth of the billionaire community increased twelvefold in 15 years, enough to eliminate absolute poverty in this country twice over. (Ibid.)

Lagarde argues that distribution of wealth matters, and, contrary to the prevailing economic orthodoxy, redistribution policies are not counterproductive for growth, 'because if you increase the income share of the poorest, it has a multiplying effect on growth … but this does not happen if you do so with the richest' (ibid.).

An honest assessment of economic reforms in India would therefore force us to admit that the movement away from public-provisioned health and education has been a step that has resulted in enormous avoidable human suffering. But there is little evidence of such soul searching. Growth by itself is no guarantee of a better life for socially and economically disadvantaged people, which surely should be both the primary objective of growth and the paramount yardstick for evaluation of its success. Unequal distribution of wealth, crony capitalism, low public investments in health, education, social protection and infrastructure, and the chronic neglect of small-farm agriculture continue to shackle millions in hunger, want, low-end and uncertain employment, footloose distress migration, damaged health and survival chances, and denial of quality education that could harness young people's full potential. And the worst sufferers are those who, in Rohith Vemula's words, are cursed by the 'fatal accident' of their births (Mander 2016).

While Dr Manmohan Singh spoke of freeing ourselves from one set of orthodoxies, market fundamentalism has taken us towards another set of orthodoxies that claim, 'There is no alternative.' New voices in many parts of the world—such as those of Bernie Sanders in the United States and Jeremy Corbyn in the United Kingdom—are speaking out against these new orthodoxies.

> Today in India we need to summon even greater courage than twenty-five years ago to liberate ourselves from these new dogmas. Only then will we muster the political and moral will to change course once again, to recognise that all people deserve decent work, health care, education and social protection; that markets cannot assure them these; and that wealth is not development unless it is shared. But to change course, more than courage we need compassion. (Mander 2018: 11)

As this study will demonstrate, the youthful bulge that India currently enjoys creates a demographic opportunity, which does not automatically translate into a demographic dividend. For this, we need to ensure much greater public spending on people, in their health, education and social protection; we need to invest far more in agriculture, and to stimulate growth from below by including more people in the market, by raising effective demand in the hands of millions.

The ways to dam the surging tides of inequality are today well known: raising and enforcing statutory wages, expanding taxation of the rich, enhancing public investments in education, health and small-farm agriculture, enlarging social protection for the aged, infirm and disabled, enhancing maternity and child benefits, protecting indigenous and socially disadvantaged groups, ensuring water, sanitation and basic utilities to the rural poor and urban slums, and protecting the rights of workers. But in India, as in much of the world today, market fundamentalism and powerful economic elites still determine state priorities and resist policies for a more equal world. We therefore remain in a world where, however hard poor people, women and socially disadvantaged communities toil, surviving with dignity remains a distant, often impossible dream for them.

CHAPTER 1

The 'Youthful Bulge' and a Hope Squandered
Understanding India's Demographic Transition

There has been a lot of optimism around the extravagant claims regarding India's demographic dividend. It is often said that India's greatest hope are its millennials. By 2020, more than 50 per cent of the population will be below the age of 25. With a large number of young workers, it has been argued that India will be propelled towards higher and even higher growth. Prime Minister Narendra Modi, with his well-known partiality for alliterations, is fond of declaring that India offers democracy, demographic dividend and demand. The image that arises is of millions of tech-savvy youth entering their cubicles with a Starbucks latte in one hand and a MacBook Pro open in the other. But if one scratches the surface of this projected imagery, we find a story that is more real and far less upbeat. A story of near-terminal despair in the countryside, the trap of low-end, low-paid, unprotected and uncertain work, and chronic jobless growth, leading to desperate efforts at survival through circulatory distress migration, and to abysmal conditions of living for the bulk of the country's youth, particularly for those coming from socially and economically deprived backgrounds. The neoliberal model of economic growth, prioritising the market over all else and built to secure the interests of big business, has in reality led to mounting inequalities. The experience of this system has not only dismantled the overblown rhetoric around India's demographic dividend, but has also muddied the essence of democracy.

There is no doubt that India is in the throes of an epochal demographic transition, having one of the largest agglomerations in history of young people in one geographical location; but a demographic transition does not automatically yield a positive demographic *dividend*. India's 'youthful bulge' is created by lags in the decline of fertility relative to declines in mortality rates. But for this to actually result in greater productive or creative capacity, one requirement is that the young people who are entering the workforce are equipped with the nutrition, health, education, training and morale to be able to contribute to their full potential to the economy and society. The other requirement is that the economy should actually create the opportunities for decent work for all of these young people who enter the workforce. As we will argue in this book, neither of these conditions that are necessary to reap a demographic windfall is met in contemporary India. Therefore, a great part of the demographic potential generated by the demographic transition is being squandered.

Before we delve into the details of this more real story, and the factors at play behind the same, it is important to understand what we mean by demographic transition and what exactly has been the larger demographic trend in India. That is what we attempt in this chapter.

Demographic transitions caused by significant movements in fertility and mortality began for different countries in different time periods. The less industrialised countries experienced such transitions driven by changes in fertility and mortality rates only in the 20th century. In the case of India, mortality decline began in the early 20th century, as a result of which overall life expectancy rose from 24 years in 1920 to 62 years in 2000. However, the fall in fertility rates began only around 1960, leading to a fall in the child dependency ratio as well as in what demographers call the total dependency ratio.

Today, in the second decade of the 21st century, India straddles the middle of what is often described as the 'first demographic dividend phase', with a high proportion of persons in the working age population, which is expected to boost levels of per capita income. The argument is that during periods of demographic transition in which a greater proportion of the population is in the productive age groups, and a smaller proportion of the population is dependent on them, the economy will benefit. But as we will argue through this study, this phase of demographic transition only creates the *potential* for reaping a demographic dividend. This dividend can only actually be realised by meeting the challenge of ensuring adequate investment in the nutrition, health, education and skill building of young people, and also ensuring the availability of enough opportunities for productive employment with adequate emoluments to all these young people. It is noteworthy that in order to reap the potential benefits of the demographic dividend, there must be a synergy between economic transition, education transition, health transition and reproductive health transition. As we will establish in this study, all of these conditions are unsatisfactorily met in India, with poor public investments and outcomes in nutrition, healthcare, education and social protections. This is further aggravated by nearly jobless growth, the transition to increasingly insecure, low-paid, unprotected and casualised employment, and the profound, chronic and unaddressed agrarian crisis. We will examine all of these claims in subsequent chapters.

We wish to introduce also at the start a conceptual caveat. The total dependency ratio is the ratio of the number of children (<15 years) and older persons (≥65 years) in the population, to the number of people in the working age group (15–64 years) However, in India, the cut-off point for older persons is set at 60 because of the lower retirement age. Our caveat is that this indicator has some limitations. It does not take into account the fact that a significant proportion of older persons continue to contribute to economic activity, both paid and unpaid. Vera-Sanso (2012) undertook research into old age livelihoods and urban poverty in the south Indian city of Chennai during 2007–10. She found that older people make significant contributions to the local and global economy through their paid and unpaid work, and through their filling of economic niches that younger people vacate in favour of more direct engagement in the global economy. She argues:

India is now entering the final stages of transition from a population with high fertility and high mortality to one with low fertility and low mortality and is doing so in the context of widespread poverty and under-developed social and infrastructural provision. The rapidly growing population of young adults, the accelerating growth of the older population and the increasing feminisation of old age have important and largely unrecognised implications for the economy, inter-generational transfers and the experience of old age that do not conform with the usual accounts of a rising burden of old age dependency. Yet most academic and policy interest in India's shifting population structure focuses on the 'working generation', defined as 15–60 years, and of these the focus is on the 'youth' who, it is thought, could potentially deliver a 'demographic dividend' of rapid economic growth. Old age, in these formulations, is seen (if discussed at all) as an uninterrupted period of dependence. In contrast to this idea, the argument here is that older people's paid and unpaid work *is* needed to realise the demographic dividend and to counter the negative consequences of the shift to low fertility and low mortality. Drawing on mixed methods fieldwork that spanned two decades, [Vera-Sanso] demonstrate[s] that older people play a key role in reducing family poverty and in supporting economic growth.

Yet older people's work is disregarded through uninformed policy and planning, exposing them to policy shifts that can threaten their livelihoods and undermine their rights as workers and their right to development under the United Nations (UN) Convention on the Right to Development. The *World Social Protection Report 2014–15* by the International Labour Organization (ILO) reveals that in India, only 24.1 per cent of the elderly population receives some kind of old age pension benefits (ILO 2014). The number is way lower than countries like China (74.4 per cent), Nepal (62.5 per cent) and Bangladesh (39.5 per cent). This report also highlights that India's social protection expenditure for older people as a percentage of GDP is merely 0.75 per cent, which is the lowest among BRICS nations (Brazil, Russia, India, China and South Africa), with Brazil spending the highest at 7.76 per cent (see the discussion in Chapter 4). Therefore, the binary that is assumed between 'working' (implying productive) and 'dependent' (implying unproductive) older populations is empirically problematic (and ageist).

Moreover, the idea of the dependency ratio does not take into consideration the fact that some of the people under 15 are economically active in developing countries like India. The latest official estimates report around five million children as economically active in the labour market, which is 2 per cent of the total child population of India in the age group 5–14. Child rights activists, however, argue that the actual numbers of child workers are much larger, because children not in school are hidden child workers, rearing younger siblings, tending the home, or helping parents earn in the fields, in home-based work or in vending. This is the much larger proportion of 'nowhere children', namely children who are not in school but also not deemed to be in work. This is hidden child labour, expanding the numbers of working children to as many as four times the population of enumerated child workers. Also, there can be a considerable proportion of the young population which is going to school and yet economically active. Here again, any claims of addressing the life opportunities of children and adolescents will prove to be a farce as long as child labour laws are moulded so as to encourage further informalisation. For instance, the 2016 Child Labour (Prohibition and Regulation) Amendment Act slashed the list of hazardous occupations for children from 83 to 3. The amendment also allows child labour in family enterprises. Considering that India's child labour is mostly occupied in caste-based work, with poor families trapped in intergenerational debt bondage, it ends up legalising almost the entire pool of child labourers.

Population growth and age structure impact all development outcomes. Migration and urbanisation add to this impact. The effect is visible in the country's consumption, production, employment, income distribution, poverty and social protection, including pensions. This, in turn, raises the stakes in initiatives for ensuring universal access to health, education, housing, sanitation, water, food and energy— all national sustainable development priorities. In India, efforts to reduce poverty and improve living conditions for a large and growing population tend to place mounting pressures on finite resources, challenging environmental sustainability and contributing to climate change and natural disasters. Also, when high fertility rates are the result of unplanned pregnancies and births, it points to the limited access women have to reproductive health services, and to imbalances in terms of women's autonomy and gender equality.

Moreover, the pace of population growth in India has been slowing down over the decades. The percentage decadal growth during 2001–11 fell by 3.9 percentage points, compared to 2.5 in the previous decade—the sharpest decline since independence. The average annual exponential growth rate in 1991, 2001 and 2011 was 2.16 per cent, 1.97 per cent and 1.64 per cent respectively.

There has been a shift in population composition across the decades. Figure 1.1 shows the trends in the distribution of population across three broad age groups in India during 1971–2011. The percentage of population in the age group 0–14, which was a little above 40 per cent in 1971, had declined by about 10 percentage points in 2011. The 'working age' population (15–59) increased continuously from 1971 to reach about 60 per cent of the total

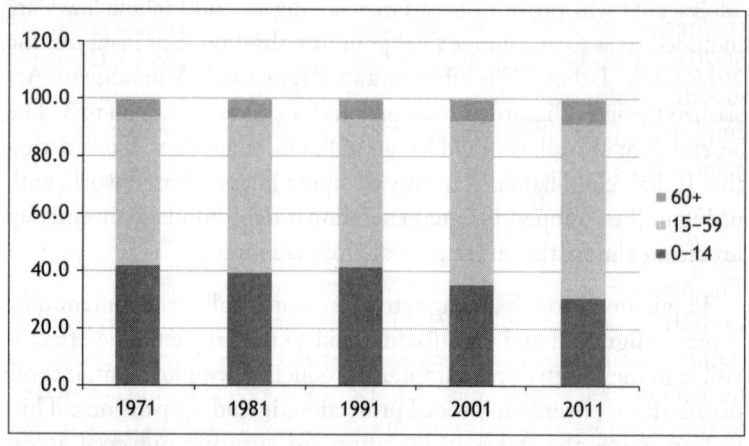

Figure 1.1 *Trends in Population Distribution by Age Groups, 1971–2011*

Source: Census of various years.

population in 2011. With the steady fall in the levels of mortality and improvement in life expectancy, the proportion of older persons increased during 1971–2011, forming 8–10 per cent of the total population. This trend clearly indicates that demographic transition is emerging in India.

According to UN estimates, India's population is expected to increase from 1,303 million in 2015 to 1,705 million by 2050. By 2050, India's population is projected to be 25 per cent higher than China's. India is expected to surpass China in 2022 in having the largest national population among all countries on the planet. There will be marked changes in the age composition of India's population by 2050. The proportion of children of 0–14 years will fall from 28.8 per cent to 19.1 per cent, and the proportion of population above 60 will more than double from 8.9 per cent to 19.4 per cent during 2015–50. The country needs to plan for ensuring just and humane social protection and free healthcare for this large older population. The proportion of population in the 15–59 age group will decline marginally from 62.3 per cent in 2015 to 61.5 per cent in 2050. In absolute numbers, it will cross the billion mark. Gainful employment will have to be found for the billion plus workforce. In a later chapter, we will describe how great a challenge this remains. As of 2016, a million people are being added to our workforce every month, yet not more than a tiny fraction of these are finding gainful employment, let alone decent work. Hence the phenomenon titled 'jobless growth'.

Figure 1.2 shows the present levels and projected changes in the age structure of India's population during 2001–26 using census estimates. The percentage of the so-called 'working age' population is expected to continue to increase during 2001–21, after which it is projected to stabilise until 2026. Also, the young population is expected to decline further until 2026, while the percentage of older population is expected to rise. Despite the reality of old age working populations, many planners are concerned about the ageing of our population because of its expected effects in terms of workforce shortage, economic growth slowdown, fiscal pressure, 'burden' of pensions and the ending of the possibilities of a demographic dividend. But it is important to look

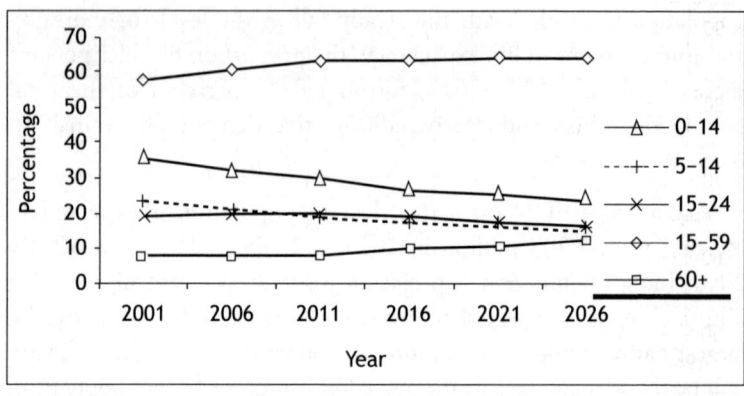

Figure 1.2 *Percentage of Population by Broad Age Groups, 2001–26*

Source: Government of India (2006a: xii).

at ageing populations, and the responsibility of extending pensions to them, not as a burden but as a social responsibility to a section of the population that has been and continues in many ways to be economically and socially productive.

A positive consequence of the demographic change is the fall in the dependency ratio, with the child dependency ratio falling more than old age dependency ratio. Figure 1.3 shows the trends in the age dependency ratio for the period 1965–2015. The dependency ratio fell by about 30 percentage points during this period, from 80.6 in 1965 to 52.4 in 2015. Most of this was accounted for by the drop in child population from 41.4 per cent in 1965 to 28.8 per cent in 2015. This window of opportunity has been open for most of the South Asian countries, which have experienced substantial falls in fertility rates. However, as stated earlier, demography by itself does not provide dividends, it only provides an opportunity. Whether we will be able to reap the dividend depends, as we emphasised earlier, on human capital investments and job creation. With the current 'growth' regime being one of jobless growth, with gainful, dignified employment being replaced by footloose migrants in distress, desperate to work even under subhuman conditions, can this be called any 'dividend'?

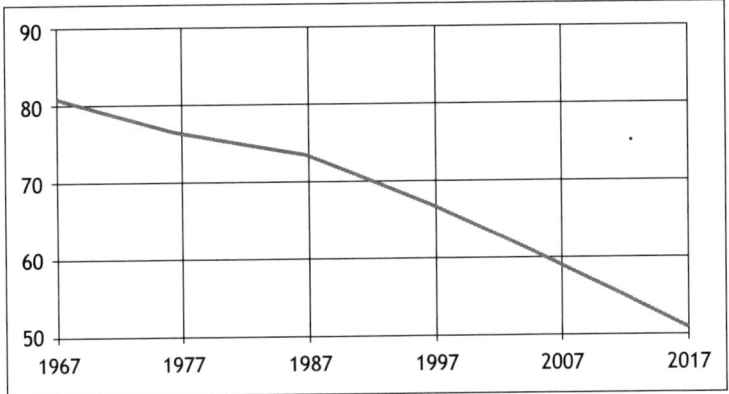

Figure 1.3 *Age Dependency Ratio, 1965–2017*

Source: World Bank staff estimates based on age distributions in the United Nations Population Division's *World Population Prospects: 2017 Revision*. See https://data.worldbank.org/indicator/SP.POP.DPND?end=2015&locations=IN &start=1965 (accessed 23 March 2019).

Note: Data are shown as the proportion of dependents per 100 working age persons; 15–64 is treated as working ages as per the United Nations Population Division.

If we are to identify the potential opportunities that our demographic transition holds in store, it is important that we first understand the changes in age structure over time.

The age structure of the population is changing rapidly with the demographic transition during the past few decades. The age structure not only reflects past trends in fertility and mortality, but also affects development opportunities. It also provides an opportunity to make provisions for healthcare and education, employment opportunities and social protection so as to facilitate 'inclusion' among all age groups. Transition in age structure occurs in two phases. In the first phase, there is an increase in the working age population with the potential to reap a demographic dividend. However, this phase is transitory and leads to a second phase with an increase in the population of the elderly.

Moreover, the transition has not been uniform throughout the country. There is evidence that suggests that most of the states of the Indian union are yet to reach the maximum working age population ratio. The median age in India in 2011 was a young 24 years, ranging from 20 in Bihar and Uttar Pradesh to 31 years in Kerala. Thus, there exists a north–south divide in the phases of demographic change in the country, with a very young/child population in the north, to a bulging young/adult national population, to an older population in the south. This in itself makes the notion of 'demographic dividend' complex as, within one nation, different demographic cycles are experienced by different states at the same time. However, there is an opportunity for the states which are greying and have gone past their first dividend phase to reap a second dividend with labour from within India to fill the working age population pool. It is important to mention that the benefits of demographic transition, economic growth and social development have been skewed in favour of the already better-off in society, resulting in unequal life chances for marginalised sections. This puts the assumptions of the demographic dividend theory to test in the context of India, as the prevalence of unequal life chances across different sections of the population slows down the capability to reap benefits from a large working population. Chapters 3, 4 and 5 of this book analyse different aspects that contribute to the perpetuation of unequal life chances for disadvantaged groups in India.

The age–sex pyramid captures the demographic development in illuminating ways. The age pyramid of developing countries today is peculiar, with a wide base, a bulge in the middle and a shrinking top. However, the shape has changed over a period of time. This can be seen from Figure 1.4 which shows the age pyramids for 1975 and 2000, and the projected pyramids for 2025 and 2050. In 1975, the pyramid was wide at the bottom, with the highest percentage of the population belonging to age group 0–4; it had shrinking sides and a pointed top. However, by 2000, there was a fall in the population of age group 0–14, particularly so among the 0–4 group, due to reduction in fertility, with the bulge moving upwards. By 2025, the bulge is expected to be at its peak with a heavy population in the middle age group (15–64), a narrower base and an increase at the top. However, by 2050, India will experience an odd-shaped age pyramid with a narrower base and a wider top and shrinking middle, signalling the closing of the opportunity to secure a demographic dividend from

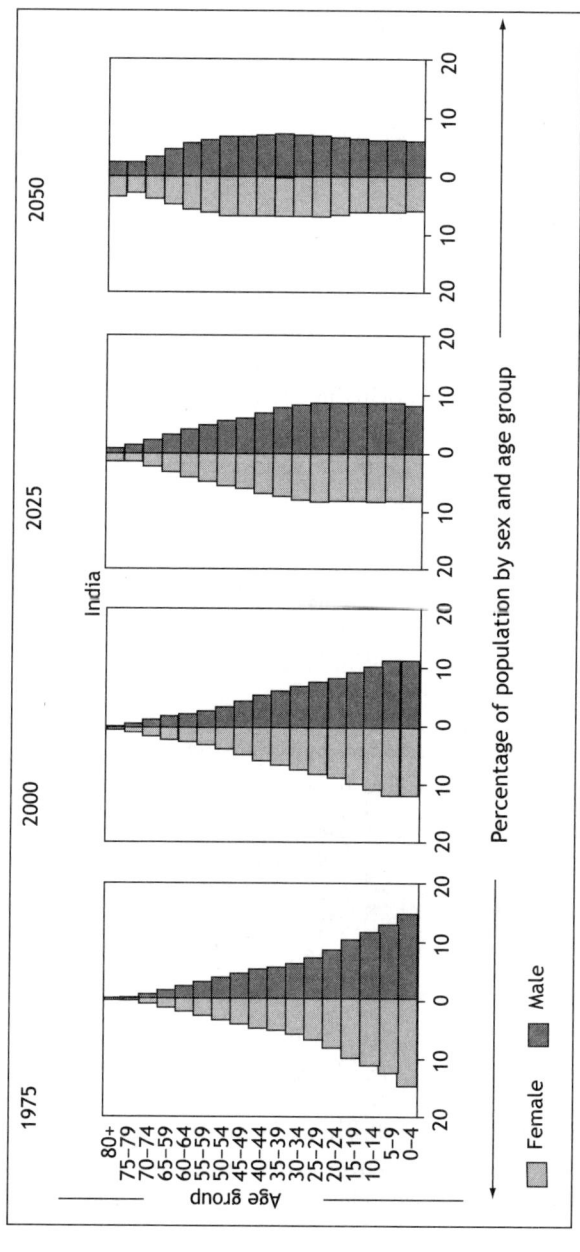

Figure 1.4 *Changing Age Pyramids, 1975–2050*
Source: WHO (2008: 38).

this period onwards. But the country can still continue to reap a demographic dividend as long as the percentage of the working age population is greater than child and old age dependency combined.

Differences in the shape of age pyramids among BRICS nations are presented in Figure 1.5, reflecting the differences in population distribution and the phases of demographic transition in these countries.

In 2016, the pyramid of China and Russia was characterised by a bulging population in the middle (15–64 age group), with a narrow base and an increasing proportion of older persons. While India and Brazil both have a wider base as compared to the rest of the BRICS countries, the transition in Brazil has begun, with a fall in the child population and the bulge moving upwards. India is yet to achieve its maximum working age population. South Africa is halfway through the demographic transition, with the youngest cohorts in the working

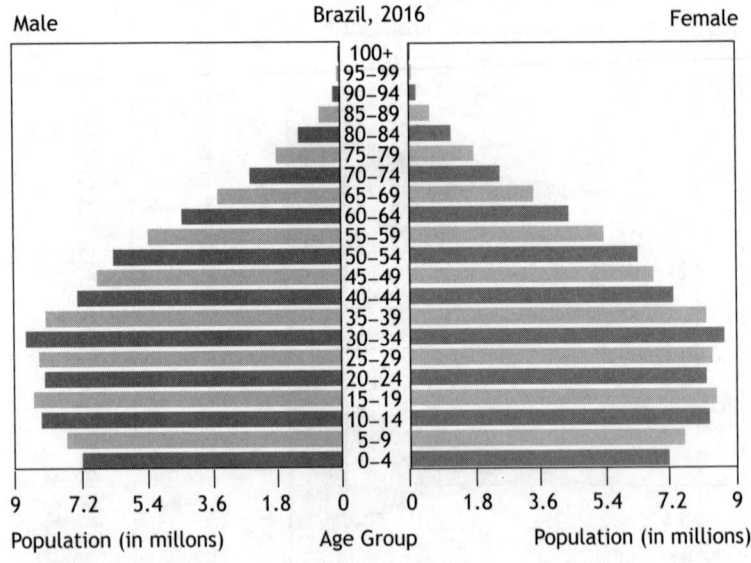

Figure 1.5 *Age Pyramid in BRICS Nations, 2016*

Source: CIA World Factbook, various countries, https://www.cia.gov/library/publications/resources/the-world-factbook/ (accessed 23 March 2019).

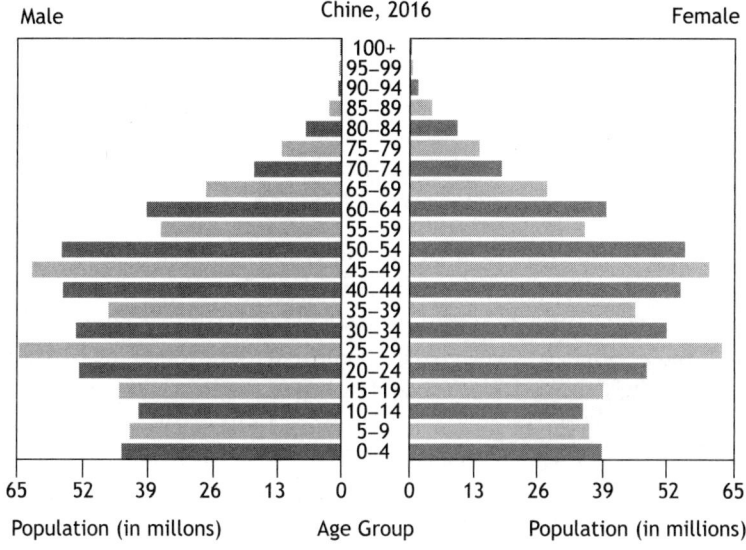

Male   Chine, 2016   Female

Population (in millons)   Age Group   Population (in millions)

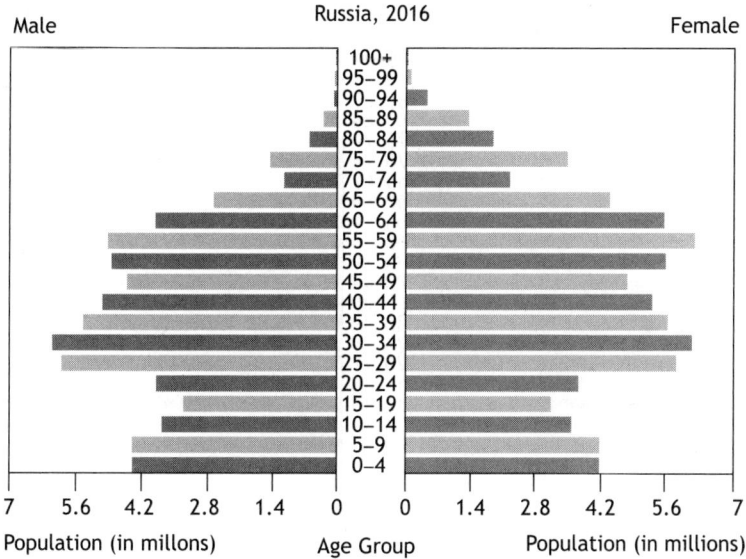

Male   Russia, 2016   Female

Population (in millons)   Age Group   Population (in millions)

Figure 1.5 *(continued)*

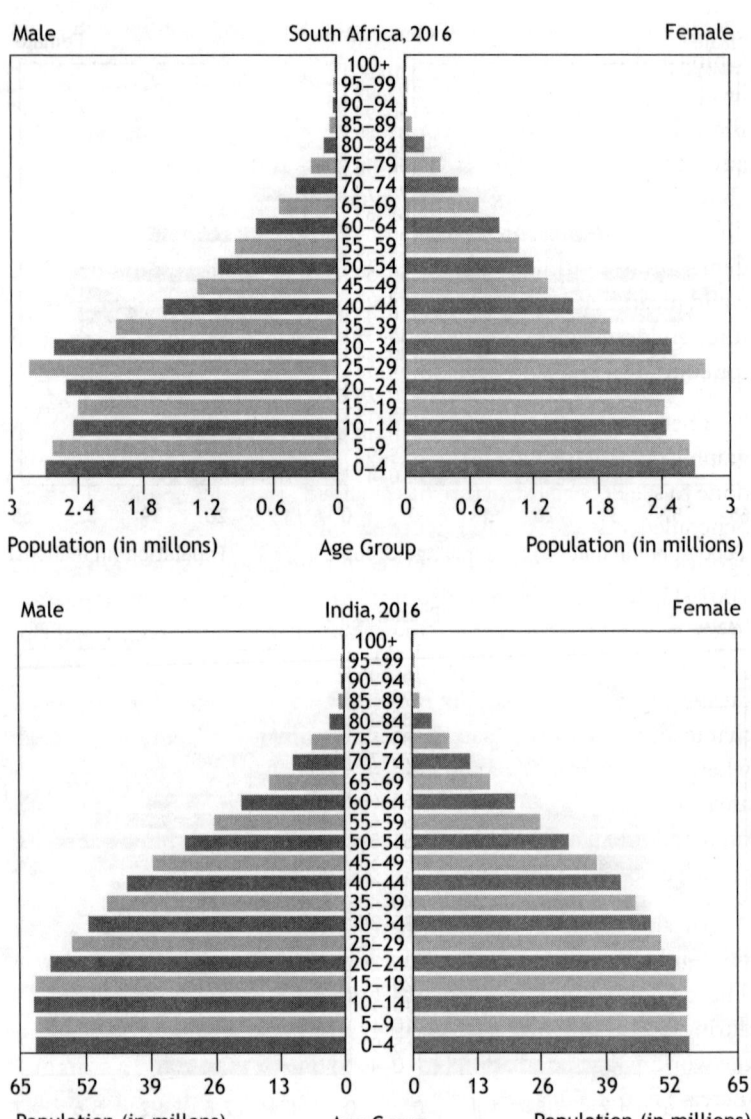

Figure 1.5 *(continued)*

age group beginning to contract. Russia had lower fertility rates, but China and Brazil have achieved fertility rates lower than replacement levels from a high total fertility rate (TFR) of 4.5 per children during the 1970s. While India will continue to enjoy a growing demographic advantage over the other BRICS nations, as its fertility rates are still above the replacement rate, reaping a dividend would seem to be difficult if the present scenario of widespread economic and social deprivation continues. However, a skewed demographic dividend could mean that in states having poor social and economic infrastructure, children belonging to richer families are sent out of the state for education and skill development.

There also exist significant inter-group variations in the demographic transition taking place in India. A disaggregated analysis may be done to see how age structure has changed across gender, rural–urban, Scheduled Caste (SC) and Scheduled Tribe (ST), and Muslim categories. The rural–urban differences in population distribution during 2001–11 shown in Figure 1.6 indicate that the percentage of population in age group 0–14 has declined in both rural and urban areas. There has been an increase in the 'working age' population (15–24 and 25–59) during this period, especially in urban areas. It should be mentioned that in 2001, the greater part of the child population lived in rural areas, whereas the majority of the working age population lived in urban areas. However, in 2011, the working age population bulged for both rural and urban areas. This is one reason why the continuing agrarian crisis has so badly hit employment prospects.

An analysis of population distribution among SCs and STs in rural–urban areas is presented in Figures 1.7 and 1.8 respectively. The demographic transition was unfolding for both SCs and STs during 2001–11, with a fall in the child population and increase in the working age population (15–24 and 25–59 years), and a marginal increase in the older population. There exist rural–urban differentials in population distribution for both SCs and STs, with a larger proportion of the population aged 0–14 and 60 and above being found in rural areas, while a larger proportion of the population belonging to the working age (15–24 and 25–59) lives in urban areas. These transitions in the age structure indicate an increasing opportunity to

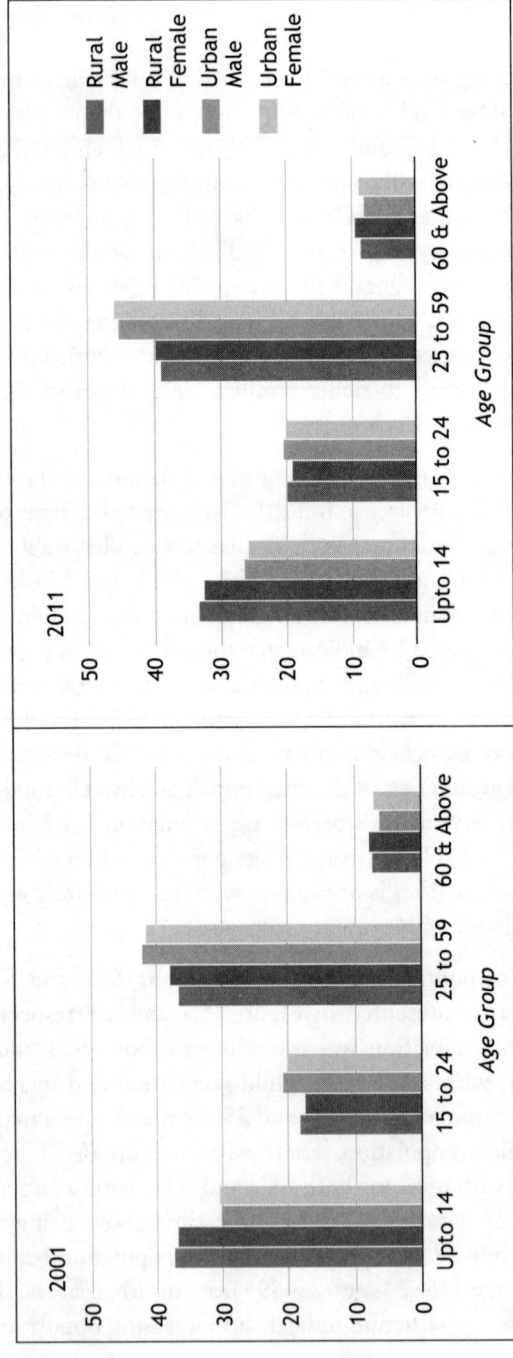

Figure 1.6 *Percentage Population Distribution by Residence and Gender, 2001–11*
Source: Census 2001 and 2011.

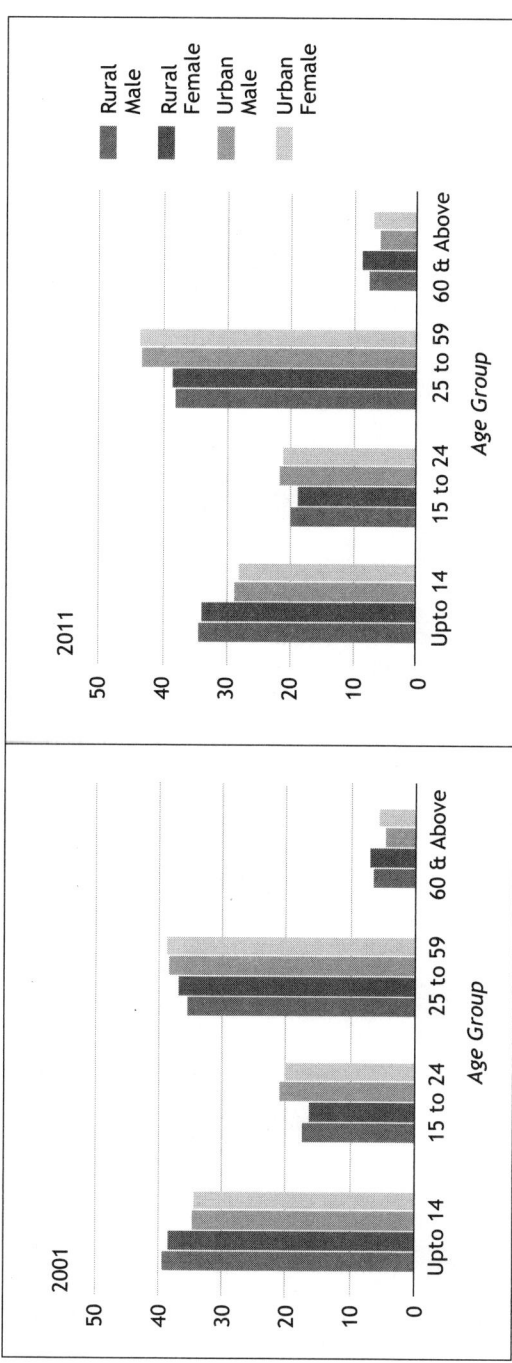

Figure 1.7 *Percentage Population Distribution among Scheduled Castes by Residence and Gender, 2001–11*
Source: Census 2001 and 2011.

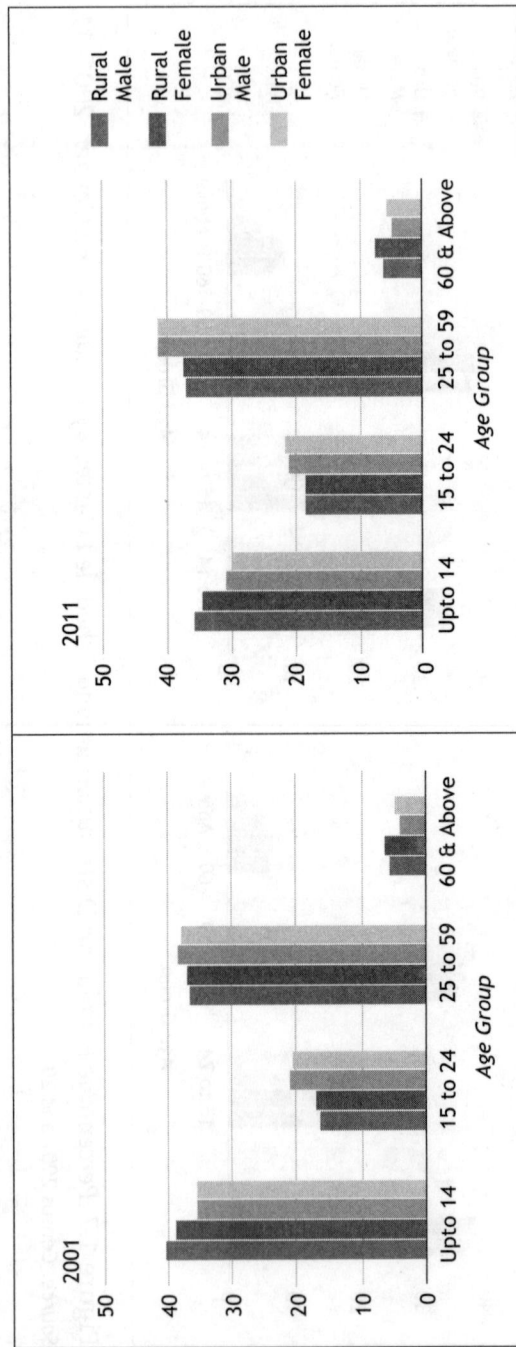

Figure 1.8 *Percentage Population Distribution among Scheduled Tribes by Residence and Gender, 2001–11*

Source: Census 2001 and 2011.

secure a demographic advantage for both SCs and STs in rural areas by providing them equal life chances in health, nutrition, education and employment, as they are yet to attain their maximum working age population. Such opportunities are nullified by facts that speak of the absence of such provisions. The SC and ST communities feature the highest infant mortality rates (IMR) (NFHS 2005–06) and maternal mortality rates (MMR) (DLHS-2 2002–04) respectively (IIPS and Macro International 2007; IIPS 2006). Also, the highest under-5 mortality rates (U5MR) (NFHS 2005–06) and illiteracy rates have been recorded among STs. In such a context (as evidenced in subsequent chapters), these historically marginalised people are also overrepresented in rural indebtedness, in seasonal migration and the casualised workforce, with little to no social security. Does the current paradigm of growth provide these vulnerable groups any opportunity to be the beneficiaries of growth prospects arising from the demographic transition?

Similarly, transition in the age structure of the Muslim population by rural–urban areas is presented in Figure 1.9. The figure shows that during 2001–11, the Muslim population in the working age group increased, but not as much as among the rest of the population. The demographic transition has been slower for Muslims in rural areas, as a large proportion of the population still belonged to the 0–14 age group in both 2001 and 2011. However, among Muslims in urban areas, the transition took place at a faster pace between 2001 and 2011.

A comparison of demographic transitions across SCs, STs and Muslims shows that the pace of transition has been slower for Muslims as compared to SCs and STs, because of high fertility rates. The transition for SCs and STs has been faster, with the population moving towards the working age group. There is still a long way to go before Muslim groups, especially those living in rural areas, attain the demographic bonus that depends on the pace of fertility reduction.

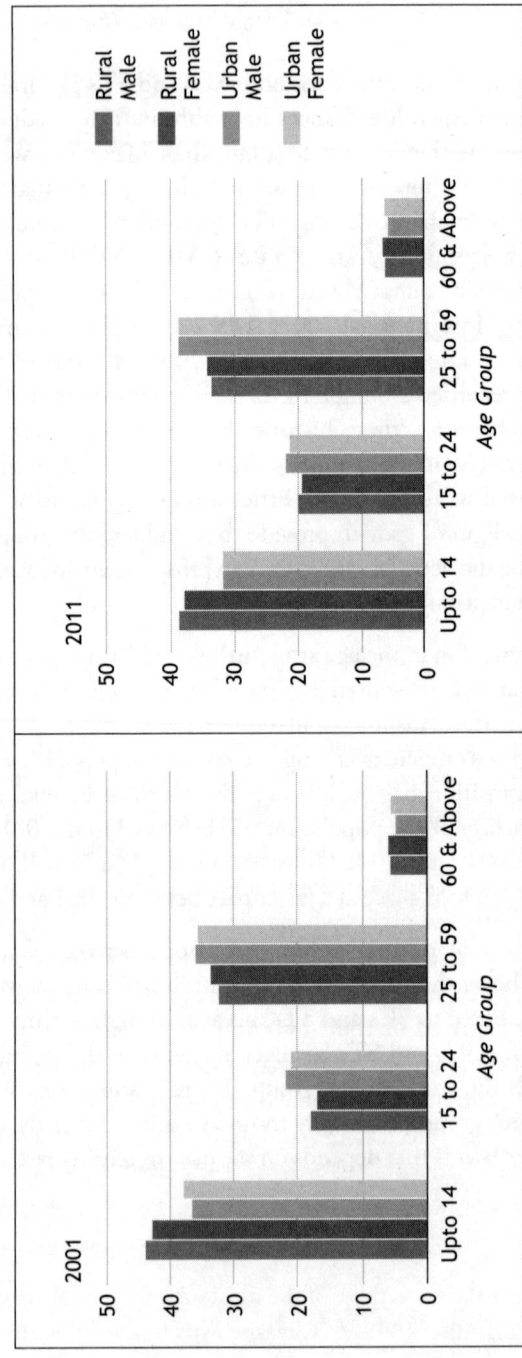

Figure 1.9 *Percentage Population Distribution of Muslims by Residence and Gender, 2001–11*

Source: Census 2001 and 2011.

CHAPTER 2

Fettered by Birth, Battered in Life

The Politics of Demographic Transition in India

The graphs around demographic transition, if seen through a strictly technocratic lens, may obfuscate the reality in all its starkness as experienced by the bulk of the bulge that is our youth. The 'youthful bulge' is not just made up of what one may simply call the 'youth of the country' in general; it includes the sum total of Dalit youth, Muslim youth, tribal youth and others who are in the margins. Given that in India, much of our so-called 'potential' or 'merit' is determined by the accident of birth, it needs to be recognised that a large share of the bulge remains deprived of equal opportunities owing to their caste, community or gender. So, more than superficial prescriptions for enhancing the yield of demographic dividend in the aggregate, what is needed is to take into account and address the particular vulner-abilities of these disadvantaged groups. It is only if the fetters can be broken here, it is only through investing in the marginalised, that the potential of the demographic dividend can be effectively unleashed.

This chapter focuses on three of the most marginalised and excluded social groups in Indian society: Adivasis, Muslims and Dalits. These three broad groups have remained at the margins of India's human development story. They are each faced with particular disadvantages that result in their members not having the requisite capabilities to better their standards of living. It is imperative to emphasise that the question of exploiting the demographic potential, which India has the opportunity to do, is not a technocratic one. Much of this potential is trapped under the ice of age-old forms of discrimination, oppressive social structures that work to exclude millions from better life chances, and regressive political projects that sustain themselves by scapegoating and brutalising the lives of particular 'others', and that are antithetical to the project of the collective self-realisation of India as a democratic republic. Thus, it follows that without tackling these essentially political questions, any talk of harnessing the demographic potential of the country is at best ignorant, if not devious and fraudulent.[1]

Before we get into a discussion of the specific groups and the particular reasons for their sustained deprivations, it is important to bear in mind that the project of an independent India was based on the promise of equal citizenship to all Indians. This meant something special, as not all to-be citizens were on an equal footing socially, economically and educationally. The prospect that the former 'untouchables' under the leadership of Ambedkar should think of themselves as Indians rested on the promise that independent India would work towards becoming a casteless society, that the state would end a social system that kept millions in a position of inferiority and suppression. Independent India was faced with the Muslim question right at its inception, and the tallest leaders of the time persevered to create an inclusive and secular country. The recognition of the rights of Adivasis to preserve and affirm their autonomy and dignity has been

---

[1] Inter-group variations in the demographic transition in India put the assumptions of the demographic dividend theory to test, as Western Europe did not factor in the prevalence of unequal life chances across different sections of the population. Such variations slow down the capability to reap benefits from a large working population. The demographic transition in India, along with a disaggregated analysis of how age structure has changed in the population across gender, rural–urban, SC/ST and Muslim categories, is shown in the Appendix (refer to sections A.1 and A.2).

an essential obligation of the Indian state, foundational to ensuring anything approximating equal citizenship. None of these promises was in the form of a concession. Honouring these promises is not a trivial milestone to be achieved; rather, each of them represents a commitment to a process. That these social groups continue to languish at the bottom with the lowest human development measures in the country is a testament to how much work needs to be done in order to honour the founding promise of the nation. The concern with harnessing the demographic potential of a young India cannot be abstracted from the foundational socio-political challenges that have always confronted the country. Any talk of the demographic dividend makes sense only when it takes these challenges into account and contributes towards overcoming them. The discussion in this chapter seeks to take this conversation forward.

Adivasis

Constructing the Adivasi Subject: Violence of the Colonial Encounter

For the colonial administration, tribals were an unreasonable and uncivilised lot who were easily incited into 'wild' and 'barbarous' rebellions. The counter-insurgency narratives of colonial officials are replete with such descriptions, either demonising or patronising tribal communities, or both. A British intelligence officer in 1916,[2] for instance, stated that they were 'extremely difficult to deal with' because of 'wholly imaginary grievances' and 'unreasonable expectations' leading up to an 'unreasoning hostility' to all existing authority. He concluded by emphasising that '[w]e are dealing with a people wholly savage and uncivilized and capable of very wild and murderous action.'[3] The Brahminical view of the aborigines and a scientific, imperialist theory of 'social evolution' converged to justify the marginalisation of the Adivasis, who were characterised as *dasa*s (slaves) or *dasyu*s (enemies)

---

[2] CID, Intelligence Branch, Correspondence dated 4/3/16, Continuous Note Sheet, Uraon Unrest, File I, File no. 239 of 1916, p. 7.
[3] Ibid.

(Banik 2012). And unfortunately, much of this attitude is still reflected in the language of counter-insurgency operations even today in the same areas, as tribal communities still remain restive against oppression, dispossession and injustice.

There was never a time when the Adivasis lived in absolute and idyllic isolation (Singh 2005) from others, and thus the colonial period was not the first time inroads were made into Adivasi society. But certainly the British brought about cataclysmic changes in the way the Adivasis related to the land and forests and wove their lives around them. The social life of the forest, Ajay Skaria says, was circumscribed by the timber needs of the Presidency. And with this, most Adivasi social practices and modes of subsistence came to be considered 'harmful' (and 'criminal') for the reproduction of the forest and its valuable timber (Skaria 1998). The forest rights of the Oraons, for instance, were fast depleted by the rampant settling of forest lands by non-tribals facilitated by landlords. The British settlement policies recognised the zamindar's proprietary rights in the land and the jungles, which curtailed the Adivasis' customary rights over the forests and its products. This systematically redefined human relations with forests, legitimising the needs of industries at the expense of the subsistence needs of agrarian resource users (Rajan 1998). An entire way of life that depended heavily on forests (with or without settled cultivation) was 'criminalised' (Sundar 1997). The repercussions of these developments contributed to building up a smouldering anger and desperation that often took the shape of rebellions against these various layers of oppression.

Continued Exclusion in Independent India: Adivasis Fare Worse Than Others in Independent India

The Indian state, after coming into being, did institute commissions and agencies to look into and ensure the welfare of tribal communities. However, not only was little headway made in terms of giving due recognition to their specific rights, even less was achieved by way of implementation. In a way, the conflict described in the previous section did not cease even at independence, and despite several legislations and committees tasked with addressing the specific vulnerabilities of tribal groups, the crisis has in fact been exacerbated over the last 70 years.

The Constitution, as per Article 342, provided for the listing of the Adivasis in a schedule so that certain administrative and political concessions or safeguards could be extended to them. There were various clashing opinions regarding the future of the Adivasis that may be categorised broadly as the isolation, integration and assimilation viewpoints. While G. S. Ghurye and the nationalists advocated for more contact with the rest of society with a push towards mainstreaming the tribal, those like Verrier Elwin strongly opposed the same, arguing for protection from non-tribal encroachers (Sundar 1997). In effect, in areas where the Adivasis were numerically dominant, two distinct administrative arrangements were carved out in the Constitution in the form of the Fifth and Sixth Schedules. These were aimed in varying degrees at providing protections to the tribal population through separate laws, including a special role for the governor, and the institution of the Tribes Advisory Council. The Panchayats (Extension to Scheduled Areas) Act, 1996, and the Scheduled Tribes and Other Traditional Forest Dwellers (Recognition of Forest Rights) Act, 2006, reinforce the provisions of the Fifth Schedule to redress the historical injustice to tribal and forest communities. The Elwin, Bhuria, Bandopadhyay and Mungekar Committees, among others, broadly dealt with the issues of development and protection. But despite these limited efforts of the state, 'the adivasis stand out as the most exploited and least empowered section of India' (Sundar 2016). The estimated gap between the human development indexes of STs and the rest of the population stands at 30 per cent at least, and about the same difference obtains in the human poverty index that measures health, education and economic deprivations (Sarkar et al. 2006). While STs are worse off in poorer-performing states like Odisha and Chhattisgarh, even in the states that are performing relatively well, they fare worse compared to other communities.

The daily per capita consumption expenditure of tribal populations is half that of the general category. The figure plummets further if we exclude the north-east. Over 40 per cent of STs in rural India have a body mass index of less than 18.5, suggesting chronic malnutrition, an issue that comes into focus only when incidents like the deaths of a hundred children in Malkangiri attract media attention briefly, before being buried and forgotten again. Just about 20 kilometres from the Malkangiri district headquarters, Palkonda village saw the deaths of 10 under-5 children, attributed to diseases like Japanese encephalitis and acquired encephalitis syndrome. This was the highest number of casualties in any single village in the district, which witnessed the deaths of more than 120 children in a month's time. Unofficial local sources estimate the figure to be in excess of 300. The prime killer was officially identified as Japanese encephalitis. Such a portrayal however hides from view the gross inadequacy of public health, chronic malnutrition, as also the general apathy towards Adivasi communities. All the 10 children who succumbed in Palkonda were undernourished and underweight. According to non-profit organisations working on the ground, 'the infection and most of the deaths occurred in the tribal villages where malnutrition is acute. Over 90 per cent of the deceased were visibly undernourished' (Mahapatra 2016). Out of a population of 80,000 under-5 children, over 1,500 children die every year in Malkangiri. In officially 'normal' times, therefore, on average more than 100 children die every month in the district not just from Japanese encephalitis or acquired encephalitis syndrome, but from undernutrition-related diseases. Such is the extent of vulnerability of the Adivasis here that normalcy has meant that 7 out of every 10 children are underweight.[4]

There is little difference in life expectancy between the poor and the non-poor when one compares STs and SCs, which shows how far the fatal accident of birth goes to determine the life chances of these communities. But the levels of life expectancy among STs are even lower than those among SCs (see Figure 2.1).

---

[4] To give a sense of the skewed priorities of the state, consider the following comparison. The understaffed government hospital in the district headquarters, the only one equipped to handle such emergencies, did not receive as much attention as the 'Make in Odisha' conference with a budget of ₹20 crore (1 crore = 10 million) intended to woo investors.

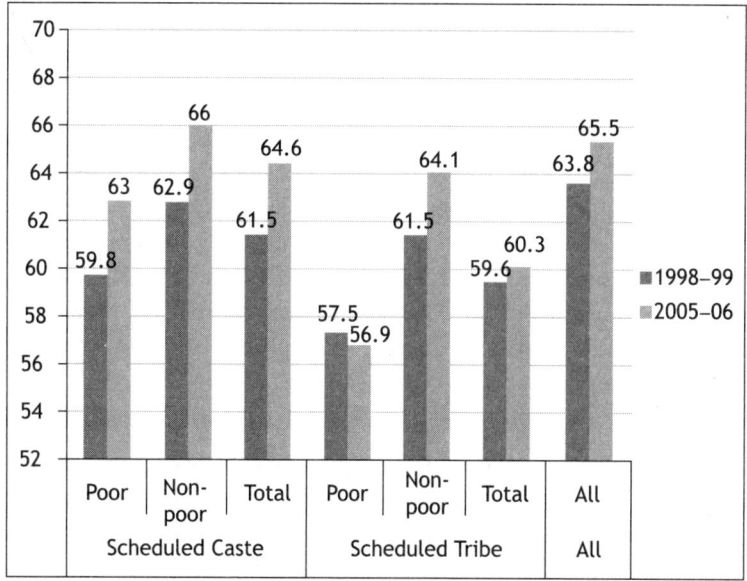

Figure 2.1 *Trends in Life Expectancy at Birth (in Years) by Poverty Level and Caste Groups in India, 1998–99 to 2005–06*
Source: Analysis based on tables drawn from Mohanty and Ram (2010).

It is alarming to note that life expectancy among STs belonging to the poor economic groups fell during 1998–2006, while SCs from the poor economic groups saw an average annual increase of 0.5 per cent over this period. Life expectancy at birth increased across caste groups and religious groups between 1998–99 and 2005–06, with the exception of the poor among the STs. This underlines the fact that the STs represent the most vulnerable social group in the country today.

As per the results of a study conducted by doctors of the All India Institute of Medical Sciences in Delhi, the average life expectancy of the Adivasis in Attappadi, Kerala, had fallen from 70 years in 1975 to 66 in 2002, plummeting further to 59 in 2010 (Jayaraj 2013). This was presumed to be due to the disappearance of traditional methods of agriculture, excessive encroachment on Adivasi farmlands by settlers from outside, and so on. This highlights how focused interventions by the state in terms of social sector spending (particularly on health and nutrition) have to go hand in hand with a model of development that is not driven by encroachment on tribal lands, displacement and forced migration.

Although data disaggregated by caste and religion is not available, various surveys and estimations in some studies indicate higher mortality among STs and SCs as compared to Muslims. P. N. Mari Bhat (2002) estimated the MMRs for caste and religious groups in rural India using National Council of Applied Economic Research and Human Development Institute survey data from 1994, and found that STs had the highest MMR at 652, followed by SCs with 584.

While specific developmental policies need to be planned to address these issues, as long as Adivasis (and Dalits) continue to top the lists with regard to landlessness, marginal farming, incidence of indebtedness, distress migration and casualised labour, policies will not yield the desired results. As long as these groups are adversely included in the ranks of a vulnerable, informal workforce, without recourse to their rightful entitlements as workers (such as maternity benefits), any efforts at improving their standing when it comes to developmental indicators such as MMR will continue to fail. The greater denial of rights and the higher incidence of their adverse inclusion in the workforce are substantiated by the fact that while there has been a decline in mortality for both SCs and STs, the decline is higher among SCs. This indicates the increased social and health-related vulnerabilities of tribal populations, which result in even more unequal life chances for them.[5]

However, it is striking to note that the sex ratio among marginalised sections—SCs, STs and Muslims—is better than the sex ratio of the overall population. The STs, India's poorest social group, have the highest sex ratio at birth across all groups, at 940 in 2001 and 935 in 2011 (see Figure A.15, Appendix). It is to be noted that though STs have the highest overall sex ratio, sex ratio at birth, and child sex ratio as per the censuses of 2001 and 2011 (see Figures A.16

---

[5] Figure A.11 (Appendix) indicates a similar trend when looking at the U5MR.

and A.17), there exist wide variations in sex ratio across individual tribal groups as revealed by the census data across tribes.[6] Thus, it is important not to consider them one homogeneous entity while framing policy directives.

Then again, the incidence of malnutrition is high among STs compared with overall malnutrition levels. The data indicates that besides stunting, more children under 5 years of age belonging to ST communities are wasted and underweight as compared to the national average.[7] About 42 per cent of children under 5 are still stunted in both SC and ST groups, which explains the unequal life chances among these populations (Figure 2.2).

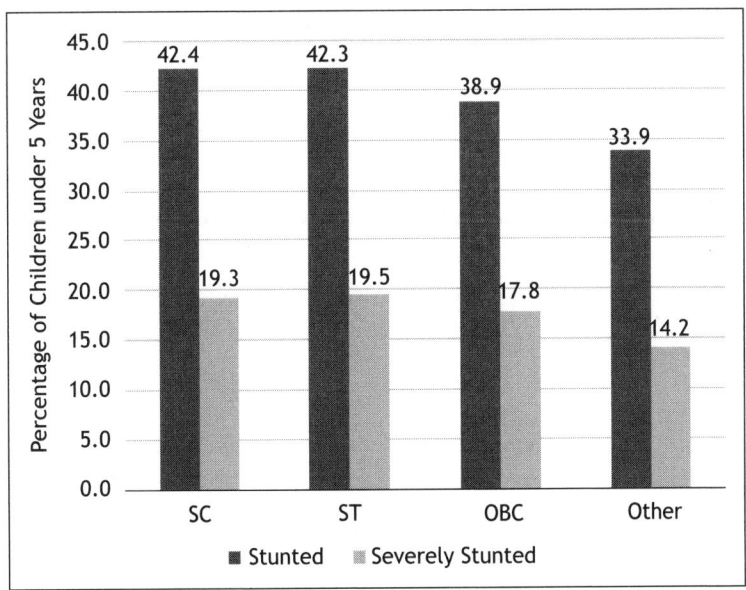

Figure 2.2 *Stunting across Social Groups*
Source: Based on India Fact Sheet, *Rapid Survey on Children 2013–14* (Government of India 2014a).

---

[6] Two out of 58 tribes have a high child sex ratio of over 1,000 (both from Odisha), while the rest have ratios as low as 879.

[7] See Appendix, section A.6; in particular see Figure A.12.

As per the *Rapid Survey on Children 2013–14* (Government of India 2014a), only 22 per cent of ST households use improved sanitation facilities, while 70 per cent of ST households still practise open defecation (see Appendix, Figure A.14 to compare with the all-India level).

In measures of household assets and facilities,[8] 52 per cent of ST households use electricity as their main source of lighting, compared to 67 per cent nationally (see Appendix, Table A.2). The lack of latrine facilities among STs is glaring: only 23 per cent of households have this facility on their premises. It may be observed that the gap between STs and the national average in access to latrine facilities on the premises has widened from 19 per cent in 2001 to 24 per cent in 2011 (see Table A.2). A large share of ST households (37 per cent) are forced to live without any assets, as per 2011 census data. The fact that STs feature disproportionately in the lowest wealth quintile (see Table A.3) does not come as a surprise, considering their overrepresentation in rural indebtedness, landlessness, seasonal migration and casualised labour.[9] In terms of educational attainment, STs rank the lowest, followed by lower-caste Muslims and SCs (see Box 2.1). During 2004–05, 53 per cent of the ST population was illiterate, a proportion that came down to 41 per cent in 2011–12. Only 2.4 per cent of STs feature in the bracket of the highly educated (see Table A.10).

---

[8] There are generally four distinct measures for assessing economic class and material well-being. These are income, consumption, expenditure and assets. For households of unorganised workers, assessing income, expenditure and consumption is a challenging task, and prone to many inaccuracies. There is evidence to support the claim that consumption-based measures of inequality often underestimate inequality. The reason for this is that consumption does not necessarily keep pace with income and wealth, and in fact tapers for the rich. We have instead chosen in this report to employ an asset-based measure of poverty.

[9] These factors are discussed in greater detail in Chapter 3.

Box 2.1: The Odds Are Stacked against the Dongria Kondhs of Odisha

Fourteen girls amongst the Dongria Kondhs created history in 2017 as they became the first girls from their community to pass the 10th grade school exam. The Dongria Kondhs are one of Odisha's most primitive and marginalised tribal communities. As per the 2011 census, the community has a population of about 8,000, with a literacy rate as low as 10 per cent. The female literacy rate is a dismal 3 per cent. Most of the girls are the first in their families to attend school. In a community where girls are seen merely as helping hands at home or in the field, and are married off at a young age, this is remarkable, says Rayagada's collector. 'It is encouraging, especially as the district has a history of high infant and maternal mortality rate propelled largely by illiteracy, early marriage, poor hygiene and superstitious beliefs,' he adds (Das Gupta 2018). However, notwithstanding a few extraordinary examples, the path to education for girls is still strewn with challenges. The dropout phenomenon is rampant. Of the 14 girls who passed Class 10 the same year, four had dropped out of higher studies. In many cases, parents force their daughters to quit school once they reach puberty. The lack of schools in the region and the paucity of state investment in education in general make it difficult to expect that people will send their daughters to those schools that exist, since they do not come across as a gainful avenue. It is imperative therefore, that the government invests more in human development instead of a 'development' model wherein it ends up siding with corporate giants like Vedanta to displace the Dongria Kondhs from their land.

As is apparent from these stark figures, Adivasis have remained outside the pale of the growth story and have consistently been at the bottom of most indices of human development. One of the most crucial contributors to this plight has been the fact that, various legislations (and protections) notwithstanding, Adivasis have continued to bear the brunt of dispossession from their land and livelihood. Private encroachment by non-tribals has continued unabated over the decades. For instance, non-Adivasis own more than half of the land in the Scheduled Areas of Andhra Pradesh (52 per cent in Khammam, 60 per cent in Adilabad, and 70 per cent in Warangal) (Rao et al. 2006).

This aside, tribal communities have also borne the brunt of the nation's 'development' in the decades since independence—a particular development trajectory in which tribes found no space for themselves except on the list of those ruthlessly displaced or dispossessed. A Planning Commission report states, 'Development which is insensitive to the needs of these communities has inevitably caused displacement and reduced them to a sub-human existence. In the case of tribes in particular it has ended up in destroying their social organization, cultural identity and resource base' (Government of India 2008: 29). Big dams, large-scale industries, infrastructure and mines came up in the mineral-rich Adivasi belts of the country, and a colonial-era law for land acquisition was used to the hilt for acquiring land and resources from the Adivasis in the name of the 'public interest' or even 'national interest' (I. Munshi 2012). From independence, till the turn of the millennium, approximately 60 million people were displaced by such developmental projects, of which at least 40 per cent were Adivasis. Considering that they constitute 84.3 million of the country's population, 'one in every four of them had suffered some kind of displacement' (Sundar 2016). This forced displacement and alienation from land resulted in the average operational landholding among STs declining from 2.44 hectares in 1980–81 to only 1.53 hectares in 2010–11 (ibid.). While the number of ST cultivators has gone down, they have swelled the ranks of agricultural labourers (ibid.).

Displacement for these communities does not only efface identities and disrupt livelihoods, it also adversely affects life expectancy, as has been noted by a DNA study on a tribal community (the Sahariyas) who were relocated from a wildlife sanctuary in Madhya Pradesh (Gandhi 2015). Deprived of their *jal-jangal-jamin* (water, forest and land) and traditional livelihoods, a large number of tribal people are forced to join the ranks of circular migrants to the cities and elsewhere, desperately searching for jobs, constituting what Breman (1996) calls 'footloose workers' in the unorganised sector. What started in the 19th century under British rule in the form of distress migration as coolies to plantations and mines, continues by other means even today in the 21st century.

Post 1991, 'the culture of unrestrained selfishness and greed spawned by modern neo-liberal economic ideology' (*Nandini Sundar and Ors v. State of Chhattisgarh*[10]) has further accelerated the process of alienation of Adivasis. This is often justified by the ruling regime as 'collateral damage' that is inevitable in the process of growth. But high growth brought about in this manner

> does not simply ignore the question of income distribution, its reality is far worse. It threatens the poor with a kind of brutal violence in the name of development, a sort of 'developmental terrorism', violence perpetrated on the poor in the name of development by the state primarily in the interest of corporate aristocracy, approved by the IMF and the World Bank, and a self-serving political class. (Bhaduri 2007)

The agenda of the state today to open up the Scheduled Areas by force through the subversion of existing legal protections and restrictions can be witnessed in the systematic widening of the ambit of what is meant by 'public purpose' so as to set up 'industrial corridors' and make possible other such initiatives of capital accumulation. This has exposed tribal groups to untold horrors of death, displacement and dispossession (Rajalakshmi 2016). There is a need to scrap the neoliberal developmental paradigm and give recognition to Adivasi agency, while squarely acknowledging this in public policy debates (see CES 2016). Unless political will is shown in undoing the 'wrong', we cannot expect Adivasi youth to harness their potential, as they will always find themselves in a disadvantageous position.

Muslims

This section examines and analyses the state of the Muslim community as judged through its performance on human development indices.

---

[10] *Nandini Sundar & Ors v. State of Chhattisgarh*, Writ Petition (Civil) no. 250 of 2007, Bench: B. Sudershan Reddy, Surinder Singh Nijjar, Supreme Court of India, 5 July 2011.

Status of the Muslim Community

The largest religious minority in India, the Muslim community, accounts for over 14 per cent of the total population. Muslims constitute close to 70 per cent of the minority population in the country. The state of the Muslim community as understood through the plain-speaking of human development indicators can be aptly described as dismal.

The Sachar Committee, instituted in 2005 to report on the educational, social and economic status of the Muslim community, submitted its final report in 2006. It was the first such report and became a policy benchmark for the status of the community. It told a story of deprivation and marginalisation faced by millions of people in the country. Some of the most striking findings of the committee related to education and employment. Muslims fared worse than all other socio-religious communities, especially as one moved upwards in terms of educational levels. Muslims lagged behind others in terms of higher education, as only 4 per cent of the community population were graduates compared to 7 per cent overall in the country. The unemployment rate among graduates was also highest for the Muslim community across the class divide. The ratio of the working population to total population was also found to be significantly lower among Muslims as compared to other socio-religious groups. The participation of Muslim women was particularly low. As far as men were concerned, a significantly high proportion of them (as compared to other groups) were found to be self-employed. As a group, Muslims were found to have the lowest representation in salaried employment (both public and private), and the average salary was found to be lower than that of other groups. In central government jobs, their representation was abysmally low at all levels, while none of the states had enough Muslim employees to even match their population share in the state.

The Sachar Committee Report also showed that areas with a concentration of Muslims were deficient in terms of infrastructure, lacking proper roads, schools, healthcare services and so on. The report further showed that Muslims fared only slightly better than Dalits and Adivasis as far as poverty measures were concerned. Thus, the Sachar Committee concretely established that the largest minority group in the country suffered from all-round deprivation and marginalisation, and that its socio-economic condition deserved special attention.[11] Along with its recommendations, the committee laid down benchmarks for further research in this area.

In the post–Sachar Committee era, limited research is available on what steps have been taken, if any, to implement the recommendations proposed in 2006. A critical body of work in this context is the Kundu Committee Report that was submitted to the Ministry of Minority Affairs in 2014 (see Kundu 2014). Among its observations and recommendations, perhaps most relevant in the context of the status of Muslims is the fact that Muslims are still underrepresented in government jobs and schools. Moreover, poverty levels among Muslims remained higher than the national average between 2004–05 and 2011–12.

The report of the Kundu Committee further pointed out that SCs and STs were able to migrate to urban areas looking for educational opportunities and jobs, made possible largely due to affirmative action and reservations; however, these avenues were not available to the Muslim community. According to the 2014–15 *All India Survey on Higher Education* (MHRD 2016), while Muslims comprised 14 per cent of the total population, they accounted for only 4.4 per cent of students enrolled in higher education. A more recent version of the survey conducted in 2016–17 (MHRD 2017) showed that Muslims had the second lowest proportional representation as teachers in higher education institutions in the country. While 8.3 per cent of SCs who formed 16.6 per cent of the total population, and 2.2 per cent of STs with their 8.8 per cent share in the total population, were employed in teaching professions, only 4.9 per cent of the Muslim population, constituting 14.2 per cent of the national population, had jobs in higher education. These figures are hardly surprising given that the 2011 census had already shown that Muslims had the highest percentage

---

[11] See Sachar Committee Report (2006) for details. For an appraisal of the Sachar Committee Report, see Robinson (2007), among others.

of illiteracy in the country. According to the census, 42.7 per cent of Muslims were found to be illiterate, a figure that was distinctly higher than the national average of 36.9 per cent.

Based on data from the two rounds of research conducted under the Indian Human Development Surveys in 2004–05 and 2011–12, Jaffrelot and Kalaiyarasan (2018) have pointed out that the socio-economic situation of Muslims has in fact deteriorated over the years. Their status vis-à-vis Hindu Dalits has declined pan-India except in the state of Uttar Pradesh. In Haryana, Muslims have dropped from 85 per cent to 68 per cent of the per capita income of Hindu Dalits; in Gujarat, from 76 per cent to 69 per cent; and in Kerala from 136 per cent to 82 per cent. The gap is even more pronounced with respect to Hindu Other Backward Classes (OBCs), a good example being Gujarat where Muslims were neck and neck with OBCs till 2004–05 but now have fallen behind, earning only 72 per cent of the annual per capita revenue of OBCs, down from 97 per cent in 2004–05.

Jaffrelot and Kalaiyarasan also draw attention to the fact that most Muslims are working as artisans and petty shopkeepers. Less than 10 per cent of Muslims have a salaried job in the three states where they are the poorest—Haryana, Bihar and West Bengal. According to a 2015 report carried in the *Economic Times* (Karunakaran 2015), corporate India also reflects the absence of Muslims. Only 2.67 per cent of directors and senior executives in BSE 500 companies were Muslims.

At the intersection of low levels of literacy and persisting poverty, Muslims also have the highest fertility rates and among the lowest levels of access to healthcare (see Appendix, section A.3). According to data from the National Family Health Survey (NFHS) 2015–16, the TFR for Muslims was 2.61 as compared to the national average of 2.2, while at the same time Muslim women had the second lowest access to antenatal care from skilled health providers, at 77 per cent. Additionally, only 69.2 per cent of Muslim women delivered babies at a health facility, as opposed to the national average of 79 per cent (see Salve 2018).

Indirect factors that have been considered as relevant in the incidence of high fertility rates are women's literacy and employment rates. The NFHS survey also pointed out that 31.4 per cent of Muslim women had had no schooling (as opposed to the national average of 27.6), and as a result only 72 per cent of currently married Muslim women were able to participate in decisions regarding their own health—the lowest figure nationally. Muslim women also had the lowest workforce participation according to the 2011–12 National Sample Survey (NSS), at 15.9 per cent for rural women and 10.9 per cent for urban women, while the national averages were 25.3 and 15.5 respectively (see Salve 2018).

The abject condition of the Muslim community is in great measure a result of the social exclusion faced by its members owing to discrimination on the basis of religious identity. This effectively results in a denial of opportunity (such as in the job market) and of access, such as access to basic services. The roots of this pervasive culture of discrimination run deep in the body politic. To understand this, one has to look back at the historical process through which nationalism and 'national culture' came to be determined in India.

National Culture and the Politics of Othering

While India officially is a 'sovereign, socialist, secular, democratic republic' as per the Preamble of the Constitution, the question of nationalism has remained a vexed one. While the Nehruvian state stood for a composite nation, built on the principles of secularism and rationality, this was not the only viewpoint in the nationalist discourse. Religio-majoritarian tendencies such as Hindu nationalism (Hindutva) were always present and found space within the state system. Organisations such as the Hindu Mahasabha and the Rashtriya Swayamsevak Sangh have long been advocating the establishment of a Hindu *rashtra* (nation). This is essentially an ahistorical and exclusivist vision of nationalism, where the nation belongs to a particular community and all others can have only secondary status in it.

This project of Hindutva depends on the success of a politics of othering, for it is only by projecting an enemy/outsider other that the claim of a singular national community can be maintained. This is especially the case given that the caste system intrinsic to Hinduism does not permit a sense of belonging and fraternity among different caste groups. The object of this politics of othering is the Indian Muslim, while its target is the body politic at large. Operating in the realm of culture, the main resource of this politics is the creation and maintenance of a deep-rooted sense of mistrust and animosity. The strength of this phenomenon lies in its ambiguity. Being supple, it has the potential to animate a wide range of situations. This basic feeling of suspicion of the other has a role to play in scenarios as diverse as job interviews/opportunities in the job market, and instances of communal flare-ups.

Keeping the Minorities in Check: Anti-minority Violence and State Complicity

The sentiment of *othering* at the heart of the cultural politics of the majoritarian right wing has always found abetment by sections within the Indian state. The strongest evidence of this can be found by examining the role of state agents in instances of what are called 'communal riots' in India. Time and again, investigations and studies have shown the complicity of state actors in the production of anti-minority communal violence. The case for this is not limited to anti-Muslim riots only, as the anti-Sikh pogrom of 1984 and the killings of Christians in Kandhamal, Odisha, in 2008 remind us. Hindu–Muslim violence, though, has a special place in the political project of Hindu nationalism; such violence is justified in the name of correcting historical wrongs, with the Muslim sought to be cast as the enemy of the nation itself.

There are numerous examples of targeted violence being condoned, supported or actively organised by state actors. One of the most striking examples is that of the Hashimpura massacre in 1987, called India's biggest instance of custodial killing. Forty-two Muslim men were rounded up by the Provincial Armed Constabulary working under the supervision of the Indian Army (which was in charge of the area when the incident happened), and were shot dead. No one was ever convicted for these killings, as the investigating agency colluded with the perpetrators owing to a shared anti-Muslim sentiment.

The case of the 2002 anti-Muslim pogrom in Gujarat is all too well known. Here too, what was deemed to be 'spontaneous' violence was actually a well-organised programme of targeted violence in which the state authorities were complicit. In the book *On Their Watch*, the contributors examine government records relating to the state's response in four of the most gruesome incidents of communal violence in India (Nellie, 1983; Delhi, 1984; Bhagalpur, 1989; and Gujarat, 2002). They find that despite rehabilitative policies being in place, state actors routinely circumvented them, thus effectively stalling or blocking the process of rehabilitation of minority victims (Chopra and Jha 2014).

Creating the villain-other is also important in order to have unity of ranks within the majoritarian fold. The construction of the majority is in itself a myth, as any sense of community is continually dispelled by the system of caste that seeks to maintain the hierarchical dominance of upper castes over those lower than them. Communal riots have become a de facto mechanism of policing the minority and maintaining the majoritarian status quo. The involvement of Dalits in the violence is of signal importance here. The displacement of caste tensions onto the field marked by religious fault lines serves the additional purpose of the unification of ranks (of different caste groups) in violent opposition to the enemy 'other'.

Ornit Shani (2007) argues that there is a dynamic linkage between the occurrence of caste contestations and that of communal violence. Exploring this linkage by analysing the case of communal violence in Ahmedabad, Gujarat, in 1985, where riots erupted over social and economic reservations for backward castes but transformed into communal violence, her study brings forth the mutually constituting role of caste and class and how tensions relating to the former (expressed in the idiom of caste politics) are sought to be displaced onto the communal arena in order to safeguard upper caste–upper class hegemony (ibid.).

Aloysius (1997) makes a similar argument when he reads into lower-caste mobilisations the particular form of the Indian class struggle—a class struggle refracted through caste. He sees the effort of

Hindutva ideology to pit against each other the imaginary monoliths of 'Hindu' and 'Muslim' as a strategy to nullify the formation of class-like organisations that would challenge upper-caste elite solidarity that cuts across religious groups.

Targeted Violence and the Creation of Second-Class Citizens

As noted earlier, discrimination on religious lines buttressed by the real threat of mass violence has been instrumental in the maintenance of a status quo that perpetuates the disadvantage of members of the Muslim community. While this continues, recent years have witnessed an escalation of hostilities based on communal lines, with organised, state-facilitated groups of fundamentalists being given free rein to polarise the body politic. There has been a spate of mob lynchings and hate crimes targeting members of the Muslim community. The perpetrators of these public crimes have almost always walked free,[12] with the investigating agencies themselves providing cover by botching up investigations and being hostile to the victims.[13] It is only in one case so far that perpetrators have been convicted.[14] Elected representatives of the ruling Bharatiya Janata Party (BJP) have gone out of their way to condone the murders and in fact have pointed the finger at the minority community as a whole for being disrespectful of the purported

---

[12] The lawlessness created by such acts led the Supreme Court to take notice and issue guidelines for such cases. See PTI (2018) for a report on the same.

[13] There are question marks over the investigation process in numerous cases of hate crimes in India. See B. Sharma (2018) for one example, where the role of the police is straightforwardly suspect. In this case of mob lynching of a hapless victim in Hapur (Uttar Pradesh), the gruesome murder was videographed and circulated over social media. Even so, the police case was riven with errors and resulted in the accused getting bail in an early judgement by the court for lack of evidence! The family and lawyers of the victim have alleged foul play and complicity of the state in ensuring that the perpetrators went scot-free.

[14] See Pandey (2018) on the verdict convicting 11 cow vigilantes, including a member of the ruling Bharatiya Janata Party, in the lynching of Alimuddin Ansari in the eastern state of Jharkhand.

majority.[15] These messages of support to murderous fundamentalists have come from the very top of the state hierarchy, with no less than union cabinet ministers making such remarks. While targeting and scapegoating the minority community for the problems faced by the country, the prime minister has not made a single remark[16] condemning the spate of brutal killings taking place under his government's rule. To the contrary, he has offered chief ministership of the populous state of Uttar Pradesh, which has a large proportion of Muslims, to a rabid fundamentalist, Yogi Adityanath.[17] The state of Uttar Pradesh has witnessed a sharp spike in police encounters (extrajudicial killings). Most of the victims in these encounters happen to be members of the Muslim community. In the name of maintaining law and order, the state government has institutionalised rule by force.

[15] There are far too many instances of this. Provided here is a brief sample: BJP lawmaker from Jharkhand, Nishikant Dubey, proactively decided to pay the legal fees of those accused of lynching two Muslim men in Godda district. See the report by the *Wire* (2018b) for details. Union minister and sitting member of Parliament Jayant Sinha went a step further and felicitated seven cow vigilantes accused of a lynching in Ramgarh by garlanding them. The Harvard-educated minister also assured financial help to the convicts for the retrial of their case. See the brief report by Saran (2018) on this. Following the hacking and burning alive of a Muslim migrant labourer in Rajasthan, which was filmed by the nephew of Shambhulal Regar, the perpetrator, right-wing Hindutva groups took out a rally in support of Regar, unfurled a saffron flag on the Udaipur court premises, and clashed with the police. See the report by Outlook Web Bureau (2017) for details. More than 500 people made donations estimated at about ₹300,000 in support of Regar. See S. Munshi (2017) for further details on the incident and the support and valorisation of the murderer by groups affiliated to the ruling BJP and members of the party.

[16] See Bhowmick (2017) among others for reportage on the deafening silence of the prime minister on the subject of mob lynchings and rising hate crimes in India.

[17] The notorious Adityanath (originally Ajay Mohan Bisht) is the *mahant* (priest) of the powerful Gorakhnath Math in the eastern part of the state of Uttar Pradesh. The leader is known for his rabid anti-Muslim stance and is the founder of the Hindu Yuva Vahini, a youth militia that has been routinely involved in instances of communal violence. His elevation to chief ministership, when the BJP won a clear majority in the most populous state of the country, was seen by most observers as a propulsion of the communal majoritarian agenda of the ruling BJP.

In doing so, the purpose has been to create an environment of fear among members of the Muslim community and crush any and all forms of assertion from within its ranks by dubbing any such instance of assertion as criminal, or even better, anti-national, and thus to be dealt with by force (either socially or through state agencies). This practice is doing irreparable damage to the idea of the collective growth and progress of Indians as a people. More specifically, it is adversely regulating the chances of young members of the Muslim community for upward mobility and achieving better standards of living

Dalits

This section explores the status of Dalits by analysing various indicators of human development among this group since liberalisation. It is crucial to discuss inter-group disparities in indicators of human development in order to understand how different historically disadvantaged groups are performing with regard to indicators of both social and economic relevance.

Dalits (also known as Scheduled Castes) continue to occupy a low position in the hierarchical structure of 'Hindu society'. Their productive and constructive role in the smooth running of the society, economy and polity (V. Kumar 2005) has been invisibilised and overlooked. Dalits have been subjected to spatial segregation, denied access to educational development, and their representation in government services and in the field of trade, commerce and industry has been inadequate (Thorat 2009). This deprivation is mainly attributed to the historical process of social and economic exclusion and the prevalence of caste-based discrimination in India. Historically, Dalits have been viewed by members of upper-caste groups as 'polluting'. Practices amounting to institutionalised humiliation—such as denial of access to the same water resources, entry into temples, and so on—were, and continue to be, deployed to maintain a social distantiation between communities. These social mechanisms work in tandem with systematic discrimination in formal and informal settings. This is compounded by incidents of caste-based atrocities against members of Dalit communities, which, it has been argued, are a way of maintaining the social power of upper-caste groups. In effect, there is a structural violence, symbolic and physical, against members of the Dalit community that perpetuates their deprivation. We explore these issues in turn below while drawing attention to the limited measures instituted by the Indian state for dealing with them. We link this up with a discussion of trends in human development indicators for the community. The section ends by arguing for the urgency of proactive state action as well as a need for social transformation if equal chances are to be given to members of the Dalit community to develop on par with others.

Systematic Discrimination

In recognition of the facts of historical disadvantage and systematic discrimination against members of SC communities, the Indian state established a framework of affirmative action.[18] This is formalised in reservation policies intended to ensure representation of the Dalit community in educational institutions and government jobs. However, the scope of reservation policies is limited to state-run and state-supported sectors, while in the private sector, which employs 90 per cent of the Dalit workforce, SCs remain unprotected from possible exclusion and discrimination (Thorat 2009). Scholars have observed statistically significant patterns that highlight that there is a lesser chance of selection of equally qualified college-educated lower-caste and Muslim job applicants as compared to their upper-caste

---

[18] The history of this framework goes back to the Poona Pact, where Gandhi forced Ambedkar to forgo the untouchable castes' demand for a separate electorate for Dalits, which had been awarded by the colonial government, in return for assured representation of the community in legislatures and the promise by Gandhi and the Congress that they would work towards ending untouchability and caste-based discrimination. 'Thus, reservation is a fundamentally political promise made in acknowledgement of the fact that caste literally excludes sizeable communities from Indian society. Since independence is demanded in the name of the Indian nation, and since the modern nation is supposed to be an egalitarian form of community, the Poona Pact is a compromise whereby the untouchables agree to forego their demand for a nation (electorate) of their own and be part of the larger nation in spite of their caste exclusion' (Deshpande 2015).

counterparts when they apply for employment in the modern private enterprise sector via mail (Thorat and Attewell 2010). In another experimental study that sought to understand the pattern of unemployment that plagues religious minorities and Dalits, 25 human resource managers were interviewed. The study reveals the prevalent culture of meritocracy, anti-reservation and caste prejudice within the private job market (Jodhka and Newman 2010). Therefore, it is important that scholars, activists, civil society organisations and others bring the discourse of affirmative action programmes into the private sector in order to combat what Ambedkarites refer to as the 'caste division of labourers' (Omvedt 2005).

Other than these limited efforts by the state to counter caste-based prejudice in society, the Government of India has at different points of time come up with various policies and schemes (both targeted and non-targeted) to cater to the needs of Dalit communities. For instance, the Planning Commission in the 1970s introduced the Special Component Plan for SCs (later renamed the Scheduled Caste Sub Plan [SCSP]) in order to provide direct policy benefits for SCs. The main objective of the SCSP was to allocate plan funds for the development of SCs in accordance with their proportion in the total population of India. However, the fund was never allocated according to the population percentage, and norms laid under SCSP were never followed. Allocation for SCs reached an all-time high at 10.43 per cent of the total allocation of the union budget of 2012–13 (revised estimate), but this was not even close to their proportion in the total population, which is 16.2 per cent (Shrivastava 2014). Further, there have been issues regarding the diversion of funds allocated under SCSP to other schemes and programmes, poor utilisation of allocated funds for the welfare of SCs, lack of transparency in the state budget, and inadequate service delivery mechanisms at the ground level (CBGA et al. 2011). These issues raise questions about governance on the one hand and the intentions of the government on the other. The exclusion of Dalits from the larger developmental process of the Indian state has thus occurred at the social, political as well as governance levels.

Despite the existence of various programmes and schemes to bridge disparities between Dalits and other, more privileged communities in education, health, income and occupational opportunities, achievement of the intended objectives is still far. Apart from lack of access to school education, language of instruction at educational institutions, and persisting poverty among Dalit communities, the poor education-related outcomes can be attributed to discrimination against Dalit children by teachers and other students in educational institutions, where Dalit children are made to sit separately during class hours and meal breaks. However, caste-based discrimination in education has never seen a mention in policy documents (Nambissan 2010). Therefore, attributing poor educational attainment merely to low enrolment, irregular attendance, dropout rates and family income is more likely to conceal the caste-based discrimination at the institutional level that children from Dalit communities face. Dalit students are often excluded from co-curricular activities, denied fair participation in classroom discourses, and often subjected to discriminatory and unequal treatment in relation to their peers. These experiences are detrimental to their self-esteem and self-worth, which also affects their learning outcomes adversely (ibid.).

Table 2.1 reflects educational attainments across different social groups, such as SCs, STs, upper Muslims and lower Muslims.[19] It can be observed that the percentage of illiterates among SCs came down from 49 per cent in 2004–05 to 38 per cent in 2011–12. However, only 3.1 per cent of SCs attained education above the higher secondary level, which possibly is one of the reasons behind their low representation in formal sector employment and overwhelming representation in the informal sector.

The condition of SC women in terms of educational attainment is even worse. Table A.5 (Appendix) shows that 47 per cent of SC women were not literate as per NSS 68th Round (2011–12) data. This proportion had come down by 12 percentage points from 59 per cent in 2004–05. Only 2.1 per cent of SC women had

[19] 'Upper Muslims' include the Muslim (general category) population except those reporting their social group as OBCs, SCs and STs. On the other hand, 'lower Muslims' include all Muslims reporting their social group as OBCs, SCs and STs.

Table 2.1 Changes in the Percentage Distribution of Population Belonging to Different Social Groups by Completed Level of Education, 2004–05 and 2011–12

Education Level	SCs		STs		Upper Muslim		Lower Muslim	
	2004–05	2011–12	2004–05	2011–12	2004–05	2011–12	2004–05	2011–12
Not Literate	49	38.2	53.6	41	42.1	33.4	47	39.1
Literate but below Primary	18.6	19.1	19.6	20.3	21.5	21.9	20.8	20.2
Primary	13.3	14.9	12	14.8	15.8	16.5	13.3	14.3
Middle	10.5	13.2	8.6	12.2	10.7	12.4	10.9	12.8
Secondary	6.7	11.6	4.8	9.3	7.4	12.2	6.3	11
Above Higher Secondary	1.9	3.1	1.4	2.4	2.5	3.7	1.8	2.6

Source: Estimates based on NSS 61st Round (2004–05) and NSS 68th Round (2011–12), Employment and Unemployment Survey.

received education up till or above the higher secondary level, which is higher than ST and lower Muslim women and lower than upper Muslim women.

Increase in wealth/income is one of the determining factors in the level of education. Figure A.20 (Appendix) suggests that during 2004–05, more than 60 per cent of the SC population in the poorest households were illiterate compared with less than 20 per cent in the richest households. The percentage had marginally decreased by 2011–12. The figure also shows that the higher income group among SCs have better education levels (over 15 per cent of this group have educational attainments above higher secondary level) than people who fall in the lowest wealth decile. Therefore, economic deprivation is a crucial indicator in improving the education level among disadvantaged communities.

Table A.7 in the Appendix shows the educational attainment among women in the reproductive age group 15–49 in 2004–05 and 2011–12. It shows that the percentage of SC women in the reproductive age group who were illiterate declined from 57 per cent in 2004–05 to 41.7 per cent in 2011–12, which was lower than the overall figure for India. Also, though the percentage of women in this age group with education level above higher education increased (from 2.3 to 3.7) during this period, it was still lower than the all-India level.

At the higher education level, as per NSS 1999–2000 data, SCs who constitute 13 per cent of the total urban population make up less than 4 per cent in all fields of higher education, and around 2 per cent in the fields of engineering and medicine. Upper castes who are little more than one-third of the urban population comprise two-thirds of all professional and higher education degree holders (Deshpande 2006). On the other hand, caste-based discrimination is a reality not just in school education, but also in institutions of higher education. As per a 2011 report in the *Hindu*, 18 Dalit students in premier institutes of higher education had committed suicide in the previous four years (Karthikeyan 2011), citing the hostile and discriminatory environment of higher education institutions. It is evident that the education level of SCs continues to lag behind other more privileged communities;

this is one of the reasons why they are overrepresented in less-skilled and low-paying jobs.

The population of SCs increased from 64.4 million in 1961 to 201.3 million in 2011 (Salve 2013). Though the sex ratio of SCs is better than the national average for India and also the averages for rural and urban India (Figure A.16), there has been a decline in the child sex ratio, which is a worrying trend. The child sex ratio declined from 938 in 2001 to 933 in 2011 (Figure A.17). Though life expectancy for SCs increased from 59.8 in 1998–99 to 63 in 2005–06, it was lower than the national average of 65.5 in 2005–06 (Figure A.7). Further, the IMR of 66.4 among SCs in 2005–06 has been observed to be higher than the national average of 57 (Figure A.9). Similarly, though the U5MR among SCs and STs has seen a decreasing trend since 1992–93, it is still higher than the U5MR for other communities— 88.1 for SCs and 95.7 for STs in 2005–06, compared with 59.2 for other communities (Figure A.11). Therefore, being an SC or ST in India is a serious determining factor for a person's health and life chances and their ability to function in society to their full potential.

Several data sources suggest that Dalits also perform worse than other communities in terms of health outcomes and access to sanitation facilities. Despite galloping economic growth, overflowing food stocks and three flagship programmes of food assistance—the Public Distribution System (PDS) for subsidised cereal supply to poorer households, Integrated Child Development Services (ICDS) to provide food and healthcare for children under 6 years of age, adolescent girls, and pregnant and nursing mothers, and the Mid-Day Meal Scheme (MDM) to end classroom hunger and improve the nutritional status of schoolgoing children—the population continues to face widespread hunger and undernutrition, with SCs faring worse than others. It has been observed that 32–33 per cent of SC/ST boys under 5 years of age are underweight, compared to 21 per cent in the general population; also, an underweight child in urban India is more likely to belong to a disadvantaged community such as an SC or ST, have an illiterate father, or live in a home without a toilet than other children (Salve 2017). Figure A.12 indicates that as per data provided by the *Rapid Survey on Children 2013–14*, about 42 per cent of under-5 children from the SC community are stunted, 16 per cent are wasted and 33 per cent are underweight, which explains the unequal life chances and resultant health outcomes among SCs. The survey also observes that 30 per cent of SC households use improved sanitation facilities, while 58 per cent of SC households still practise open defecation.

Apart from what government data suggests, there has also been scholarly research analysing the extent of discrimination against SCs and STs by health service providers in government healthcare facilities. A study exploring this issue shows that, when Dalit children accessed healthcare services, on more than 93 per cent of these occasions, they experienced discrimination by auxiliary nurse midwives and anganwadi workers; and on 59 per cent of the occasions on which they accessed healthcare services, they experienced some kind of discrimination by doctors and lab technicians (Acharya 2010).

Caste-Based Violence

The poor performance of the Dalit community across human development indicators cannot fully be explained without factoring in the role of caste-based violence—both symbolic and physical—that is periodically meted out to members of the community. This factor is crucial for understanding the perpetuation of the status quo, as it is a mechanism that sustains the disenfranchisement of the community and the maintenance of the social power of upper castes over them. We now briefly discuss this phenomenon and the recognition of it which led to constitutional safeguards against such atrocities.

In addition to the constitutional safeguards for Dalit communities against discrimination (discussed previously), there are several anti-discriminatory measures that criminalise the practice of untouchability and discrimination in public places, and also provide legal protection to Dalits against violence and atrocities by members of the upper castes—for instance, the Untouchability Offence Act, 1955 (renamed as the Protection of Civil Rights Act in 1976), and the Scheduled Castes and Scheduled Tribes (Prevention of Atrocities) Act, 1989 (Thorat 2009). Despite these legal safeguards, studies have found that crimes against SCs have increased over time. Of 47,064 crimes against SCs in 2014, representing a 44 per cent rise over five years from 2010 to 2014, 40,300 cases were reported under various sections of the Indian Penal Code and the Prevention of Atrocities Act. It has also been observed that sexual assaults against women and rape are the top crimes against SCs (Mallapur 2015). An analysis of cases filed under the Scheduled Castes and the Scheduled Tribes (Prevention of Atrocities) Act, 1989, suggests that there has been a massive spike in the number of pending cases and a steady decline in the number of cases that complete trial; also, there has been a fall in the conviction rate between 2010 and 2016 (S. Nair 2018).

Structural violence is a key component of caste oppression, as we have established in the preceding discussion. What are referred to in the literature as 'atrocities' are instances of naked violence and humiliation that are used to keep Dalits in their place. While most such atrocities are not even reported, a few have been able to catch the eye of mainstream media. For instance, in 2006 in Khairlanji district of Maharashtra, four members of a Dalit family were murdered by members of the politically dominant Kunbi caste (Ghoshal 2016). In another instance, as recently as 2015, in Jat–Dalit violence in Dangawas village of Nagaur district of Rajasthan, 4 Dalits were killed and 13 were injured in a clash between the two communities (Husain 2015). These are examples of several such cases in which members of the Dalit community have been harassed, humiliated and murdered. Recently, there has been an effort to dilute the provisions of the act, after the Supreme Court of India in a judgement stated that the anti-atrocities act has become an instrument to 'blackmail' innocent citizens and public servants, and issued guidelines to protect public servants and private employees (Rajagopal 2018). Such judgements can potentially affect already marginalised communities that face discrimination on an everyday basis, and result in the further marginalisation of Dalits and Adivasis.

The preceding discussion provided a snapshot of the lives and the extent of exclusion of members of Dalit communities, and their differential treatment in various spheres of life. It described how the maintenance of a hierarchical social order contributes to their deprivation and denial of rights. Therefore, apart from interventions at the policy level, it is crucial to ensure that constitutional and legal safeguards for SCs are implemented so as to prevent a complete breakdown of legal, education, healthcare and other public systems vis-à-vis Dalit communities.

Equal Opportunity: Imperative for Realising the Demographic Dividend

As should be evident to the average observer, the status of the three communities discussed in this chapter needs to be addressed urgently. It is also the case that the fate of these communities will in great measure determine the progress of the Indian people as a whole. This is so from two angles. First, the normative imperative. The measure of success of any human development effort must be judged for the good it brings to the most marginalised subjects. Adivasis, Dalits and Muslims represent the three broad demographics in the country who suffer (and have suffered) systemic discrimination and exclusion from the conditions of possibility of self-realisation as citizens of a democratic nation-state. Undoing this systemic discrimination is the test of India's existence as a democratic republic. This was indeed the implicit promise of independent India, that all citizens, irrespective of caste, religion or ethnicity, would be equal. We clearly have not accomplished this precondition of being a democratic republic, and much more effort needs to be made in this direction.

Second, the potential demographic dividend that India seeks to exploit in the coming years is not going to be realised unless the youth from these three groups are given their fair share of chances. If the opportunities afforded to a large segment of the youthful working population are stifled by oppressive social structures, their potential for collective human development will never be realised. Given that the youth from these social groups represent a segment of population ranked lower than the rest in terms of development indices, the aim should be to enable them to improve their position. This would contribute tremendously towards overall development, as it would mean the reduction of poverty and the elimination of the lowest ranks that currently present us with a scenario of acute inequality. If the idea is to create better standards of living and greater prosperity overall, then it makes complete sense to focus on moving people from the lowest levels upwards. The gains made by a mass movement from the lowest rungs into the middle of the pyramid would far outweigh those made by investing in a select few at the top.

CHAPTER 3

Vicissitudes of Growth
The Precarity of India's Labouring Lives

Development: Contested Meanings

'Development': the frequency with which this word is used is matched only by the multiple points of contention among theorists in arriving at a definition of it. In this chapter, we discuss contending views on the trajectory of India's economic development. Different schools of thoughts advocate different means of reaching the common goal of achieving 'development'. There are difficult theoretical questions about what development really means and how we should understand it. Is a certain basic quantum of economic growth necessary for human development? Does development mean increasing some economic indicators, or should it have broader, more abstract but meaningful goals, such as expanding 'human capabilities', as Amartya Sen (1999) propounds in his book *Development as Freedom*?

The debate between Amartya Sen and Jagdish Bhagwati, two eminent Indian economists, revolves around different understandings of what constitutes development. While Bhagwati considers economic growth as a precondition of poverty reduction, Sen on the other hand advocates for policies that are welfare oriented, and explains why India should invest more in the social sector and in building the capabilities of its citizens. The fundamental difference between economic growth and human development is that economic growth focuses on the expansion of only one human aspect, that is, income, whereas human development looks at the expansion of all human choices—social, economic, political and cultural (Haq 1995). It is pertinent to look at the debates around India's growth trajectory to understand the priorities of the Indian state.

In their book *Why Growth Matters*, Jagdish Bhagwati and Arvind Panagariya (2012) describe the role played by economic reforms in reducing poverty and accelerating growth. Poverty here is understood as a measure drawn from the consumer expenditure surveys conducted by the National Sample Survey Organisation. The claim of poverty reduction has been vehemently questioned and criticised for being too narrow in its understanding of a complex reality. A second order of criticism is that the poverty line is fixed at abysmally low levels, with some commentators calling it the destitution line (Bhan 2014) As per the recommendations of the Tendulkar Committee (Planning Commission 2009), as little as ₹27 in rural areas and ₹33 in urban areas (in 2011–12) qualify as the poverty line based on spending on food, education, health, electricity and transport. This can be understood as a deliberate attempt by the government to keep the poverty line abysmally low in order to present a picture of 'poverty reduction'—one of the buzzwords of the global developmental lexicon.

Absolute poverty measures only count poverty reduction in absolute terms. It is important to understand that even if absolute poverty has declined since liberalisation, vulnerability has increased. Further, any serious stocktaking needs to consider the deleterious consequences of economic reforms, like uneven growth, sharp increase in social and economic inequality, privatisation of natural resources—land and water among others (Sood 2016). The *World Inequality Report 2018* highlights that since 1980, income inequality has increased rapidly in India (Alvaredo et al. 2018). The top 1 per cent in India accounted for 22 per cent of the national income in 2014, up from about 14 per cent in 1980, while the share of the bottom 50 per cent decreased from almost 24 per cent to below 15 per cent in the same time period (see Figure 3.1). The average national income of the top

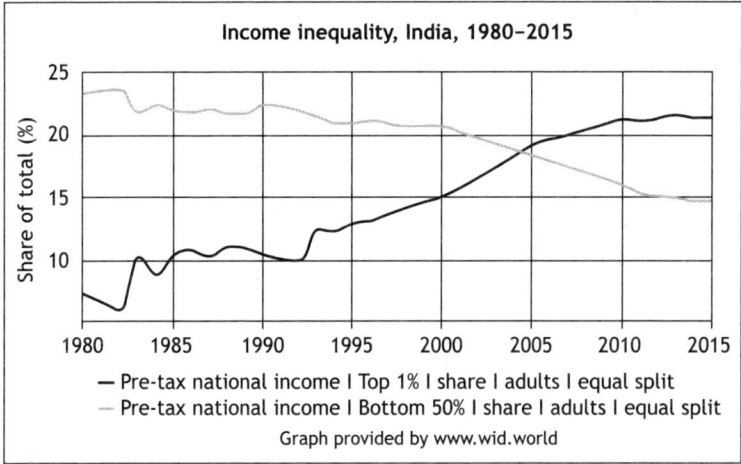

Figure 3.1 *Share of Top 1 Per Cent and Bottom 50 Per Cent in National Income*

Source: World Inequality Database, https://wid.world/country/india/ (accessed 26 March 2019).

1 per cent has increased by approximately 355 times since the initiation of economic reforms (ibid.).

The proponents of economic liberalisation advocate market-led growth as providing the means of tackling the socio-economic problems faced by Indians ('capitalism with a human face'). They champion the idea that high economic growth will lead to increased revenue generation in the state's exchequer, which will then allow the state to engage in redistribution through various social sector programmes to cater to the needs of disadvantaged populations. (In the next chapter, we will discuss the trends in social sector spending in India in the post-liberalisation period.)

In reality, however, things have played out rather differently, as welfare has become disjointed from growth under the prevailing pro-liberalisation orthodoxy. This conceptual break has had a systemic material impact, and provides us with insight into the concrete consequences of different ways of conceptualising 'development'. We may consider the following instance of this seismic shift.

The miserable state of 'pro-poor' policies in India can in part be attributed to the acceptance of the Fiscal Responsibility and Budget Management Act, 2003, by successive governments. The act restricts deficit spending and promotes the idea that government should raise resources through privatisation and public–private partnerships (Bhaduri 2008). This approach to the fiscal deficit has become a dogma of the global capitalist economy, with the spectre of capital flight ever present for states that think otherwise, thus constraining their capacity for investing in people's needs. In this way, what started out as a justification for increasing the state's resources to tackle socio-economic issues has become the very albatross that prevents it from doing so.

The champions of economic growth have consistently pushed for changes in laws and policies that are supposed to protect the interests of the marginalised sections. The changes suggested in the Land Acquisition, Rehabilitation and Resettlement Act, 2013, and the recent proposed changes in labour laws, are examples of the increasingly heavy impact of dominant private economic interests on state policies. Michael Levien (2015) explains the shifts in the purpose of land acquisition, and the resultant dispossession, from state-led projects of industrial and agricultural transformation to projects that serve private actors, particularly in post-liberalisation India, with an increasing rate of dispossession under the neoliberal regime. This is disastrous for a country already going through agrarian distress and rampant farmers' suicides. Similarly, the recently suggested substantive changes in existing labour laws is a way to grant more power to private corporations (in the name of rationalisation and ease of doing business), thus tilting the scales of employer–employee relations in favour of the former. As discussed later in this chapter, this will lead to the erosion of labour rights and the establishment of even more exploitative conditions.

From the perspective of human development, the efficacy of the neoliberal growth regime and the increasing reliance on private actors to provide social services while constantly exploiting both natural and human resources should be investigated seriously. The evidence suggests that the 'growth first' model of development is more prone to producing inequality and distress in the lives of the already disadvantaged sections of our society. The mainstream Sen–Bhagwati debate should be probed further to get a deeper understanding of what kind of 'development' we should seek to attain in a country like India. In this chapter, we try to take a deeper look into the state of the Indian economy in the context of agrarian distress and increasing precarity of work.

Agriculture: A Harvest of Despair

In this section we turn to agriculture, the most populous sector in the economy, and discuss the state of affairs from the perspective of the majority of those engaged in it. We discuss how the majority are unfavourably placed to benefit from the model of economic development that delivers high growth rates. It follows that the benefits of growth (or surplus value created) are cornered by a narrow stratum. We pay attention particularly to the role of policy in contributing to such an unjust state of affairs. An account of the change in policy orientation in the sector post liberalisation is provided. Further, we look at the consequences of these changes for the sector as a whole, and for the lives of half of India's workforce who rely on agriculture for their primary source of income.

Though increasingly removed from the imagination of middle-class Indians, it is worth repeating a commonly known fact. *Agriculture continues to employ the majority of the working population of India.* This makes it imperative for any worthwhile analysis of economic development to start with a discussion on this sector.

A Distress-Ridden Countryside

The most basic thing to consider when understanding the opportunity structure in a system is the initial endowments of the participants. In the case of agriculture, the centrepiece is land. Therefore, let us begin by looking at some numbers regarding land.

The landholding pattern we witness today is reflective of the highly skewed nature of property ownership in the sector. Looking at trends from NSS data, we see a massive increase in the marginal holding

Table 3.1 *Population and Agricultural Workers in India*

Year	Cultivators (%)	Agricultural Labourers (%)
1951	71.9	28.1
1961	76	24
1971	62.2	37.8
1981	62.5	37.5
1991	59.7	40.3
2001	54.4	45.6
2011	45.1	54.9

Source: Table 2.3(a), 'Population and Agricultural Workers', Government of India (2018).

category,[1] from 39.1 per cent of all operational holdings in 1960–61 to 71 per cent in 2003 (see A. K. Singh 2013). All other categories show a significant decline in their percentage share of total holdings over the same period, reflecting the fact that labour is being tied down in agriculture with no other alternatives, leading to the fragmentation of holdings under population pressure. The decrease in the percentage of small holdings (from 22.6 to 16.6 over the same period) is relatively small, and, along with the sharp increase in marginal holdings, it reflects the fact of proletarianisation. Small and marginal holdings combined (87.6 per cent) account for only 43.5 per cent of the total operational area, while at the other end, medium and large holdings combined (5.1 per cent) account for 34 per cent of the total operational area (see Table 1.5 in Reddy and Mishra 2012).

Seen alongside officially available agricultural statistics on the share of cultivators and labourers in the agrarian economy, the picture becomes starker. As shown in Table 3.1, between 1951 and 2011, the percentage of cultivators shrank from 72 per cent to 45 per cent, while the share of those relying on agricultural labour increased from 28 per cent to 55 per cent. That is to say, the proportion of people

---

[1] Holdings less than 1 hectare are counted as marginal. Those between 1 and 2 hectares are taken as small.

in the agrarian economy reliant on income from land has decreased by over a third, while the proportion of those reliant on performing labour on someone else's land has increased by half.

Recently released preliminary results from the Socio-Economic Caste Census (SECC), 2011, paint a rather grim picture of life in the countryside.[2] The data evokes a massive hinterland still imprisoned in persisting endemic impoverishment, want, illiteracy and indeed hopelessness. It tells a story which every thinking and caring Indian must heed. Official enumerators with handheld laptops were commissioned to ask members of all households in the country a few basic questions, including what they owned, how they earned a living, how much they earned, and how far they had studied. The findings tell us, first, that in three out of four rural households, no one earns more than 5,000 rupees a month. More than 9 out of 10 rural households have no one earning over 10,000 rupees a month. This forces more members of each household to work—even the children and the old. Thus, we have a picture of labour supply outstripping demand, where lack of remunerative work opportunities result in multiple members of the poorer households working for depressed wages. The aspect of economic deprivation is made further evident if we look at asset ownership in rural households. As per census 2011 data, 23 per cent of rural households do not possess any assets, so to speak.

The SECC survey also reveals that 56 per cent of rural households own no land. Around half of all rural households report that they depend primarily on manual labour to survive. Economist Prabhat

---

[2] The SECC mandates officials to survey every single household in the country, which contributes to its importance and credibility. It is a census, not an estimate. All large official surveys, however, tend to neglect invisible populations, such as forest dwellers, nomadic communities, footloose distress migrants, bonded workers, and people stigmatised by their vocations, sexuality or ailments. These populations are invisible to state officials because of their extreme vulnerability and powerlessness; as a survival strategy, they are also often forced to hide from the state. Moreover, although rules require that the survey results be ratified in open community meetings, this is rarely done. Far from overstating the situation, therefore, it is likely that in fact the SECC has significantly underestimated levels of poverty and deprivation in the countryside.

Patnaik (2015) observes: 'the share of cultivators has actually fallen [since 1951]. A whole lot of people, who might have been independent peasants ... have been pushed into the ranks of agricultural labour.' According to Patnaik, 'They have no rights, no security of income, they are subject to the worst kind of drudgery because it is all manual work: they cannot be organized. It's just a miserable state of existence' (ibid.).

Agriculture in the Era of Economic Reforms

Having established that the majority of those engaged in agriculture start with a very low threshold of economic capacity, we look now at the changes in policy and what they have meant in terms of the performance of agriculture since economic liberalisation.

Let's start with some broad facts.

- Agriculture's contribution to overall GDP has been declining, whereas there has not been a commensurate drop in the number of people dependent on it. As shown in Figure 3.2, while the share of agriculture in total GDP has reduced to 15.5 per cent,

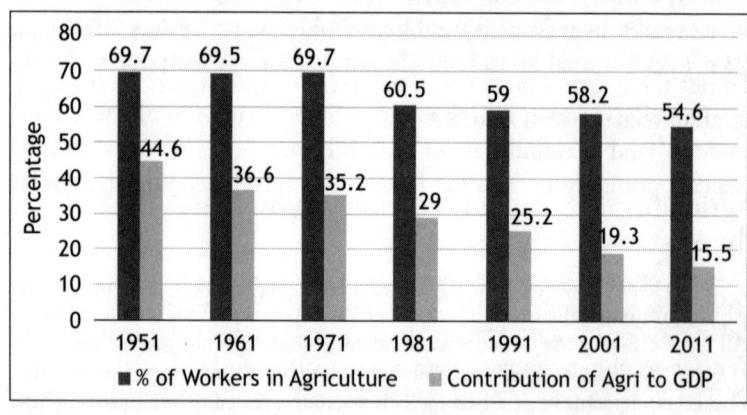

Figure 3.2 Agriculture: Share of Workers Compared with Contribution to GDP

Source: Government of India (2017) for percentage of workers in the agricultural sector; Planning Commission (2014: 5–6) for contribution of the agrarian sector to GDP.

54.6 per cent of the population still depends on it as their primary source of income. This is indicative of severe stagnation as far as the question of opportunities for gainful employment is concerned. A huge number of people are tied to a sector that is stagnating. We shall return to this point later.

- The post-reforms performance of the sector, as compared to the decade preceding economic reforms, has deteriorated. While the growth of agricultural output stood at 3.45 per cent during the 1980s, a sharp slump in the decade following liberalisation saw it plummet to 1.96 per cent between 1990 and 2004.

- A spate of farmers' suicides in the last two decades—the number of farmers who have committed suicide since 1995 officially crossed 300,000 in 2014—has been the most telling example of the sector being in the grip of a crisis.

- Between 2004–05 and 2011–12, five million persons exited agriculture per year. This net movement out of agriculture is a historically unprecedented occurrence. Subsequent years have seen a rapid decline in the number of people leaving agriculture, with a worrying trend, an increase in the share of youth (15–29 years old) in agriculture, being reported.

To put these facts into context, we have to understand the changed agrarian scenario post reforms.

Agricultural Policy in the Reforms Era: A Break from the Past

Economic liberalisation did not entail a new agricultural policy, as it did in the case of commerce and trade, or even industry for that matter. Yet, far-reaching changes were made to the working of the sector. The basic argument for reforms in agriculture was that opening up the sector to global trade would result in a correction of prices (artificially distorted thus far, to the detriment of farmers), which would be beneficial for farmers as they would reap the profits of comparative advantage. Getting prices right, by allowing exposure to global prices for inputs and output, was the mantra that would supposedly create prosperity for an encumbered peasantry. This implied an end to state 'interference' in the form of input subsidies, price support, procurement and so on. Such interventions on the part of the state were deemed harmful for the health of the sector.[3]

This approach marked a fundamental break with earlier thinking on the issue, which maintained a concern with the institutionalist transformation of the sector.[4] In the period up till the 1990s, measures were employed that sought to increase efficiency and production by focusing on the aspect of production, by altering the property structure (land reforms) or by improving the technological mix applied (green revolution). Policy prescriptions for agriculture in the reforms era banked on what proponents of reform thought was the radical potential of open trade in creating conditions for positive change. The thinking was that openness to the global market would fetch higher returns for commodities in which Indian farmers had a comparative advantage. This would lead to a change in the incentive structure, which would in turn lead to a more rational allocation of resources on the part of cultivators (crop diversification). Cultivators would then plough back their earnings into the sector, compensating for the retreat of the state. It was argued that state intervention in procurement (just as in pricing) was an inefficient mechanism. Private trade, along with a futures market in agro commodities, would be a preferable way of ensuring a better match between supply and demand across domestic and offshore markets. This turned out to be wishful thinking, as borne out by the dismal performance of the sector. The point that we wish to emphasise is not that the policy prescription was flawed, but that it was partisan in terms of whose interests it sought to further. We shall return to this point shortly.

Other propositions that characterised the policy outlook towards agriculture were: deregulation of the credit market; the move towards enabling concentration of landholdings for the purpose of contract

[3] Proposing amendments to land ceiling laws—in other words, promoting land concentration for contract farming of cash crops to be sold in export markets—on the other hand, was just considered 'good governance' (and not interference).

[4] Even though the emphasis on institutional transformation had diminished, it continued to remain a part of official policy till then.

farming; at the cost of publicly funded research; and the reconfiguration of the agricultural extension system through public–private partnerships and reliance on NGO-based networks.

Were Reforms Beneficial for Indian Farmers?

Largely, the answer is no. But a powerful minority of large farmers have benefited from the policy changes. While the sector as a whole recorded declining output growth, large farmers outperformed the rest. The unequal impact of the reforms in agriculture has been asserted by economists Vamsi Vakulabharanam and Sripad Motiram (2011), among others. They have shown the continuing good performance of larger cultivators in the post-reforms era while, at the same time, the performance of all other classes declined.

Analysing NSS data on consumption from the 38th (1983–84), 50th (1993–94) and 61st (2004–05) Rounds, Vakulabharanam and Motiram (2011) are able to show that during the 1980s, average consumption was increasing for all classes. The growth rate for classes other than the larger farmers was in fact much higher during this period. In the next period, there is a reversal of this process, with the growth rate of average consumption dropping for all classes except large farmers, for whom it increased from 1.65 per cent in the first period to 1.87 per cent in the second (Figure 3.3). The overall average rate of growth of consumption, however, fell from 1.68 per cent previously to 0.94 per cent in the post-reforms period. Therefore, even as agricultural growth has declined since the 1980s, a narrow upper section in the sector has grown faster than the rest.

Survival with Dignity? An Unviable Proposition

To better comprehend the situation of small and marginal cultivators, as well as the conditions faced by agricultural labourers, it is important to understand the post-reforms policy prescriptions for agriculture in conjunction with the effect of what has been termed the 'lagged green revolution'. The term is used to describe the expansion of green revolution technology to rain-fed and drought-prone regions,

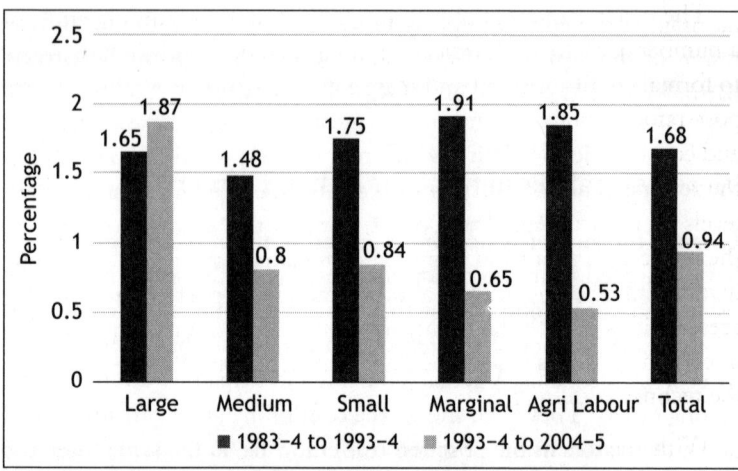

Figure 3.3 *Growth in Average Monthly Per Capita Expenditure for Various Classes (2005–06 Values)*

Source: Vakulabharanam and Motiram (2011), Table 7.3.

Note: Large = self-employed in agriculture, land possessed more than 10 ha; Medium = self-employed in agriculture, land possessed 2–10 ha; Small = self-employed in agriculture, land possessed 1–2 ha; Marginal = self-employed in agriculture, land possessed 0–1 ha; Agri Labour = self-employed in agriculture with no land or those who define themselves as agricultural labourers.

which started taking place in the 1980s. This was in keeping with the productivist mindset that sought to overcome the challenges of the agrarian economy by avoiding tackling its structural problems, such as inequality of access to productive resources, through advocating a technological solution. This had the result of inducing changes in agricultural practices in the rain-fed regions, without a corresponding rise in yield that could offset the increased input costs. Notwithstanding the belief of its proponents, the opening up of agricultural markets did not bring forth a technological innovation for the dry regions that took to green revolution technology despite its fallouts in terms of excessive costs and subpar output.[5]

---

[5] The case of irrigation exemplifies the interplay of reforms and a lagged green revolution post the 1990s. The green revolution areas had benefited from

The increase in input costs is caused by the compounding effect of a number of factors. Significant among them is the decline in access to formal credit for small and marginal cultivators, as a fallout of the post-reforms policy agenda. This means having to take cultivation and consumption loans from informal sources, which has resulted in the re-emergence of usury in the countryside. The increasingly high levels of rural indebtedness point towards this fact. Also harming the interests of small and marginal cultivators is the decline in public investment in agriculture—another fallout of post-reforms policy prescriptions. This has not only resulted in an increment in costs, but in certain instances has also created imbalances in the application of the technological mix.[6]

With the extension of green revolution technologies to rain-fed areas alongside the privatisation of input markets, there is need for the dissemination of know-how regarding these technologies. This role of information dissemination.that should ideally accompany the introduction of new inputs is often appropriated by private input dealers, given the lack of public investment in the extension system. This strengthens the position of the input dealer, who often doubles up as the local moneylender as well.[7]

---

the perennial availability of water, which was largely due to the substantial state investments in major and medium irrigation projects such as canals. In the post-reform period, we note a decline in the expansion of major irrigation works, which had accounted for 38.49 per cent of total irrigated area in 1970–71. This had decreased to 27.11 per cent by 2003–04, with negative rates of increase setting in from the 1990s. Tubewell irrigation, which is mostly privately financed and used, grew at more than 4 per cent per annum in this period, increasing its share of the total irrigated area from 14.34 per cent in 1970–71 to 43.86 per cent in 2003–04. The requirement of water for the technological mix being employed, and the slowdown in major irrigation projects by the state, have meant that the rain-fed areas where green revolution technologies continued to be used had to rely increasingly on the intensive exploitation of groundwater resources, adding to cultivation expenses. See Vakulabharanam and Motiram (2011) for an elaboration.

[6] The haphazard reduction of fertiliser subsidy led to a distortion in the mix employed by several cultivators. See Vakulabharanam and Motiram (2011) for an elaboration of this point.

[7] See Vasavi (1999) for this point.

The incidence of indebtedness among all rural labour households, defined as the percentage of indebted households to total rural labour households, increased from 25.0 per cent in 1999–2000 to a towering 47.3 per cent in 2004–05. The average debt per indebted rural labour household (₹10,259) in 2004–05 recorded an increase of 69.6 per cent over the level of debt (₹6,049) in 1999–2000. An analysis of total outstanding loans reveals that about 97 per cent of the debt raised by the rural labour household was contracted, and a small proportion of the total debt (3 per cent) was inherited. Moneylenders continued to remain the major source of debt (44.2 per cent), followed by banks (16.5 per cent). Other sources, such as shopkeepers (6.1 per cent), friends and relatives (12.8 per cent), and cooperative societies (9.3 per cent) were also significant contributors of loans to rural labour households.

The burden has been most crushing on the already disadvantaged and deprived. Over the high 'growth' period from 1999–2000 to 2004–05, the incidence of indebtedness grew from 25.30 per cent to 48.04 per cent in case of SC households; from 22.60 per cent to 46.67 per cent in the case of OBC households; and from 22.90 per cent to 39.39 per cent in the case of ST households. The average amount of debt per SC household at the all-India level in 2004–05 had increased to ₹3,767 from ₹1,283 during 1999–2000. If this is the picture of rural labour households, the picture of agricultural labour households in particular is in fact marginally worse. The incidence of indebtedness among agricultural labour households was 48.40 per cent in 2004–05, while that among rural labour households was 47.30 per cent. The incidence of indebtedness among SC, ST and OBC agricultural labour households was reported at 49.41 per cent, 41.20 per cent and 47.25 per cent respectively.

The figures from the *Rural Labour Enquiry Report on Indebtedness* brought out by the Ministry of Labour and Employment in 2009–10 (Government of India 2010) indicate that the incidence of indebtedness saw an overall decrease from 47.30 per cent to 34 per cent. Indebtedness decreased from 48.04 per cent to 34.60 per cent in SC households, from 39.39 per cent to 27.50 per cent in ST households, and from 46.67 per cent to 33.70 per cent in OBC households. However, the incidence of indebtedness remained high. Despite the

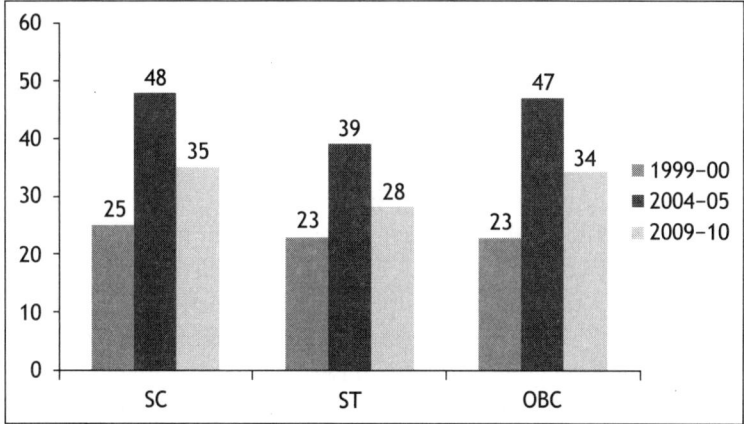

Figure 3.4 *Incidence of Indebtedness across SC, ST and OBC Households, 1999–2000, 2004–05 and 2009–10*
Source: Government of India (2010).

decrease compared to the previous survey in 2004–05, the 2009–10 report found that while the incidence of indebtedness had fallen, the average debt per indebted household rose sharply from ₹10,259 to ₹16,265 at the all-India level. In keeping with the all-India trend, the average debt per indebted household spiked from ₹7,845 to ₹13,671 for SCs, from ₹4,735 to ₹6,547 for STs, and from ₹14,086 to ₹19,912 for OBCs, all in the span of four years between the consecutive surveys in 2004–05 and 2009–10 (see Figure 3.4).

An Epidemic of Suicides

The prevailing circumstances characterised by stagnating incomes, increasing levels of indebtedness, the individuation of cultivators (Vasavi 2012), and declining public investment in agriculture have led to a scenario where over 300,000 agriculturists have committed suicide over the last two decades.[8] Srijit Mishra (2006) identifies the leading causes as indebtedness, sudden fall in the household's economic status

---

[8] The official count is hotly debated. See Sainath (2015) for an incisive critique of the politics of numbers behind reporting farmers' suicides in India.

on account of crop failure, and consumption expenditure towards a marriage in the family. Other causes of farmers' distress as outlined by the Reserve Bank of India in its report (2007) include falling profitability of cultivation, increased volatility in global prices and non-implementation of the minimum support price.

What is surprising is that this situation has not resulted in a policy effort to transform the conditions faced by cultivators. Suicide has been interpreted as the last act of defiance by a distressed peasantry. From time to time, as protests peak or when elections come closer, governments (both state and central) announce farm loan waivers in a bid to quell the growing sigh of misery. We can contend based on this observation that as far as the state is concerned, it is no longer a question of positively transforming a sector that impacts the lives of millions, but one of managing a crisis with palliative measures.

In such a scenario, the net movement of people out of agriculture cannot be understood as a positive development as the orthodoxy of developmental literature would have us believe. We are witness to a situation that is better understood as distress migration. This might very well give us the clue to understanding the seemingly apathetic inaction on the part of the state in responding to the epidemic of suicides in agriculture—the creation of a huge class of footloose migrant workers who keep circulating between town and country in search of work.

These are the reserves that are mobilised for casual work through extralegal or pre-capitalist means, using caste, kinship and religion. This is the vagrant populace that is 'willing' to work at any rate for any number of hours under conditions to which local labourers would never agree. For as long as the countryside in despair can provide these teeming millions in circulation to be mobilised by subcontractors at cheap rates using extra-economic means, employers will never feel the dearth of labourers ready to work in subhuman conditions in open defiance of all legal and mandatory safeguards. It is the despair in the countryside, the stagnation and indebtedness that sustain the model of rampant casualisation and informalisation of the labour market and the depletion of organised employment avenues. It is this reserve pool churned out by the wastelands of distress that enables employers to sack workers with ease when demands for unionisation or better conditions crop up from among them. There are always plenty ready to work for less and for longer. And it is precisely this subhuman exploitation and erosion of rights of labourers that sustain today's model of 'market growth'. It is to a discussion of these dynamics that we turn to in the next section.

Informalisation and Chronic Underemployment

The Indian countryside, as we have observed, has been transformed increasingly into a wasteland of near-terminal despair by forced integration with globalised markets, an uncaring state, and crushing indebtedness. The gap, in such circumstances, between existence in 'normal' conditions and what one may call 'distress' conditions has become rather thin. It is the massive reserve of the underemployed and unemployed among agricultural labourers (including also unviable small and marginal farmers and artisans escaping another dying sector) who, in their desperation to eke out a living, are willing to go the distance in order to just survive. In order to stay alive, they will go to any corner of the country, to do any work, for any remuneration, on any terms. These are the floating footloose labourers who flock to cities and live invisibilised behind the epic growth story. In Jan Breman's (1994) evocative words, these are 'the hunters and gatherers of work'.

Hence arises the synonymy of 'growth' and casualisation as observed at the outset of this chapter. The pauperisation in the countryside, the casualisation of labour, the erosion of the latter's hard-earned rights are not the *unintended consequences* of a flawed model of development. This particular model of development or 'growth', rather, is *made possible* by the despair in the countryside and the precarity of labour under conditions of acute informalisation and casualisation.

The Whopping Rise of the Informal

Of the 60 million new jobs that were generated in 1999–2004, 52 million were in the unorganised sector. Moreover, the increase in employment opportunities in the organised sector has primarily been

Table 3.2 Sector-wise Distribution of Workers by Formal–Informal Employment, 2004–05 to 2011–12 (in Millions)

Sector	2004–05		2009–10		2010–11	
	Formal	Informal	Formal	Informal	Formal	Informal
Agriculture	0.3	268.2	0.4	244.5	0.6	231.3
Manufacturing	5.6	48.3	5.7	45	6.5	53.3
Non-manufacturing	2.1	27.3	2.9	45.4	2.9	52.3
Services	20.6	86.7	24.1	92.2	25.4	101.9
Total	28.6	430.5	33.1	427.1	35.4	438.9

Source: Mehrotra et al. (2014); authors' estimates based on NSS rounds.

in its share of informal workers. Their share rose from 32 per cent in 1999–2000 to 54 per cent in 2004–05, and to 67 per cent in 2011–12 (Mehrotra et al. 2014). Thus, workers in the unorganised sector and informal workers in the organised sector put together make up the overwhelming majority of India's workforce that is most vulnerable and insecure (ibid.). Table 3.2 shows the trend towards informalisation in the sector-wise distribution of workers in formal and informal employment.

In 2012–13, only 16.5 per cent of the workers in the country were wage/salary earners. In another estimate, about 78 per cent of households had no wage/salary-earning members. On the contrary, the proportion of casual labourers in the workforce is supposed to be a considerable 30.9 per cent, and still rising. Although labour law prohibits the appointment of contract workers for perennial tasks, these years saw sharp growth in contract and casual work, at the expense of regular employment. The share of contract workers in total organised employment rose from 10.5 per cent in 1995–96 to 25.6 per cent in 2009–10, while the share of directly employed workers fell from 68.3 per cent to 52.4 per cent in the same period. Even regular workers were appointed increasingly on short-term contracts, with little or no social security, as termination of their employment was not legally barred because they were contract and not regular employees. This is how the increasing informality in the organised labour market has blurred distinctions between formal and informal labour. This is what one may call 'reform by stealth'; that is, even without the laws changing, fewer and fewer workers enjoy the protections of secure employment and social security as mandated by law on paper.

Today, written job contracts with formal agreements and associated legal responsibilities (at least on paper) are already an endangered or near-extinct mode of employing workers. As per government estimations, labour relations—where they exist—are based mostly on casual employment, kinship or personal and social relations rather than contractual arrangements with formal guarantees. About 82 per cent of the employed persons in the AGEGC (agriculture sector excluding only growing of crops) and non-agricultural sector were reported to be working without any written job contracts. About 93 per cent of casual workers do not have any written job contracts, while the figure for contract workers is 68.4 per cent. Even among the supposedly more formal wage/salaried employees, about 66 per cent were reported to be working without a written job contract.

Kompier et al. (2014) cite the 2009 report of the National Commission for Enterprises in the Unorganised Sector, which found that the vast majority of jobs created in recent years have been in the informal sector, in the absence of a legal framework for labour protection and social security. Out of every 100 workers, the report revealed, around 90 per cent work in the informal economy producing half of India's economic output. This implies that out of the current total workforce of around 475 million, around 400 million workers, considerably larger than the total population of the US, are employed with little or no job security, protection for health (sick or maternity pay), retirement benefits or any formal entitlements to call upon the protection of the labour law regime (Mander 2014).

The brunt of this casualisation is of course borne by the most oppressed sections. That is, workers who are SC, ST or Muslim would be considerably more likely than others both in rural and urban locations to end up with casual jobs instead of contractual ones. Muslims in general seem to be the worst sufferers of rampant casualisation among all the oppressed categories. The proportion of urban Muslims in casual labour seems to be particularly pronounced. And then again, it is the lower Muslims who are more likely to be casual workers than even SCs and STs. In 2005–06, 76.8 and 70.7 per cent of SCs and STs respectively working in urban areas were in casual employment. Among all others, the proportion was 63.9 per cent. And the corresponding figures for upper and lower Muslims were a staggering 81.4 and 86.6 per cent respectively. And this mounted further to 86.6 and 90.2 per cent respectively in 2011–12.

Dilution of Labour Laws Aiding Further Informalisation

There have been strong recommendations in favour of strengthening the labour laws so as to check this constant move towards informal and insecure employment. But what has been happening is exactly to the contrary. Industry, however, has continued to complain about the Indian government's less-than-satisfactory efforts to introduce what it called labour 'reforms': labour reforms were one of the promises of the avowedly capital-friendly government. The term 'reform' is misleading, because what is sought is not a better deal for the labouring class but, rather, the further weakening of the already infirm framework of labour regulation in our country. This would perhaps attract more investment, but would damage further the promise of assured, dignified and safe work for the aspirational young. Leo Panitch notes in the *Guardian*: 'For most of the 20th century, the word "reform" was commonly associated with securing state protection against the chaotic effects of capitalist market competition. Today, it is most commonly used to refer to the undoing of these protections' (Panitch 2014).

It has been expected that avowedly industry-friendly governments would muster the political will to 'reform' labour laws to render these more 'flexible'. The rigidities of the current labour regulatory regime, it is alleged, are major hurdles to attracting private investment into manufacturing. Greater freedom to hire and fire workers, a less intrusive labour welfare supervisory regime and the reduced power of unions would, it is argued, actually benefit workers as greater private investment would result in higher economic growth and, therefore, more jobs.

In this light, the labour law amendments introduced in June 2014 by the then newly elected Vasundhara Raje government in Rajasthan were widely seen as establishing the template for 'labour reforms' to be undertaken nationally. These amendments, first, reduced the application of the Contract Labour Act to companies with more than 50 workers, against the then current minimum of 20. This statute prohibited engagement of contract labour in tasks requiring perennial work in the production process, and prescribed a mechanism for the registration of contractors. The amendments likewise restricted the protections of the Factories Act to units employing 20 workers with power supply and 40 workers without power supply, down from the existing norm of 10 and 20 workers respectively. This, in effect, reduced the protections of workers with regard to health, safety and welfare standards which employers were earlier legally bound to ensure.

The legal changes further exempted factories employing 300 (up from 100) workers from the protections of the Industrial Disputes Act, which protects the rights of collective bargaining, and raised the minimum numbers of workers required to register a trade union from 15 to 30 per cent. Labour economists estimate that after this amendment, around 57–60 per cent of workers in the formal sector could be fired, or subjected to suppressed wages and degraded work conditions. The cumulative impact of these amendments has been to free more employers from even the poorly enforced and modest obligations they currently hold for ensuring the job security, health and social protection of their workers.

High GDP, Few Jobs and Falling Real Wages

As per the government's own reluctant admission, 'the economy has indeed experienced high rates of growth in the post reforms period [but] the optimism on employment creation, however, has not been realised to the fullest extent' (Mishra and Bhattacharya 2017). In the decade 1999–00 to 2009–10, while GDP growth accelerated to 7.52 per cent per annum, employment growth was just 1.5 per cent, below the long-term employment growth of 2 per cent per annum over the four decades since 1972–73.

In the period from 2004–05 to 2009–10, a tectonic shift was in evidence as 23.7 million of India's agricultural workforce abandoned agriculture, that is, 10 per cent of India's agricultural workforce. Non-agricultural jobs grew by 7.5 million per annum on an average between 1999–2000 and 2004–05, but this growth was not rapid enough to absorb the 12 million joining the workforce during this period. Given the exodus from agriculture since that time, it has become a more daunting task than ever before to absorb both those entering the labour force and those leaving agriculture (Mehrotra et al. 2014).

More recent data reveals that the rate of creation of jobs deteriorated substantially during the period 2013–14 through 2015–16. While real GDP grew at a faster 7.8 per cent per annum, jobs grew at a meagre 0.2 per cent per annum during this period, realising what many have termed as the perpetuation of jobless growth. According to the *India Employment Report 2016* (Ghose 2016), almost 13 million are openly unemployed, some 52 million are in conditions of 'disguised unemployment', and 52 million women are not part of the labour force due to fewer opportunities. That makes for a bulk of virtually 117 million unemployed people (Natti 2017).

Looking at the share of labour in real gross value added, one finds that it declined considerably in the period between 1980–81 and 2012–13 from about 60 per cent to below 20 per cent (Abraham and Sasikumar 2017). This shows that the major share of surplus generated from increase in labour productivity has been cornered by owners, and the workers have received less than half the share of increase from their increased productivity. This is significant when one is trying to understand the low level of wages. This suppression of wages in the organised sector in turn is bound to have a negative impact on the wage levels in the unorganised sector, where labour protections and security are virtually non-existent. The share of profits in this time period, on the other hand, has shown a sizeable increase, thus confirming the claim that reforms have benefited owners of capital much more than they have the workers.

It is worth noting that while the Indian economy is generally seen to have 'taken off' in terms of transcending the 'Hindu rate of growth' to move to a higher growth trajectory, in terms of the overall net domestic product (NDP), there has been an uneven decline in the share of compensation of employees, especially marked in the most recent years. If one looks at the organised sector NDP, the decline is striking, with the share falling from 75 per cent in 1980–81 to 69 per cent in 1990–91, to 60 per cent at the turn of the century, and to as low as 46 per cent in the late 2000s, recovering slightly to 51 per cent in the most recent year, 2009–10. At the same time, what is most notable is the very significant increase, within the organised sector's NDP, of the share of surplus which now accounts for nearly half of the income accruing to that sector. This is a substantial increase over a period of three decades since the neoliberal shift. Clearly, in the period of rapid growth, the greater part of the growth has accrued to the surplus takers. 'This confirms the reality that is increasingly apparent within Indian society, of a growth process that has generated significant economic inequality and concentrated the gains among those who do not have to work as employees in the organised sector or as self-employed workers in the unorganised sector' (Chandrasekhar and Ghosh 2012).

Feminisation or Expulsion from the Labour Force for Women?

The toll of informalisation is unfairly borne by women, as a steady widening of the gender gap is visible over the years. If one compares the estimates of NSS 2004–05 and NSS 2011–12 (Government of India 2006b, 2013), one finds that in the informal sector in urban areas, the relative shares of men and women shifted from 81.3 per cent and 18.7 per cent to 83.1 per cent and 16.9 per cent respectively. If one includes both urban and rural areas in the informal sector, the shares shifted from 71.5 per cent and 28.5 per cent for men and women respectively to 77.7 per cent and 22.3 per cent over this period. This marks a significant pushing out of women from the labour market. Even the marginal share of migrants for employment in the female population declined from 1.9 per cent in 1993 to 1.2 per cent in 2007–08. Employment data from the NSS for the period in question also showed a fall in female work participation rates in both rural and urban areas. Between 2004–05 and 2011–12, while the labour force participation rate for women in rural areas dropped from 39.3 to 27.1, for urban women the decline was from 21.8 in 2004–05 to 19.3 in 2011–12. The decline was sharper for women in rural areas, and specifically for women belonging to the age group 15–29. In 2004–05, the workforce participation of women in the age group 15–29 was reported to be 30.9, and in 2009–10, the same fell to 23.3. In absolute terms, there was a withdrawal of around 21 million women workers. Out of this, 19.8 million were from rural areas. The fall, in fact, continued even between 2009–10 and 2011–12 (Mehrotra et al. 2014).

Data from the ILO on female labour force participation corroborates this finding. We see a sharp decline in the participation of young women aged 15–24 in the workforce (see Figure 3.5). Their rate of participation has halved since liberalisation in 1991, from about 30 per cent in 1991 to about 15 per cent in 2017. This is an extremely worrying trend, as it indicates a lack of suitable jobs for young women. What makes it even more worrisome is that the same period has witnessed an increase in enrolment in higher education, which implies that this group of women are gaining education,[9] but are not finding jobs, thus exemplifying the squandering of the demographic potential they embody.

The diminishing scope for gainful employment in agriculture has led to the loss of employment for both women and men. From rising rural wages to growing mechanisation, a range of factors has contributed to this decline. The employment elasticity in the construction sector seems to have mitigated the situation for men; however, for whatever reasons, this sector has not absorbed as many women yet.

---

[9] 'Women enrolment in higher education which was less than 10 per cent enrolment on the eve of Independence has risen to 41.5 per cent in the academic year 2010–11. Out of 169.75 lakh students enrolled in higher education in higher education in 2010–11, almost 70.49 lakh were women as compared to just about 47.08 lakh women enrolled in 2006–07, reveals the University Grants Commission (UGC) report' (P. V. Nair 2012).

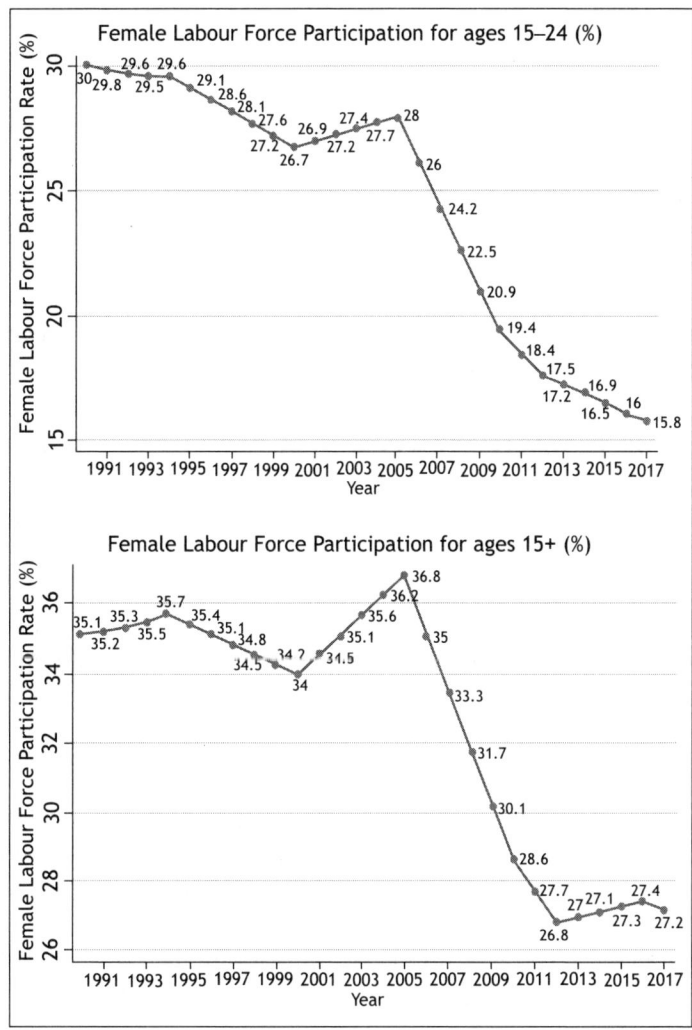

Figure 3.5 *Declining Labour Force Participation of Women*

Source: For the 15–24 age group, see World Bank, 'Labor force participation rate for ages 15–24, female (%) (modeled ILO estimate)', https://data.worldbank.org/indicator/SL.TLF.ACTI.1524.FE.ZS?locations=IN&view=chart (accessed 27 March 2019). For the 15+ age group, see World Bank, 'Labor force participation rate, female (% of female population ages 15+) (modeled ILO estimate)', https://data.worldbank.org/indicator/SL.TLF.CACT.FE.ZS?locations=IN (accessed 27 March 2019).

The expectations that expanding employment opportunities would generate demand for women workers under a liberalised policy regime, and that this would fuel gainful labour migration, are not borne out by the NSS data on either employment or migration. Vast economic reforms over two decades in a society deeply entrenched in patriarchal structures are bound to have a cumulative effect on women. The household is not a unit where one can assume there to be equitable distribution of resources. In such a context, being pushed out of the labour market, or steady informalisation and the resultant erosion of legal protections (for instance, the right to maternity leave), can accentuate women's vulnerability in an already unequal society.

Seasons of Despair and Migration

The millions being forced to look for work—often seasonally—beyond the stagnant countryside hardly ever have a notion of 'choice margin', wherein they engage in a marginal calculation involving free choice between two possibilities. Rather, the reason behind this form of distress labour migration lies in subsistence agriculture itself. A labourer moving from agriculture to wage labour hardly ever makes a rational choice between different possibilities. Making a significant and relevant distinction between a peasant and an agrarian proletarian (or landless agricultural labourer), Lalita Takravarty (1978) contends that while the aforesaid choice margin may be relevant for a peasant, it does not apply to the agrarian proletariat who constitute the majority of migrant workers in India. For most such migrants who are members of the agrarian proletariat, the choices are more often than not between either barely subsisting by working with their bare hands, or dying of slow, invisible starvation.

These are the migrant workers toiling in the prosperous rice, wheat, sugarcane and cotton farms of Punjab, Haryana, western Uttar Pradesh and Maharashtra, construction workers building high-rise structures in cities across the country, semi-bonded workers in the brick kilns that pockmark the country, workers building roads in frontier states with endemic conflict, and so on. Often boys barely in their teens set out to distant lands to earn some money to keep their families alive.

This is evidenced by a major clustering of the 16–40 age group among migrants. But now increasingly families migrate along with women and children, interrupting children's schooling, forcing women to bear and raise children on dusty city streets and in shanties, and leaving behind old people in the village to starve, beg or die. Many of the older generation too are forced to migrate to work in brick kilns or as agricultural labourers.

It is not that the subcontinent is new to migration. Mines, plantations and factories through the years of colonial rule had been fed by distress migration consequent upon famines, the loss of forest rights and land settlement policies. There was also a time in the early 20th century when metropolises like Calcutta and Bombay, or industrial centres like Kanpur, invited and sheltered hundreds of thousands of such impoverished migrants as the aspirant industrial workforce. The condition of these labouring masses in colonial India was abysmal. But certainly there has been a marked shift in recent decades, a noticeable worsening of the lot of these millions living in the long, dark shadows of growth. The twin phenomena of rural distress and rampant casualisation of labour have drastically swelled both the ranks of migrant labourers and the uncertainties they face.

Expelled from an agriculture sector that is being starved and poisoned into a wasteland of despair, these are the teeming millions of young people, the hidden faces of India's youth bulge, who are hopeful that they will be able to build a new future in the cities. But they are increasingly unwelcome in the cities to which they throng, forced to confront a hostile state that treats them as illegitimate citizens of the city. Even as the city consumes their dirt-cheap labour through growing informalisation, they are condemned to living rough on city pavements, or in illegalised shanties without tenure, clean water, sanitation or even a roof and walls to protect them from the elements. Trapped in low-end, unprotected work, these are India's nowhere people—neither gainfully employed in the countryside, nor able to find decent work in cities.

There is an inbuilt assumption promoted by the 'growth' story that this massive human movement from village to cities is actually a sign of good health, that it is an inevitability and is in fact a symptom of India's 'successful' growth policy. Former finance minister of the United Progressive Alliance government P. Chidambaram said in an interview that his dream for India was a country in which 80 per cent lived in cities. However, there is much in these assumptions that needs to be interrogated, not just regarding the sustainability and desirability of this transition, but also the exact facts on which such assumptions rest. We do need to ask that if it is the unprotected drudgery and enforced footloose existence of migrant labourers that feeds this 'development' paradigm, then whose 'development' are we talking about? We do need to ask that if millions of youthful aspirations for better, dignified living are to be sacrificed at the altar of 'growth', then who is earning the dividend out of India's so-called demographic dividend?

The Swelling Reserve of the Footloose

The despair in the countryside, the considerable failure of land reforms and the incumbent landlessness, compounded by crushing debts in the era of globalisation, have made agriculture increasingly unsustainable as a year-round and decent-paying employer. Growth in real wages in agriculture was 5 per cent in the 1980s, but fell to 2 per cent in the 1990s, and virtually 0 per cent in the 2000s. The 2011 census shows that the percentage of the country's population engaged in agriculture is shrinking. An estimated 10 million people abandoned rural India forever in the last decade, but 58 per cent of the country is still employed within the agricultural sector.

As agriculture plays an increasingly small role in GDP (estimates for 2018 indicate a contribution of 14 per cent [at 2011–12 prices] for agriculture and allied services), there are fewer incentives for farmers to stay in the sector. As the costs of inputs increase, agriculture is increasingly getting concentrated in the hands of a small group of dominant-caste feudal landholders who have the capital and the influence to remain in agriculture. As seen from Table 3.3, today, 84.87 per cent of the total holdings belong to marginal farmers who own less than 1 hectare (10,000 square metres), and just 7 per cent own more than 2 hectares as per NSS data on household landownership

Table 3.3 Landholding Pattern in India

Category of holdings	percentage of households		percentage of area owned	
	2002–03 (59th round)	2012–13 (70th round)	2002–03 (59th round)	2012–13 (70th round)
(1)	(2)	(3)	(4)	(5)
landless	10.04	7.41	0.01	0.01
marginal*	69.63	75.42	23.01	29.75
small	10.81	10.00	20.38	23.54
semi-medium	6.03	5.01	21.97	22.07
medium	2.96	1.93	23.08	18.83
large	0.53	0.24	11.55	5.81

Source: As per data on household landownership from *Key Indicators Land and Livestock: NSS 70th Round*, 2013 (MSPI 2014).

*In 2002–03(59th round), the 'marginal' category of land holding included the 'landless' category also. In the above table, for better comparability, the estimates of the round for 'landless' is shown separately and excluded from 'marginal'.

(see MSPI 2014). Tribal people are overrepresented among the landless, SCs among marginal landowners, and 'upper' castes among medium and large landholders. Across the country, in every state, landholdings have decreased in size, almost halving in the last 20 years. The 'growth' years that saw drastic cuts in the government budget for agriculture were accompanied also by a steady diminishing in the size of the average landholding. In 1992, the average rural household was a small landholder with over 1 hectare of land, as compared with 2013, when the average rural household was a marginal landholder with 0.59 hectares of land.

Migration, one might assume, would be relatively rare among agricultural households, but in fact is very high among households with marginal landholdings unable to provide the family much income; over 75 per cent of all migrants come from marginal landowning households. That is to say, while more people who are landless are prone to migrating, the contribution of marginal landholders to total migrants is higher. Seasonal migration is critical to the livelihoods of a vast number of landless labourers and also the vast numbers of partially employed workers in the rural sector. These are people from rural areas who generate a continuous stream of outmigrants destined for cities, numbering around two million a year.

It is therefore the marginal farmers along with the landless—whose numbers have proliferated over the 'growth' decades—who are swelling the ranks of migrant casual workers. Many of them living under crushing debt are prone to getting locked into a debt–migration cycle through some form of labour bondage, where earnings from migration are used to repay debts incurred at home or in the destination areas, thereby cementing the migration cycle and resulting in conditions of neo-bondage in informalised settings propped up on caste/kinship equations.

Over time, the census shows an increase in urban migration and in inter-state migration. Total urban migration as a percentage of total migration increased from 28.7 per cent in 1981 to 29.5 per cent in 1991 and further to 32.85 per cent in 2001 (as calculated from Table 3.4). As a correlate, migration to rural areas declined. Ravi Srivastava (2012) points out that there has been a noticeable increase in rural–urban and urban–urban migration streams. Rural–urban migration increased from 18.8 per cent of total migrants to 19.5 per cent of all migrants between 1999–2000 and 2007–08. In absolute terms, net rural to urban migration rose from about 11 million during 1981–91 to 14 million during 1991–2001 and to about 19 million during 2001–11 at the all-India level.

About 35 per cent of India's urban population is constituted of migrants, according to the NSS survey of 2007–08 (Government of India 2012). Both the census and the NSS confirm an increase in long-distance (inter-state) migration in recent years. Census results show that inter-state migrants as a proportion of total migrants declined marginally from 12.02 per cent in 1981 to 11.82 per cent in 1991, and then increased to 13.31 per cent in 2001. The NSS data specifically shows an increase in inter-state migration between 1999–2000 and 2007–08 in the two urban streams; in the rural–urban stream, the percentage of inter-state migrants increased from 19.6 per cent to 25.2 per cent. But there is a need to examine the trend more closely to arrive at nuanced conclusions.

Table 3.4 *Number of Migrants and Migration Rate, Census Figures, 1981–2001*

Census Year	Place of Resident	Number of Migrants			Migration Rate		
		Persons	Male	Female	Persons	Male	Female
1981	Total	201607061	59235306	142371755	30.3	17.2	44.3
	Rural	143583222	31354273	112228949	28.3	12.1	45.3
	Urban	58023839	27881033	30142806	36.8	33.2	40.8
1991	Total	225887846	61134303	164753543	27.0	14.1	40.9
	Rural	159190095	31196064	127994031	25.6	9.8	42.5
	Urban	66697751	29938239	36759512	31.0	26.3	36.2
2001	Total	309385525	90677712	218707813	30.1	17.0	44.1
	Rural	207773661	42528896	165244765	28.0	11.1	45.8
	Urban	101611864	48148816	53463048	35.5	32.0	39.4

Source: Internal Migration in India Initiative, National Workshop on Internal Migration and Human Development in India (UNESCO and UNICEF 2012).
Note: The Migration figures for 1981 exclude Assam and the 1991 figures exclude J&K.

There is a debate regarding the exact contribution of migration to growth in urban areas. Some have argued that owing to policies promoting 'exclusionary urbanisation', a declining trend is in fact observable in urban migration. Kundu (2009) shows that the three mega cities of Mumbai, Kolkata and Delhi have demonstrated low rates of growth in the last decade, and hence it is not that the cities are going to be inundated by poorer migrants as predicted by the likes of Chidambaram. Recent UN projections have also, in fact, revised their projections of urban growth in India downwards. These contradictory sets of data seem perplexing, but closer observation may provide some answers.

The urban environment and the policy environment have both contributed to an inhospitable rise in the cost of urban migration for the poor. Within total urban migration, the component of urban–urban migration has increased. Since 1992–93, labour market changes along with changes in the urban environment have tended to increase the relative magnitude of the migration of the better off. The poor are finding it more difficult to get a toehold in urban areas. So who, after all, are filling this gap between the rising ranks of the rural destitute and the faltering ranks of permanent migrants to the cities? They are the phenomenally swelling seasonal or circulatory labour migrants who remain virtually invisibilised, informalised and unenumerated—the footloose migrants who make ends meet by combining their seasonal remittances and income from the shrinking agriculture sector. Income from agriculture or land is also used to justify lower wages, helping to keep the labour cost low and thereby contributing to the 'growth' of super-profits.

The NSS 55th Round at the turn of the millennium attempted for the first time to give us an estimate of the number of short-duration outmigrants. It estimated that around 12.24 million people were seeking work for two to six months annually. Of these, 77 per cent are resident in rural areas. The NSS results were suggestive of some increase in seasonal migration, but since the results are not strictly comparable, there was no firm evidence of this. While most migrants were from rural areas, more than two-thirds migrated to urban areas. By 2009–10, some estimates showed that about 35 million to 40 million labourers—almost half the number of casual labourers outside agriculture—and 10 per cent of agricultural labourers (about 9 million) could be seasonal migrants (Srivastava 2012). The linkages between casualisation and seasonal migration are becoming evident, with some studies estimating that 90–95 per cent of casual workers are migrants. The majority of seasonal and temporary migrants are casual workers (31 per cent) or self-employed (26 per cent) in urban areas. About 23 per cent of them are regular workers, 11 per cent were not in the labour force, and 8 per cent were reported to be unemployed. The casual workers and self-employed seasonal and temporary migrants are found to be the most vulnerable to the vagaries of the labour market as they are made to work with no social protection (ibid.).

Seasonal migratory labour is preferred in a large number of industries, but the largest sectors are agriculture, construction, brick kilns, textiles, mines and quarries, large-scale and plantation agriculture, sericulture, head-loaders and coolies, rice mills and other agro-processing industries, salt pans, rickshaws and other types of land transportation, leather manufacture, diamond cutting and polishing, and other unorganised industries that have a seasonal nature. Circulatory labour is concentrated in many other industries including textiles (power looms and garments), manufacturing, domestic and other support services, land transport, head-loaders and others.

Most seasonal/short-duration circulatory migrants are in casualised work, but in some sectors, they could be counted as self-employed (for example, rickshaw pullers or head-loaders) or regular workers (for example, garment workers). The 'growth' years have made the construction sector emerge as the principal industry employing short-duration outmigrants almost entirely as casual labour (see Figure 3.6). Outmigrants constituted 36.2 per cent of those employed in the construction industry, followed by agriculture (20.4 per cent) and manufacturing (15.9 per cent). The nationwide employment data shows

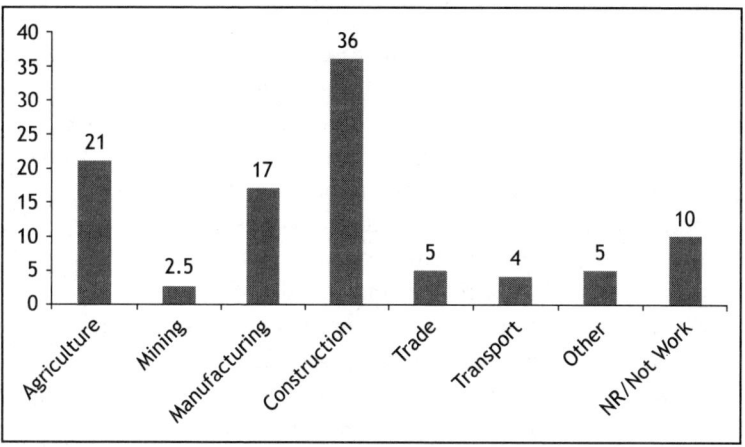

Figure 3.6 *Percentage Distribution of Short-Duration Migrants by Industry in Principal Destination, 2007–08, as per NSS 64th Round*

Source: NSS 64th Round, 2007–08 (Government of India 2012).

Note: The 64th Round of the NSS considered the people who stayed away from their universal periodic review for work/seeking work for a period between one month and six months as short-duration outmigrants, provided further that they had stayed away for more than 15 days in any one spell.

that in 2009–10, there were an estimated 91.4 million casual workers in agriculture and 58.6 million casual workers in non-agriculture. Of the latter, 32 million were employed in the construction industry alone.

The quantitative change over time in seasonal migration in recent decades is difficult to establish in the absence of firm data. However, micro studies based on resurveys indicate an increase in seasonal migration over time. Deshingkar et al. (2008) in their study of villages in Andhra Pradesh and Madhya Pradesh between 2000–01 and 2006–07 indicate an increase in seasonal migration. The percentage of households involved in seasonal migration grew from 40 per cent to 52 per cent over the survey period. Mosse et al. (2005) also report an increase in seasonal migration in the Bhil villages studied by them. As observed earlier, labourers in the construction sector are principally seasonal migrants, and the total number of such workers alone has increased by 26.5 million in the decade 2000–10. This is clear evidence of the increasing currency of seasonal migration in the 'growth' years.

The increasing preference for seasonal migrants is related to the cost-cutting 'free'-market mantra of growth. Employers under this regime are 'free' from responsibility, provision of social security, certainty and adherence to legal guidelines that could determine working hours/conditions. Migrant workers best suit this search for cheap labour, since they have virtually no claims of social or wage security from their employers. The employers also find it easier to discipline migrant labour (that is, the transaction cost of dealing with them is low). And finally, desperate masses of migrant workers with virtually no organisation or bargaining leverage are often more ready to work in areas where local labourers are sometimes unwilling to work because of preferences or because of the hazardous or arduous nature of the work. Studies show that the seasonal and migrant labour supply is highly flexible in terms of work intensity, payment regimes, working hours and so on. Migrant labourers work for long and odd hours. Moreover, payments are not made on time. Piece rates are prevalent, which provides greater flexibility to employers. It has been pointed out that migrants in the urban informal sector often receive lower wages compared with non-migrants. The low wage structure of seasonal work is the result of instability of demand, segmented labour markets, the unregulated nature of seasonal work, the dominance of labour contractors and the vulnerability of these workers.

Figure 3.7 shows a large share of circulatory longer-duration, circulatory shorter-duration, irregular short-term, short-term seasonal and medium-term migrants among both men and women. In the traditionally outmigration-endemic rural areas of central India and tribal-dominated regions such as Andhra Pradesh, north Bihar and eastern Uttar Pradesh, among other areas, the incidence of families with at least one outmigrant ranges from 30 per cent to 70 per cent. Deshingkar et al. (2008) in their survey of villages in Madhya Pradesh find that 52 per cent of households were involved in seasonal migration in 2006–07, mainly to the construction sector. Mosse et al. (2005) find that in 42 Bhil villages studied by them in central-western India, at a conservative estimate, about 65 per cent of households

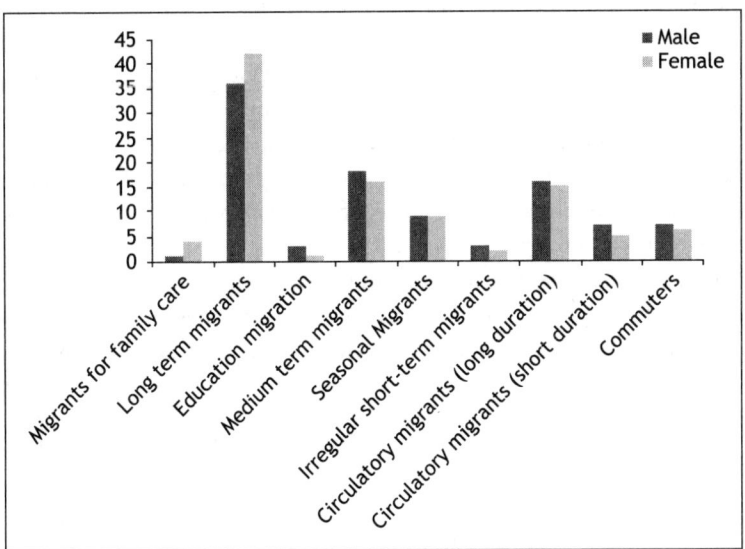

Figure 3.7 *Distribution of Male v. Female Labour Migrants by Type of Migration (Village and Sector Sites Combined)*

Source: Internal Migration in India Initiative, National Workshop on Internal Migration and Human Development in India (UNESCO and UNICEF 2012).

(up to 95 per cent in some villages) and 48 per cent of the adult population were involved in seasonal migration, overwhelmingly for casual urban construction work.

Who Are the Migrants in Seasonal Circulation?

As officially recognised by the *National Commission for Rural Labour Report*, 1991, labourers and farmers with little or no land have a high propensity to migrate as seasonal labourers. There is a preponderance of illiterates among seasonal migrants. Data on individual migrants from micro surveys shows a significant clustering of migrants in the 16–40 age group, in particular among poorer semi-permanent or temporary labour migrants. Further, ST and SC migrants are more often involved in short-term migration (NSS 2001). Both macro data and field studies show that seasonally migrant labour belongs to the most poor and deprived sections of society, such as SCs, STs and OBCs. These migrants are a product of individual and household livelihood deficits (generally due to the absence of assets) and regional resource and livelihood deficits as discussed in the previous chapter. Scheduled Tribes are especially involved in short-duration migration; 18.6 per cent of such migrants were short-duration, compared with only 6 per cent of long-term migrants. Similarly, a higher proportion of SCs were short-duration migrants. Migration of this sort provides subsistence to the workers and their families, but exposes them to a harsh and vulnerable existence, in which working and living conditions are very poor. Jobs in the urban informal sector are highly segmented, and access to them is often based on networks of caste, religion and kinship.[10]

The relative share of women's participation in migration is difficult to gauge, but, if looked into closely, we do see certain disturbing trends. Adding to the lack of recognition given to women's economic activity, an underestimation of female labour migration appears to be inbuilt into the available macro data. Several decades of macro data on migration have, for instance, presented a largely unchanging picture

---

[10] On this, see Vijay (2005) among several others who have studied labour migration and informal sector work in India.

of women's migration mainly for social (largely marital) reasons and men's migration for economic reasons. So, it is male migration that has been used as the primary indicator in development-oriented discussions on migration, instead of a nuanced gendered analysis. This is an important knowledge gap that requires to be overcome by innovation on the part of analysts.

The pattern displayed by male migrants is distinct from that of female migrants. For male migrants, the rural-to-urban migration stream was the most dominant one, comprising nearly 39 per cent of total male internal migrants, while for females, rural-to-rural migration was the dominant stream, comprising nearly 70 per cent of total internal female migrants. Within this, the NSS migration surveys show a fall in employment-oriented migration rates for women, from 3.3 per cent in 1993 to 0.3 per cent by 2008 in rural areas. In urban areas, employment-oriented migration by women has always been marginal, but even this marginal share declined from 1.9 per cent in 1993 to 1.2 per cent in 2008. The employment survey that was conducted in tandem with the 2007–08 migration survey seems to reveal that between 2004–05 and 2007–08, some 13.3 million women were pushed out of the paid and unpaid workforce, around 1.8 million from the paid workforce (Agnihotri 2011).

The share of female migrants in migration-based employment is found to be even lower (15 per cent) than the share of all female workers in the total paid workforce, which stood at 22 per cent by 2008. The only sector in which there has been a concentration of women migrant workers is agriculture. At 34.3 per cent, the share of female labour migration was almost half of the 65 per cent share of agriculture in the country's income-earning female workforce in 2007–08. That apart, there is a clear male domination in the overall migrant workforce: 95 per cent of all migrant workers in trade were male. One finds the same story in manufacturing, where men commanded 88 per cent of migrant jobs. In 2008, migration for construction too seemed to be overwhelmingly male, with the share of women workers being just 10 per cent. This relatively greater male bias in migration for employment implies that the dynamics of labour migration may be playing a role in enhancing gender biases in employment.

An intersectional analysis of the categories of women and other oppressed groups gives a clearer picture of the labour market and the labour relations prevailing therein. Fifty-nine per cent of migrant women workers from STs and 41 per cent from SCs accounted for short-term and circulatory migration. More than 22 per cent of SC women migrants were in brick making, while 28 per cent of ST women migrants were construction workers.

So, the alarming devaluation of women's traditional work along with the endemic stagnation and despair in agriculture is today compounded by the narrow range of options in paid employment opportunities for women. The crisis in the countryside is not being adequately compensated by any diversification in opportunities for women. The predominance of temporary and circular migration, in fact, indicates structural limitations in the possibilities migration has opened up, and thus in effecting durable sectoral/occupational shifts away from agriculture and the degradation of semi-feudal social relations, more so for women migrant workers.

CHAPTER 4

Misplaced Priorities

*Social Sector Expenditure in India—A
Comparative Perspective*

The strongest finding of our study of demographic trends in India in
the 21st century is one of great and persisting if not growing inequality. It tells a story of highly unequal life chances for persons on the
lower rungs of the social and economic order, of growing gender gaps
in life chances even with growing wealth and education, of agriculture
turning into a wasteland of despair, of jobless growth, and a growing
army of young workers desperate for any work on any terms in any
corner of the country.

It is interesting to observe that in the past 15 budget speeches,
the term 'inequality' appeared only twice. The term was mentioned
in the budget speech of 2008–09 and again in the budget speech
of 2016–17. However, according to a recent report published by
New World Health, India is the 12th most unequal country in the
world. Also, as per the Credit Suisse *Global Wealth Databook 2015*,
the richest 1 per cent of India owns 53 per cent of the country's
wealth, and the share of the top 10 per cent is 76.30 per cent (Credit
Suisse 2015).

These contrasting realities make India a unique and challenging country to govern. In this chapter, we will look carefully at the

changes over time in India's public spending, especially in the social sector (education, health and social protection), from an international, comparative perspective. We demonstrate that India can and must spend more on these sectors, and on agriculture, failing which it will continue to squander a great part of its potential demographic dividend.

In other words, we believe that India must strengthen and expand the welfare state for greater justice, but also to realise its growth potential by reaping its full demographic dividend. In simple terms, a welfare state should ensure the equitable distribution of resources and opportunities among citizens in order to maximise their well-being and happiness. Such a state collects adequate taxes from the better-off sections of the country through different means to fund the necessary levels of public spending. The process of collection and distribution of resources may be understood through an analysis of planning and budgeting processes.

In India, both the central and state governments collect funds through taxes, duties, grants and loans, rents on services, etc., and prepare their annual financial statement which is also called the 'budget', that provides details of the expected receipts and estimated expenditure of governments for a definite period of time. The terminologically incomprehensible and vague nature of budget documents makes it extremely difficult for common people to engage with this important aspect of governance, and excludes them from using the budget as a tool to make government more accountable.

The budget also reflects the priorities and ambitions of a government. Given the unique diversity of India, it becomes even more important to understand whether the priorities of the government are equitable and just or not. Who benefits? Who is excluded? How much is spent on different activities that the government is undertaking? What has been the fund utilisation pattern and is it in harmony with the objective of reaping the demographic dividend? These are the questions that one can explore by conscientiously engaging with the planning and budgeting processes of a government.

Government Revenue and Expenditure

We begin with a broad comparison of government revenue and expenditure as a percentage of GDP in India's South Asian neighbourhood as well as across the BRICS nations.

We analysed revenue and expenditure as a proportion of GDP during 2013–16 for the governments of five neighbouring countries in South Asia, namely Bangladesh, Bhutan, China, India and Sri Lanka. We also examined the social sector spending in these countries as a percentage of GDP. Figure 4.1 shows that the revenue generated and expenditure incurred by the Government of India has been less than those of Bhutan and China. China is as populated as India, yet it has managed to generate revenue between 28–29 per cent of its GDP. The Indian government's revenue, on the other hand, is still below 20 per cent of its GDP.

As Figure 4.1 shows, it is clear that China's expenditure is less than its revenue, whereas India spends more than it generates. This has made the difference between revenue generated and expenditure the highest for India among these five countries. This is more likely to enhance India's debt burden and may further adversely affect the budgetary allocation in the social sector and other essential services.

In comparison with BRICS nations, India turns out to be the lowest-performing country both in terms of revenue generated and expenditure incurred as a percentage of GDP. Figure 4.2 shows that both Brazil and Russia are able to generate revenue to the tune of approximately 34 per cent of their GDP. All countries except India maintained a difference of approximately 3–4 per cent between revenue generated and expenditure incurred. It is evident that countries like Brazil, Russia, China and South Africa are able to spend more because they are generating more revenue as compared to India.

It is crucial to understand that greater revenue generation by the government makes room for greater expenditure in the social sector. Unfortunately, overall social sector spending as a percentage of GDP could not be determined for these countries. Also, different countries have different determinants of social sector spending, which becomes

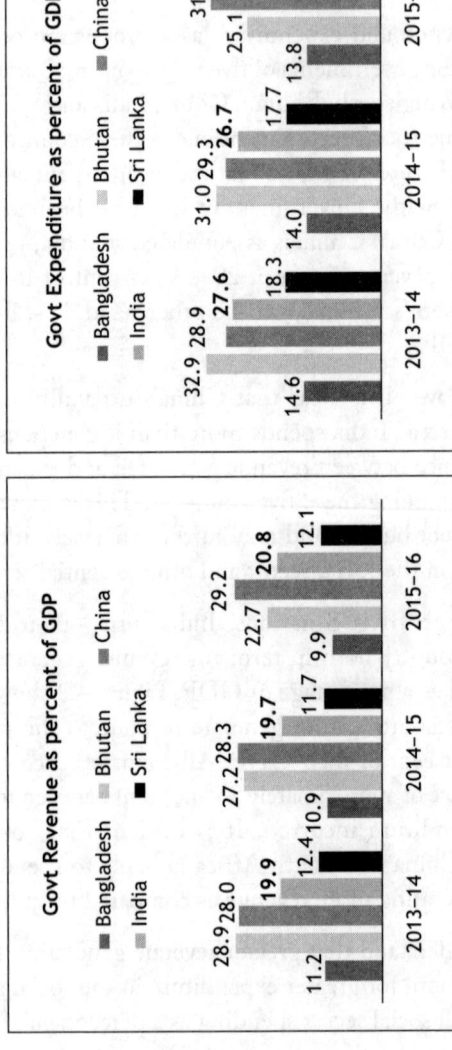

Figure 4.1 *Government Revenue and Expenditure (Percentage of GDP) in India and Neighbouring Countries*

Source: Based on IMF World Economic Outlook Database, 2015.

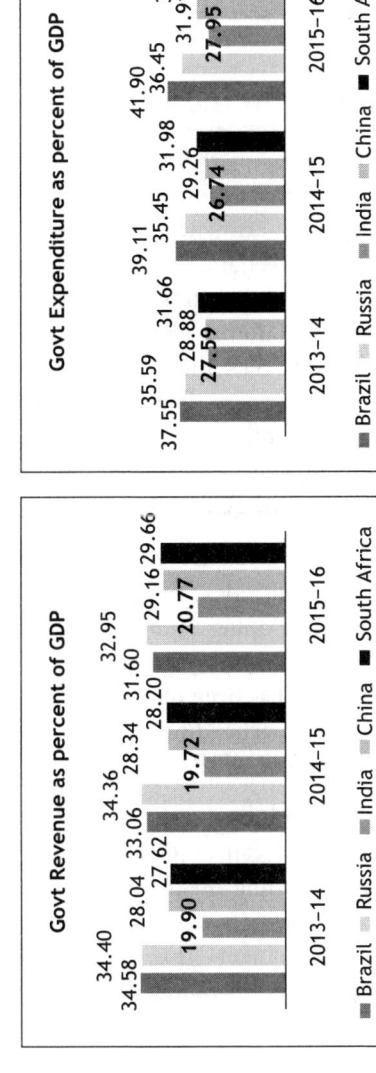

Figure 4.2 *Government Revenue and Expenditure (Percentage of GDP) among BRICS Countries*
Source: IMF World Economic Outlook Database, 2015.

a constraint in undertaking a cross-country comparison of overall social sector spending, for it may cause inconsistency of information. However, the following sections will take up cross-country comparisons of public expenditure as a percentage of GDP in vital social sectors such as education, health, social protection and agriculture.

Social Sector Financing in India

The social sector consists of services that are directed towards the overall development and welfare of society. This sector includes services provided by government departments, such as the departments of education, health and family welfare, nutrition, youth affairs and sports, arts and culture, drinking water and sanitation, social security, housing and urban development, information and broadcasting, labour and employment, welfare of SC/STs and OBCs, and others. This section examines social sector budgetary allocation in India since 1990 as a percentage of GDP; it also offers a cross-country comparative overview of overall government revenue and expenditure as a percentage of GDP in South Asian and BRICS nations.

According to the UNDP's *Human Development Report 2015*, in terms of the human development index, India is ranked 130 out of 188 countries, behind other developing countries such as China, Sri Lanka, Brazil and South Africa. Despite its consistently poor ranking, India's focus on the social sector has been inadequate for many years. Figure 4.3 reflects the change in expenditure on the social sector in India since 1990 as a percentage of GDP.

The data reflects the disappointing state of expenditure on the social sector overall in India. It can be observed that in the last 25 years, overall budgetary spending on the social sector as a percentage of GDP has increased by only 2 percentage points—despite significant levels of poverty and hunger. Also, the contribution of the union government in social sector spending has not increased substantially; over the period 1990–2015, it has increased by a meagre 0.3 per cent of GDP. The contribution of the union government has declined constantly since 2008–09. The current proportion of budget that is being spent on the most vital of the human

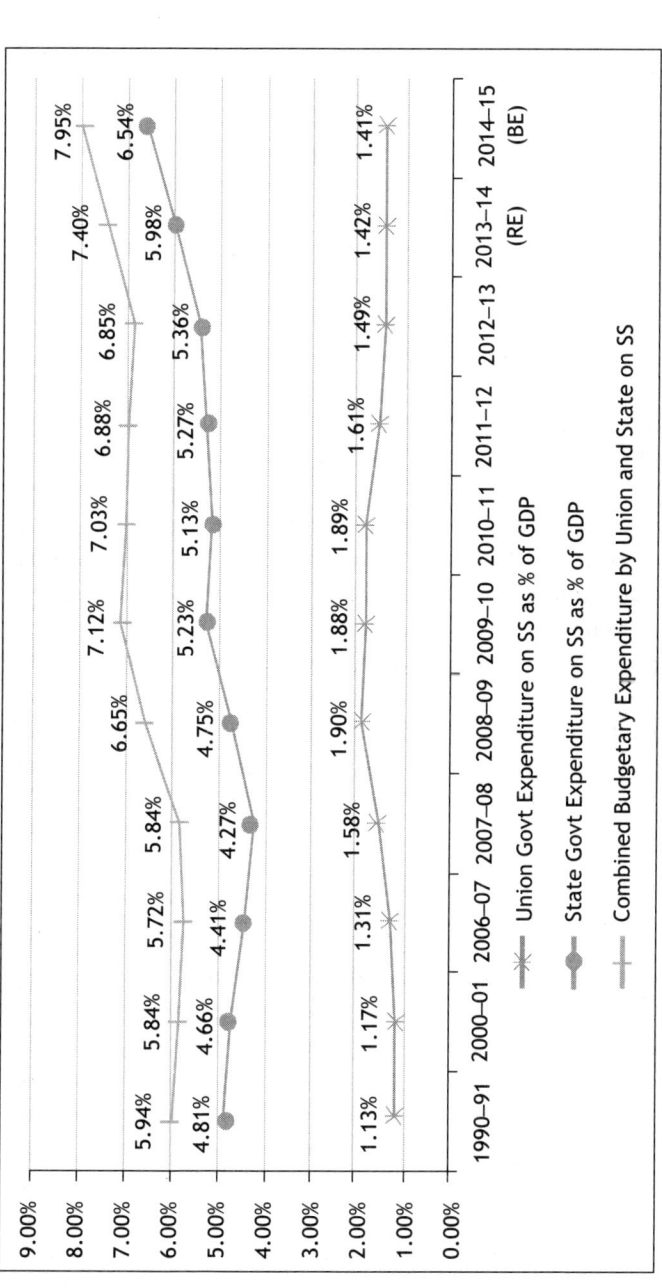

Figure 4.3 *India's Budgetary Spending on the Social Sector (Percentage of GDP), 1990–91 to 2014–15*

Source: Compiled and calculated by the authors from Indian Public Finance Statistics 2014–15.

development indicators in India is significantly lower than that of many developing countries.

Sector-wise Allocation of Funds

As mentioned earlier, the social sector comprises many important sectors that are central to human development—for instance, education, health, drinking water and sanitation, social protection, and housing. Here, four areas—education, health, social protection and agriculture—are taken into consideration, because we regard these as the most critical sectors for public investment in order to realise India's demographic dividend and ensure more equitable life chances. We examine the changes in their respective budgetary allocations over time, and undertake a cross-country comparative analysis among South Asian and BRICS nations. Although agriculture comes under economic services, for a country like India where the majority of the population is still dependent on agriculture for survival, it is important to understand and assess the priorities of the government with respect to this sector, and the sensitivity of our decision makers towards those who are completely dependent on agriculture for their livelihood. Therefore, we also discuss public expenditure in India on agriculture and allied services, and compare this with expenditure on agriculture in other nations.

Education

Education can be one of the most effective instruments of change and equity, as it can ensure greater equality of opportunity, and at its best also encourage the scientific temper for enhancing well-being and free and critical thinking. However, the dismal condition of government schools in India is a reflection of the unsatisfactory efforts in the direction of improving the education system—despite finance ministers invoking education reforms in their budget speeches almost every year. Shortage of both physical and human resources in government schools, poor quality of teachers, the unconducive atmosphere for girls, Dalit, tribal and Muslim children, and for children with disabilities, the lack of provision for clean drinking water and functioning toilets, poverty and migration have been major roadblocks in delivering a decent education to the children of the country.

The *Annual Status of Education Report* (ASER Centre 2015) states that the learning levels of students in both government and private schools are not improving. The UNDP's *Human Development Report 2015* raises serious concerns about the miserable condition of education in India in terms of expected years of schooling and mean years of schooling. According to the report, the expected years of schooling for female and male children in India are 11.3 and 11.8 years respectively, which is lower than in neighbouring countries like China, Sri Lanka and Nepal, and also in other developing nations like Brazil, Russia and South Africa. Similarly, the figure for mean number of years of schooling for females in India is disappointingly low at 3.6 years, while for males it is 7.2 years. The report also reveals that only 27 per cent of women above the age of 25 have at least some secondary education; the corresponding figure for males is almost double at 56.6 per cent (UNDP 2015). Although India has claimed to have achieved a literacy rate of around 74 per cent, the *Human Development Report* and other similar studies such as the *Annual Status of Education Report* put a question mark on the country's achievements in the education sector since independence.

In order to improve the quality of education service delivery, it is very important to allocate sufficient resources—financial, physical and human—to this sector. Figure 4.4 reflects the trends in budgetary spending on education by the union government, state governments, and total spending as a percentage of GDP. It may be observed that the share of the union government in the education budget has not increased much since the 1990s, and has remained constant for almost a decade since 2006. Total public spending on education since 1990 has seen a rise of only 0.62 per cent of GDP. These poor education-related outcomes can certainly be attributed to inadequate allocation of the budget to the sector.

Interestingly, the share of education in overall social sector expenditure has decreased over time since 1990—from 51.4 per cent in 1990 to 46.2 per cent in 2014 (budget estimate [BE]) (see Figure 4.5).

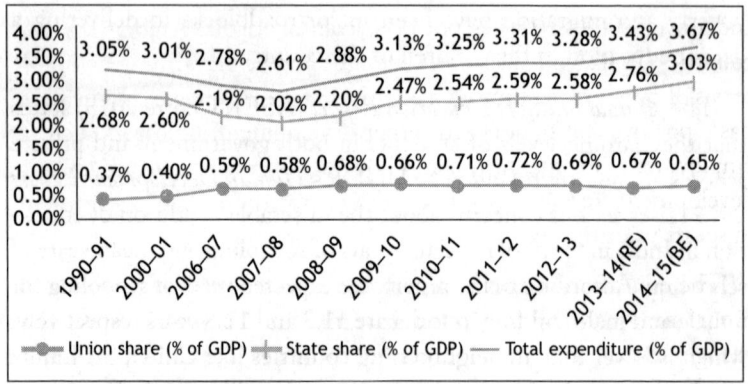

Figure 4.4 *India's Budgetary Spending on Education (Percentage of GDP), 1990–91 to 2014–15*

Source: Compiled and calculated by the authors from Indian Public Finance Statistics 2014–15.

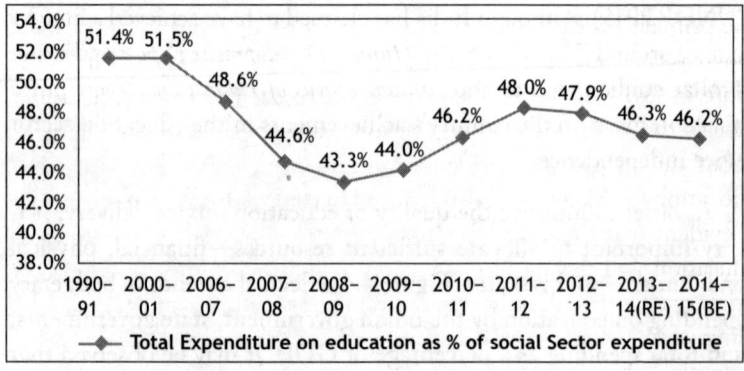

Figure 4.5 *Total Expenditure on Education (Percentage of Social Sector Expenditure)*

Source: Compiled and calculated by the authors from Indian Public Finance Statistics 2014–15.

If we compare the performance of India with its neighbours in terms of public expenditure on education as a percentage of GDP, we find that India ranks behind countries like Nepal, Bhutan and China in its financial priorities with regard to the education sector. Similarly, when compared with BRICS countries, the trend in

India over 2000–2015 has not been commendable. Among BRICS countries, India has consistently been the lowest-performing nation in terms of public expenditure on education (see Figure 4.6). Education has a positive correlation with other development indicators such as employment, income, health and housing. In order to ensure holistic development for all, it is very important for the Indian government to set its priorities right.

The education budget is distributed across multiple schemes and programmes run by the union government. Table 4.1 shows the changes in the budgetary allocation for these schemes and programmes over 2014–17. The table presents the actual expenditure on the respective schemes for 2014–15, the BE and revised estimate (RE) for the year 2015–16, and also the BE for the year 2016–17.

It is clear from the table that most of these schemes experienced a budget cut in 2016–17 (BE) as compared to the actual expenditure in the financial year 2014–15. The SSA, which is directed mainly towards the primary education arena, saw a reduction of about ₹1,500 crore, whereas the allocation for higher education was increased from ₹417 crore in 2014–15 to ₹1,300 crore in 2016–17 (BE). This certainly reveals the priorities of the government and should create concern about the state of primary education in the country. Similarly, the allocation for MDM was also reduced by approximately 9 per cent. It is evident that the government is investing relatively more in higher education and paying less attention to improving the condition of primary education. Public-funded higher education is critical to enabling young people from disadvantaged backgrounds to achieve their potential, but this has to be built on a robust foundation of public-supported universal elementary education.

The illiterate and those educated below the primary level together still make up 50 per cent of the country's population. The SCs and STs continue to feature in abysmally large proportions in the remaining population of uneducated or undereducated. The overrepresentation of such vulnerable groups in the vast reserve of unskilled, casualised workers is hence neither surprising nor unconnected. How budget cuts in the education sector in such a context can ameliorate this condition is a pressing question when one talks of reaping demographic dividends.

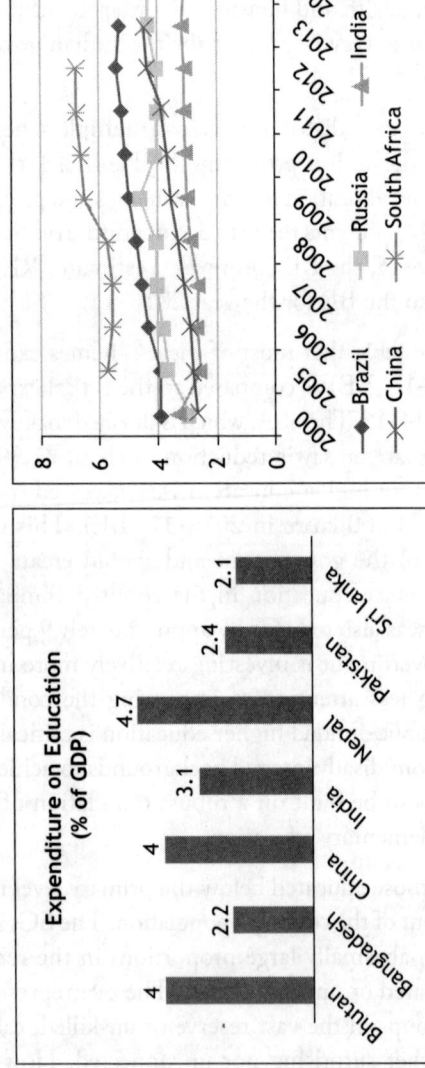

Figure 4.6 Total Public Expenditure on Education (Percentage of GDP), Neighbouring Countries and BRICS

Source: Compiled from UNDP (2013); BRICS Joint Statistical Publication 2015; Statistics of Russia 2015.

Table 4.1 *Budgetary Allocation for Select Schemes in Education (in ₹Crore)*

Schemes	2014–15	2015–16 (BE)	2015–16 (RE)	2016–17 (BE)
NEM: Sarva Shiksha Abhiyan (SSA)	24,097	22,000	22,015	22,500
NEM: Rashtriya Madhyamik Shiksha Abhiyan	3,398	3,565	3,565	3,700
NEM: Rashtriya Uchchatar Shiksha Abhiyan	417	1,155	1,055	1,300
NEM: Teacher Training and Saakshar Bharat	1,158	1,397	1,203	879
Scheme for Providing Education to Madrasa and Minorities	119	376	336	120
Kendriya Vidyalaya Sangathan	3,243	3,278	3,278	3,795
Navodaya Vidyalaya Sangathan	2,013	2,061	2,285	2,471
Mid-Day Meal (MDM)	10,523	9,236	9,236	9,700
Indian Institutes of Technology and Indian Institutes of Management	4,273	4,949	4,463	5,714

Health and Family Welfare

In the established Indian federal arrangement, health is a subject in the state list of the Indian Constitution (Schedule 7, List II, Clause 6), which implies that the primary responsibility of delivering health services lies with state governments. However, the central government also contributes resources for improving the public health system of the country, by initiating new schemes and sponsoring various existing schemes related to public health and family welfare.

The ailing state of healthcare in India becomes clear from a recent incident. An impoverished man named Dana Manjhi of Odisha was forced to carry his wife's dead body for 12 kilometres after the hospital refused to provide him an ambulance to carry the corpse back home (Sahu 2016). Such is the condition of our healthcare and the apathy of health service providers towards powerless people. This is only one of many such incidents that the disadvantaged sections of society experience on a regular basis. There are stories of women delivering their babies outside health centres because the latter were not equipped to carry out the delivery process, because of which the women did not get the requisite medical attention in time (Rozindar 2016). Lack of resources and insufficient funds to cater to the demand for public healthcare are often cited as excuses for this situation. Those who cannot afford expensive private hospitals or cannot purchase costly insurance policies for themselves and their families are largely dependent on relatively cheaper public health facilities for their health-care needs. Improper healthcare services for the poor push many of them back into poverty because of high out-of-pocket expenditure on health, which adds to their debt burden. The miserable state of public healthcare in India increases the reliance of people on private practitioners, who charge huge amounts as consultation charges—not including the cost of medicines. Lack of resources—financial, physical, human—is directly related to the funds that government allocates for public health delivery.

Public health commentator Vikram Patel says:

> Put simply, India's healthcare system is one of the greatest stains on the conscience of our modern State, for it is one of the most regressive in the world. At one end of the healthcare spectrum, people get pampered in hospitals, which could comfortably double-up as luxury hotels, receiving unnecessary interventions aimed primarily at recouping the investments of their promoters, while at the other end, people who desperately need medicines or surgeries are denied their basic right to life. (Patel 2015)

Patel observes that in human development, India lags behind even 'Iraq, which despite a decade-long conflict enjoys a higher life expectancy than India' (ibid.). The solution, he says, is universal health coverage: 'a national healthcare system which integrates both the public and private sectors, operating with a common set of standards and regulations, where all citizens are guaranteed accountable and quality care which is free at the point of delivery is one practical concept among many others' (ibid.).

The answer to the question of how to go about this is also patently clear from countries around the world which have fixed their health-care systems in recent decades. This section examines the state of healthcare financing in India and the trend in the past few years in the budgetary allocations for health and family welfare. A comparison with neighbouring countries and BRICS nations highlights the position of India and the seriousness of our political representatives with regard to one of the gravest human development issues.

Figure 4.7 reflects the budgetary expenditure since 1990 on health and family welfare, including the water supply and sanitation budget. The figure shows that the share of the union government in public healthcare financing in India has remained constant over 1990–2015. The share of government is also much below satisfactory levels. The overall public spending on health increased from 1.42 per cent of GDP in 1990 to 1.54 per cent of GDP in 2014–15 (BE)—this is after India's GDP had grown, the country's overall wealth had increased, and per capita income saw a tremendous rise since the economic reforms of 1991.

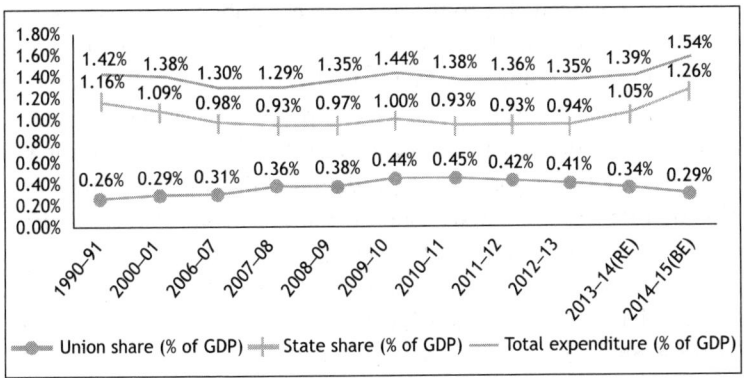

Figure 4.7 *India's Budgetary Spending on Health and Family Welfare (Per Cent of GDP)*

Source: Compiled and calculated by the authors from Indian Public Finance Statistics 2014–15.

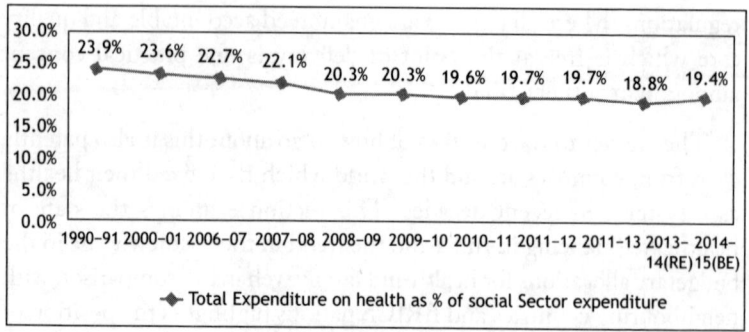

Figure 4.8 *Total Expenditure on Health and Family Welfare (Percentage of Social Sector Expenditure)*

Source: Compiled and calculated by the authors from Indian Public Finance Statistics 2014–15.

It is disheartening to see (Figure 4.8) that the share of health and family welfare in overall social sector expenditure has been declining since 1990—from 23.9 per cent of the total to 19.4 per cent of total social sector spending. This unfortunate trend is contrary to what the current public healthcare system demands. It also reflects the misplaced priorities of the Indian government. After 71 years of independence, India has not been able to provide a decent public healthcare system to its people. It is understood that merely increasing the amount of allocation is not going to solve the problems of the public healthcare system, but it is certainly the first step towards satisfactory public health service delivery to people who are highly dependent on it and who also are the majority of the Indian population. It is unfortunate that despite the celebrated economic reforms of the 1990s, subscription to the millennium development goals and the current focus on sustainable development goals, the state of the public healthcare system in India has remained abysmal, with people positioned at the bottom of the economic pyramid being the worst hit.

Figure 4.9 attempts to position India among its neighbours and BRICS nations in terms of public health expenditure as a percentage of GDP. It can be observed that the situation is terrible in India. Among its neighbours, India is far behind China, Bhutan, Nepal and also

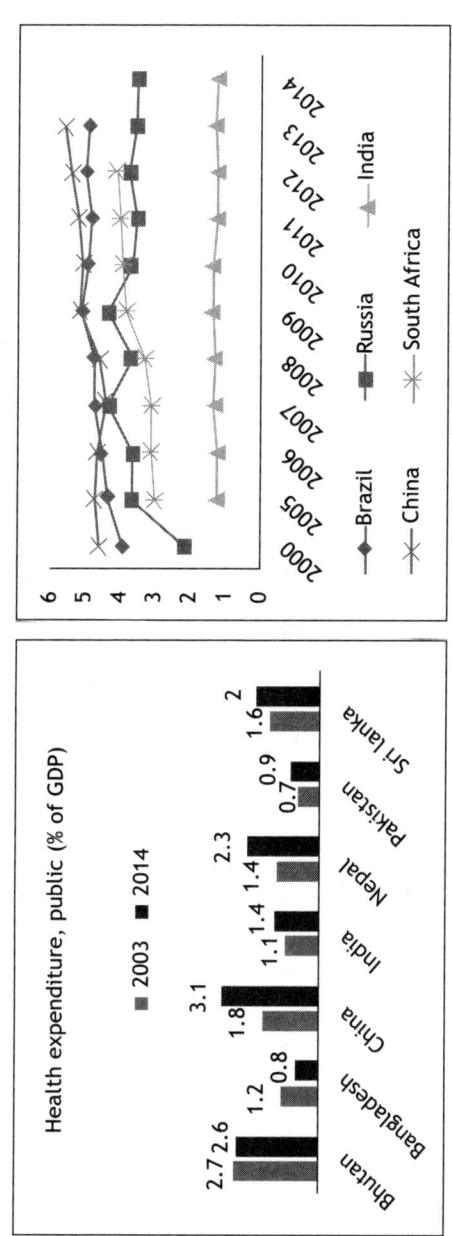

Figure 4.9 *Total Public Expenditure on Health (Percentage of GDP), BRICS and Neighbouring Countries*

Source: WHO Global Health Expenditure Database; BRICS Joint Statistical Publication 2015; Statistics of Russia 2015.

Sri Lanka in terms of public health spending. India also occupies the lowest position among BRICS nations in its financial responsiveness towards the public healthcare system. Brazil, Russia, China and South Africa are much ahead of India in financing their public healthcare systems. Also, basic health-related indicators like IMR, MMR and malnutrition levels are worse in India compared to other South Asian countries such as Bangladesh and Sri Lanka. The public health infrastructure is in crisis because of inadequate human resources, especially in rural areas. It is time that our political representatives realise the role of a good healthcare system in the overall development of a country and its economy. An anaemic woman cannot give birth to a healthy child, a malnourished child cannot become a responsive citizen, and an unhealthy labourer cannot be industrially productive. Therefore, attention needs to be directed towards providing sufficient healthcare services to people and also ensuring that everyone has access to safe drinking water and sanitation facilities.

Table 4.2 presents the changes in the budgetary allocations of a few health sector schemes being run by the union government—the National Health Mission (NHM), the Pradhan Mantri Swasthya Suraksha Yojana, the Rashtriya Swasthya Bima Yojana and the Jan Aushadhi Scheme. The table presents the actual allocations for the financial years 2012–13, 2013–14 and 2014–15, and also the RE for 2015–16 along with the BE for 2016–17.

The NHM, which consists of the National Rural Health Mission and the National Urban Health Mission, is a national-level programme to ensure effective healthcare for everyone, and primarily for people living in rural areas. Under this initiative, the government runs various schemes for children and women and to improve healthcare systems in the country. The budget for NHM is shared between the central and state governments. The core strategies of NHM as per the government documents are: decentralised village- and district-level health planning and management, appointment and training of ASHA (accredited social health activist) workers, mainstreaming of AYUSH (Ayurveda, Yoga and Naturopathy, Unani, Siddha and Homoeopathy), improved management capacity of health systems, improved intersectional convergence, and strengthening the responsibility of Panchayati Raj

Table 4.2 Allocations across Select Schemes in the Health Sector (in ₹Crore)

Schemes	2012–13 (Actual)	2013–14 (Actual)	2014–15 (Actual)	2015–16 (RE)	2016–17 (BE)
National Health Mission (NHM)*	18,046.70	18,633.80	19,751.40	19,122.01	19,037
Pradhan Mantri Swasthya Suraksha Yojana**	989	1,273.20	822	1,621.00	2,450.00
Rashtriya Swasthya Bima Yojana (RSBY)***	1,001.7	887.5	550.6	658.8	1,743.70
Jan Aushadhi Scheme#	1.7	15.2	–	16.9	35

Source: CBGA (2016: 16–18).

* The figures for 2016–17 include only the NHM component of the umbrella programme NHM including AYUSH NACO and Medical Research, as mentioned in the NITI Aayog report. Thus, figures do not include Human Resources in Health & Medical Education, National Mission on AYUSH including Mission on Medicinal Plants, and National AIDS & STD Control Programme.

** PMSSY is the scheme for 'establishment of AIIMS type super-speciality hospitals-cum-teaching institutions and upgrading of State Government hospitals'.

*** The figures include the allocations for RSBY under both the Ministry of Health and Family Welfare and the Ministry of Labour and Employment. Since 2015–16, RSBY has been divided into two distinct components—social security for unorganised workers and provision for health services. The card would be provided by the Ministry of Labour and Employment and the health services would be provided by the Ministry of Health and Family Welfare.

The Jan Aushadhi scheme is under the Department of Pharmaceuticals, Ministry of Chemicals and Fertilisers.

institutions to increase community ownership in the effective delivery of healthcare services. Although the absolute amount allocated for NHM increased between 2012–13 and 2016–17, it is important to note here that the amount allocated in the BE of 2016–17 was less than the actual amount spent on NHM in 2014–15, and also the RE of the previous financial year, 2015–16. The allocation for the other three schemes, that is, Pradhan Mantri Swasthya Suraksha Yojana,

Rashtriya Swasthya Bima Yojana and Jan Aushadhi Yojana, increased compared to previous years' allocations.

Increase in the allocation amount is certainly a welcome step, but the next big challenge that confronts the implementers of the programmes is the utilisation of the allocated funds. A report by the Comptroller and Auditor General of India mentions that in 2014–15, nearly 70 per cent of savings (or unutilised funds) remained under the head 'Establishment of AIIMS Type Super-Specialty Hospitals-cum-Teaching Institutions and Upgrading of State Government Hospitals'. Therefore, there is now a double challenge before India: to allocate sufficient amounts to different healthcare schemes that are meant to benefit the most disadvantaged of our society, and also to make sure that the allocated amount is spent judiciously in order to bring necessary changes in the healthcare system.

Social Security and Protection

The contribution of labour in an economy cannot be overstated, as workers are the backbone of a productive economy. However, the labour force in general, and those who are part of the unorganised sector in particular, need some sort of social security in terms of better living conditions, healthcare, pension provisions and so on, to remain productive in their lives and to continue to contribute effectively to the growth of the economy. Apart from workers, there are other sections of society, for instance, senior citizens (approximately 8 per cent of the population), persons with disability, children and widows, who need an adequate support system from the state. Many of these people are also workers, although they work most often in invisible, undervalued, unpaid or low-paid work. The government budget for social security is meant to cater to people who are disadvantaged and need social support to live with basic dignity and security. This section discusses past trends and the current situation of public expenditure on social security along with labour and employment in India.

The total combined budget for social security, labour and employment of the union government and state governments is presented in Figure 4.10. The figure reveals the expenditure on social security and

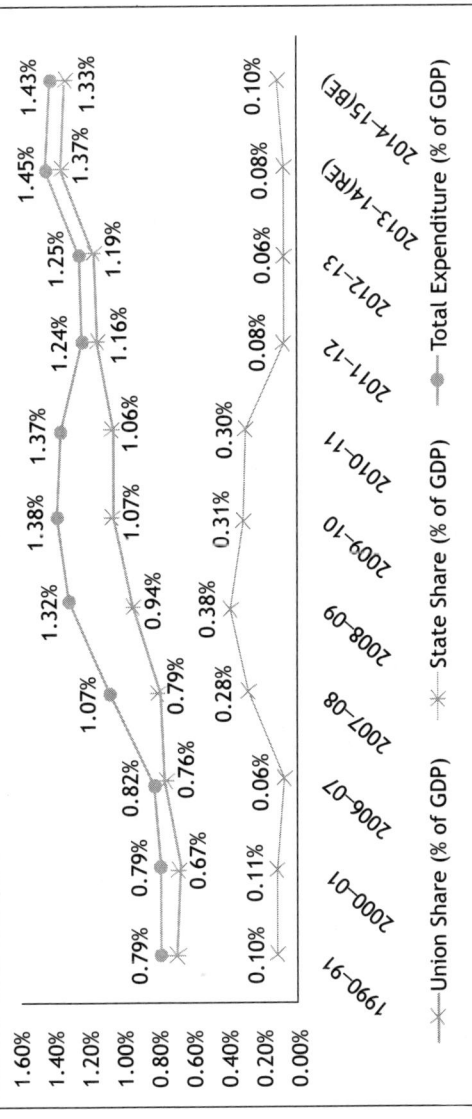

Figure 4.10 *Public Expenditure on Social Security and Welfare and Labour and Employment in India (Percentage of GDP)*

Source: Compiled and calculated by the authors from Indian Public Finance Statistics 2014–15.

welfare, and labour and employment, in India as a percentage of GDP since 1990. It can be observed that the share of the union government in social security spending has remained constant, except for a small increase during a brief period (2006–07 to 2008–09). On the other hand, the share of states has increased from 0.69 per cent in 1990–91 to 1.33 per cent in 2014–15 (BE).

As enunciated in a report published by the ILO in 2003, a well-designed system of social protection contributes through enabling people to enhance their well-being and security by protecting them from life's dreaded vulnerabilities and threats. It also provides access to basic survival needs to all citizens of a country, and helps unleash fuller human potential.

The ILO publishes reports on the state of social protection-related schemes and provisions in countries across the world. Figure 4.11 indicates the state of public spending on social protection in India's neighbouring countries and also in the BRICS nations, as a percentage of GDP. The figure also reveals how expenditure on social protection is distributed between children, people in their active 'working' age, and senior citizens.

It can be observed from Figure 4.12 that India's performance has been consistently poor for all age categories in comparison to most of its neighbours, and especially China. Whereas India spends only 2.46 per cent of its GDP on social protection-related schemes, countries like China, Bhutan, Sri Lanka and Bangladesh have been spending 6.83, 4.77, 3.14 and 2.56 per cent of their GDP respectively on social protection.

India also lags behind China and Sri Lanka in taking care of its senior citizens in terms of public spending on social protection for elderly people. The ILO's social protection report (ILO 2014) reveals that only 24.1 per cent of the elderly population receives some kind of old age pension benefits. This number is way lower than in countries like China (74.4 per cent), Nepal (62.5 per cent) and Bangladesh (39.5 per cent).

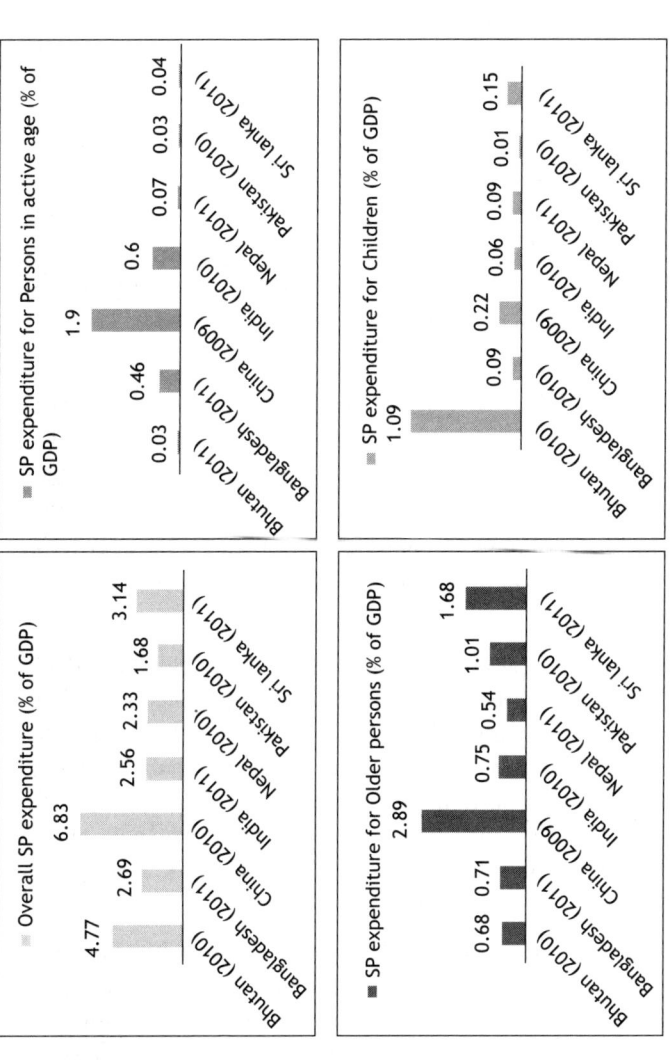

Figure 4.11 Public Social Protection Expenditure (Percentage of GDP), Neighbouring Countries and BRICS

Source: Compiled by the authors from ILO (2014).

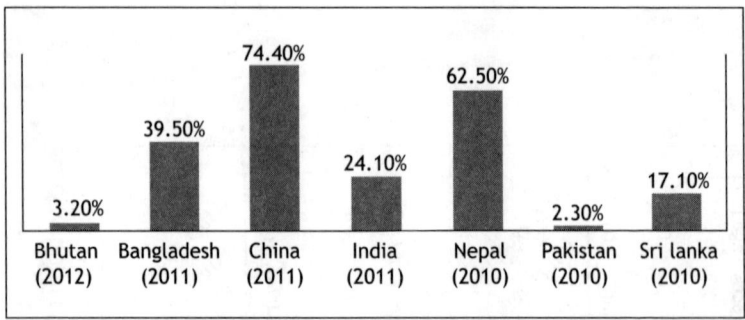

Figure 4.12 *Old Age Effective Coverage: Old Age Pension Beneficiaries (as Percentage of Population above Statutory Pension Age), Neighbouring Countries*
Source: ILO (2014).
Note: The data is for the latest available year (mentioned in parentheses).

Similarly for children, the situation in India is not satisfactory. Compared to India, all other countries except Pakistan are spending more on their children as a percentage of their GDP, in order to provide them state support to enhance their survival chances, education and well-being.

If we compare the public spending on social protection for BRICS nations (Figure 4.13), we find that India is lagging compared with all other nations, namely Brazil, Russia, China and South Africa, in its spending commitments on social protection. Brazil, Russia and China are spending huge proportions to the tune of 29.29 per cent, 15.97 per cent and 9.79 per cent of their GDPs respectively. India on the other hand allocates only 2.56 per cent of its GDP on social protection expenditure.

As is evident, social spending on labour in India has remained highly inadequate. However, while stating this, it ought to be kept in mind that we are here referring to a miniscule number of dwindling formal sector workers. Nine out of 10 workers in India work in the informal sector with no social protection whatsoever.

Among the BRICS nations, India's commitment towards the social protection of its senior population as reflected in public spending as

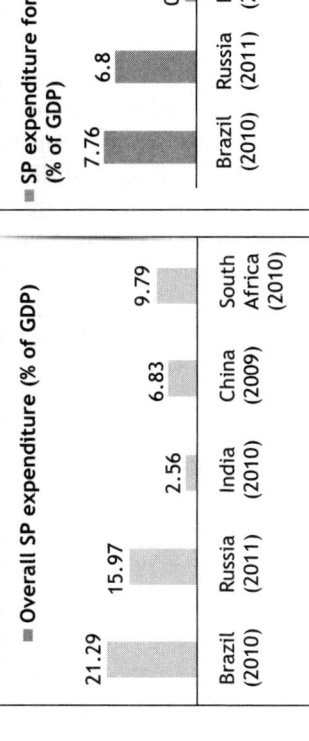
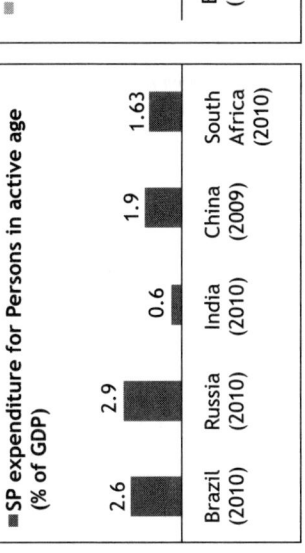
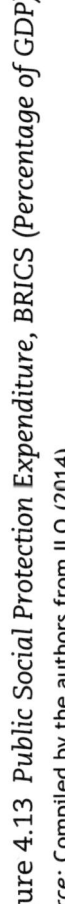

Figure 4.13 *Public Social Protection Expenditure, BRICS (Percentage of GDP)*
Source: Compiled by the authors from ILO (2014).

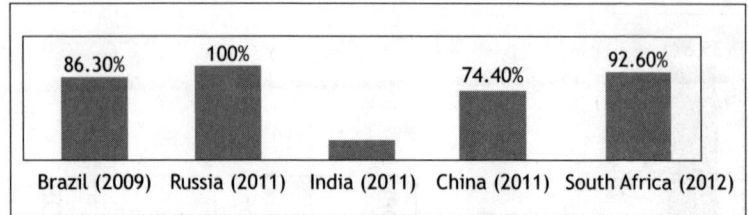

Figure 4.14 *Old Age Effective Coverage: Old Age Pension Beneficiaries (as a Percentage of Population above Statutory Pension Age), BRICS*
Source: ILO (2014).
Note: The data is for the latest available year (mentioned in parentheses).

a percentage of GDP has been abysmally low. The proportion is not even 1 per cent for people who constitute 8 per cent of India's population. However, as mentioned earlier, only 24.1 per cent of people of statutory pension age are getting some kind of old age pension benefits in India—the number is way lower than in countries like Brazil (86.3 per cent), Russia (100 per cent), China (74.4 per cent) and South Africa (92.6 per cent) (Figure 4.14).

It is projected that the youth bulge will eventually fade and there will be an increase in the elderly population. However, a second phase of the demographic dividend will be possible if adequate social protection could be ensured today for our ageing population. The absence of such protection will only bring more hardships and lack of opportunities for them in the future.

Mahatma Gandhi National Rural Employment Guarantee Scheme

The National Rural Employment Guarantee Act led to the establishment of NREGA in 2005. The scheme was initiated to grant legal rights to people, particularly in rural areas, who are unemployed. The scheme entitles an individual to demand 100 days of employment per year. Under this scheme, if the work is not provided in the legally stipulated time frame, then the person is entitled to unemployment

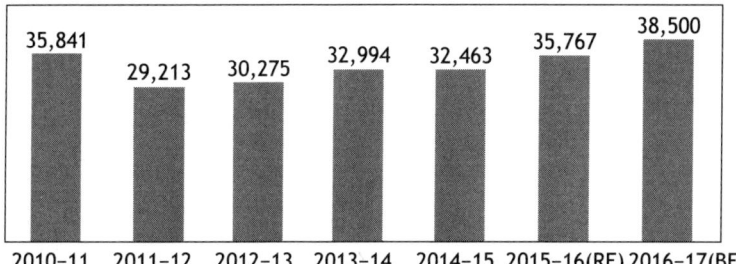

Figure 4.15 *Union Budget Allocations for NREGA (in ₹Crore)*
Source: Compiled by the authors from Government of India, *Budget Book*, vol. II, Department of Rural Development, 2010–11 to 2016–17; CBGA (2016).

benefits. Acknowledged as one of the largest rights-based integrated employment and social protection initiatives in the world, NREGA covered close to 50 million rural households—approximately 30 per cent of rural households—in 2012. Figure 4.15 presents the actual allocations on NREGA for the financial years 2010–11 to 2014–15 and the RE and BE for 2015–16 and 2016–17 respectively.

The finance minister claimed that he had allocated the highest ever resources to NREGA in the 2016 budget. However, allocations have actually fallen significantly in real terms from the peak of 0.6 per cent of GDP in 2010–11 to 0.26 per cent of GDP in 2016–17. Also, if the 2010–11 allocations are adjusted for inflation, allocations in 2016–17 should be higher than ₹66,000 crore to actually qualify as the highest ever. The allocations made in the budget of 2016–17 were ₹38,500 crore. Of this, as much as ₹12,590 crore is required to meet the record high of pending liabilities at the end of the financial year 2015–16. Therefore, the amount of resources available to meet wage demands in the current year is only ₹25,910 crore.

What does this huge bill of pending liabilities represent? It means simply that workers have not been paid wages for work done, often for several months. If wages are delayed so extensively, then a precariously surviving impoverished person cannot rely on NREGA to extend wage and social protection in normally lean times—even less in times of acute distress during drought scarcity. In effect, by deliberately delaying fund releases to states, the central government ensures that fewer and fewer workers actually demand work under the programme. This is, under the law, a demand-led programme, in which the central government is legally bound to provide all the resources needed to meet demand for work up to 100 days per rural household. Chronically delayed payments amount to a killing of demand for work, and thereby a subversion of the purposes of the law.

Agriculture and Allied Services

According to the census of 2011, approximately 54 per cent of India's population is engaged in agriculture and allied services. Agriculture also contributes 17.4 per cent of the country's gross value added (current price 2014–15, 2011–12 series). We have already observed the depth of the chronic agrarian crisis, and seen that the failure of land reforms, extreme and mounting indebtedness, landlessness and unviable holdings, unequal integration with global markets, and the agro-ecological crisis are some of the reasons for this crisis. It is aggravated by extremely low public investments in agriculture.

We therefore place very high stress not only on higher social spending but also greatly enhanced public spending in agriculture, to protect farmer incomes, promote small-farm sustainable agriculture and build rural infrastructure. The bottom line is that in order to reverse the decades-old agrarian crisis, the problems pertaining to agriculture and the distress experienced by people associated with farming, the government needs to invest more in policies that are favourable to farmers, especially small farmers, farm workers and artisans in rain-fed regions of the country. Figure 4.16 reveals the share of the union government and state governments as a percentage of GDP in overall budgetary spending on agriculture and allied services in India. It is evident that in the sector on which at least 54 per cent of our population is dependent, and that contributes 17 per cent of our gross value added, overall government spending is just 2.92 per cent of GDP. Although there has been an increase in both the union and the state shares in spending on agriculture and allied services since 1990, it is

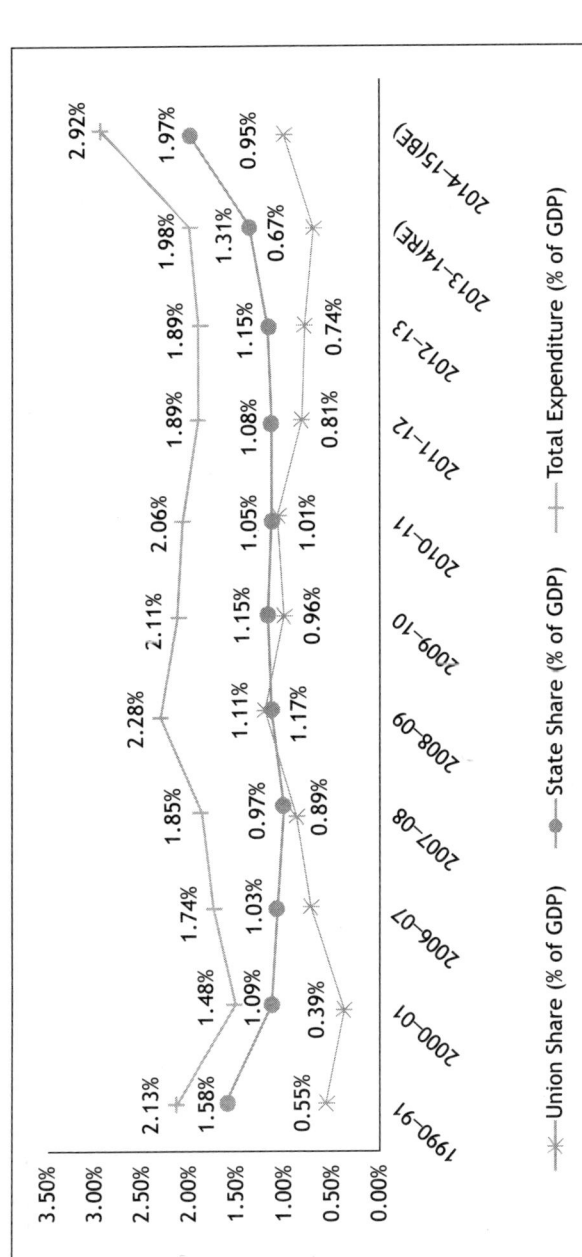

Figure 4.16 *India's Budgetary Spending on Agriculture and Allied Services (Percentage of GDP)*

Source: Compiled and calculated by the authors from Indian Public Finance Statistics 2014–15.

still woefully inadequate for the farming community, which is in grave distress—distress that if not addressed could become terminal, with calamitous human and social consequences.

Table 4.3 looks at a few schemes run by the Ministry of Agriculture and Farmers' Welfare. The table contains the actual expenditure data for the financial year 2014–15, budget and RE data for the year 2015–16 and the BE data for the year 2016–17 for these schemes.

It can be observed that except the Pradhan Mantri Fasal Bima Yojana and Pradhan Mantri Krishi Sinchai Yojana, the allocated amount under all other schemes has decreased since 2014–15. It is interesting to note that the allocation for an insurance scheme has

Table 4.3 *Allocations across Select Schemes under the Ministry of Agriculture and Farmers' Welfare (in ₹Crore)*

Schemes	2014–15	2015–16 BE	2015–16 RE	2016–17 BE
Pradhan Mantri Fasal Bima Yojana*	2,598	2,589	2,955	5,501
Rashtriya Krishi Vikas Yojana	8,443	4,500	3,900	5,400
Krishonnat Yojana	9,823	9,056	8,884	7,580
National Food Security Mission	1,873	1,300	1,137	1,706
Paramparagat Krishi Vikas Yojana	NA	300	250	297
Pradhan Mantri Krishi Sinchai Yojana	NA	1,800	1,550	2,340
Pradhan Mantri Krishi Sinchai Yojana **	2,319	3,530	6,040	3,427

Source: CBGA (2016).

* Pradhan Mantri Fasal Bima Yojana includes the existing National Agriculture Insurance Scheme, weather-based crop insurance scheme, the Modified National Agricultural Insurance Scheme being implemented through the Agriculture Insurance Corporation, and the Coconut Palm Insurance Scheme.

** These are provisioned under the Department of Land Resources and Ministry of Water Resources, River Development and Ganga Rejuvenation.

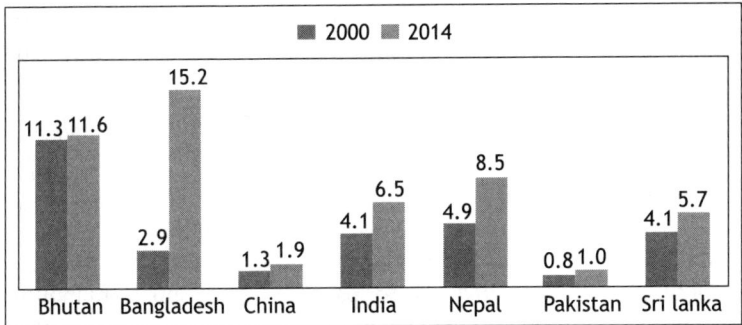

Figure 4.17 *Government Expenditure on Agriculture (Per Cent Total Outlays)*
Source: FAO (2015).

doubled in the past two years. The amount under the National Food Security Act has meanwhile seen a reduction of more than ₹100 crore between 2014–15 and 2016–17.

Figure 4.17 depicts the government expenditure on agriculture as a percentage of total government outlays for the years 2000 and 2014. Although government expenditure on agriculture as a percentage of total outlays has increased, India is still behind countries like Bhutan, Bangladesh and Nepal. The chronic agrarian crisis, mounting suicides, indebtedness and swelling of the ranks of agrarian labourers feeds the pool of those forced to migrate, often seasonally, in search of work under any conditions in the growing casualised sector.

Budgets for Different Marginalised Communities

SCs and STs

According to census 2011 data, the proportion of SCs and STs in the country's population is 16.2 and 8.2 per cent respectively. We have discussed the highly unequal life chances for SCs and STs across all aspects of social and economic life. In addition, the Ministry of Rural Development recently published the results of the SECC. The data primarily reveals the status of SCs and STs in India. The SECC data highlights the harsh realities in which SC and ST populations live. The data reveals that in 83.55 per cent of rural SC households, the monthly income of the highest-earning member is less than ₹5,000, and in 11.74 per cent of households, the income is between ₹5,000 and ₹10,000—which means that in 95 per cent of rural households, the monthly income of the highest-earning member is less than ₹10,000. The data also highlights that approximately 55 per cent of rural SC households derive a major part of their income from manual casual labour. Only approximately 5 per cent of households have members with salaried jobs either in the public or the private sector. Approximately 18 per cent have unirrigated land. Similarly, the data for rural ST households indicates that in approximately 87 per cent of households, the monthly income of the highest-earning member is less than ₹5,000 and approximately 96 per cent of rural ST households have highest-earning members with monthly income less than ₹10,000. The report also highlights that as many as 43 per cent of households own unirrigated land.

The SC and ST communities are among the most disadvantaged in India. The persisting reality of backwardness of these communities rings alarm bells for the need to provide special and timely attention in order to deal with the issues of exclusion and discrimination against them—both at the policy and at the societal level. India's Planning Commission in the 1970s introduced special plan strategies—the SCSP and Tribal Sub Plan (TSP)—for directly benefiting these communities. These sub-plans were aimed at channelling funds for the development of these communities at levels of budget expenditure that at least matched their proportion in the overall population of the country (see Figure 4.18).

Figure 4.18 reveals the budgetary outlays during 2012–17 under SCSP and TSP. The BE amount for 2016–17, when compared to the actual allocations of previous years, appears high. However, a report prepared by the Centre for Budget and Governance Accountability states:

the outlays in the Scheduled Caste Sub Plan (SCSP) have also witnessed a steep decline since 2014–15 (BE) when it was around

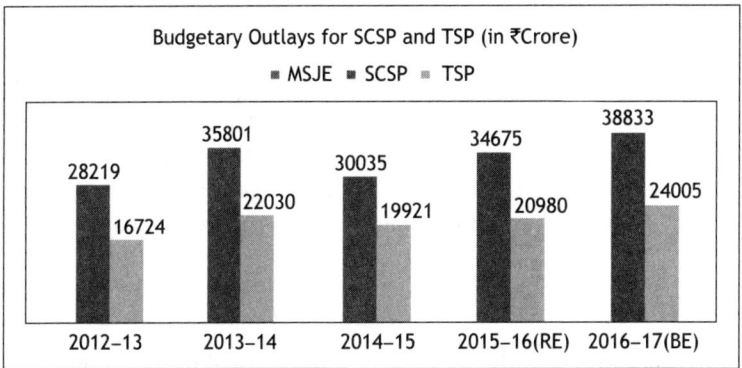

Figure 4.18 *Government Expenditure on the Scheduled Caste Sub Plan and Tribal Sub Plan*
Source: CBGA (2016).

Rs. 43,000 crore. This is primarily owing to (i) overall decline on the Union Government's Plan outlays on social sector schemes, and (ii) Reduced share of the Union Government in majority of CSS [centrally sponsored schemes] which are reported in SCSP. (CBGA 2016: 34)

It usually happens that the actual amount spent on a programme or scheme is less than the BE for that year. Paying attention to the BE of a year reveals a lot about the real intentions of the government. Underutilisation of funds brings down the actual amount spent on a particular programme. This should be a serious concern, apart from the poor budgetary allocation. It is also important to make sure that, in handing out 'incidental' benefits to these communities, the actual budgetary commitment does not remain inadequate.

A report by John Kumar (2013) on the Special Component Plans (SCP) in Tamil Nadu also reveals the lopsidedness of the claims of increased allocation under the SCSP and the TSP. The report states that 'what had been so far general/common programme meant for all (poor/marginalised) people, have been brought and shown under the SCP with a certain proportion of fund culled out of general schemes, and categorised with the budget code of the SCSP and the TSP.'

This is the sad reality of how these sub-plans have been subverted, not just in terms of poor allocations, but also in how expenditures are 'booked' that have no relation to the welfare of these communities. It is also to be noted, as evidenced in earlier chapters, that only budgetary allocations for SCs and STs would not suffice to address their physical and economic deprivation as long as they are concentrated in insecure employment with no social protection, as is the trend today.

Muslims

Muslims suffer from being treated as 'the Other' in their own land, and experience everyday discrimination because of their religious identity. This in a country whose Constitution prohibits discrimination on the grounds of religion and grants freedom of religion to its citizens. Muslims of India face diverse issues at the social, economic and political levels. Poverty among Muslims is higher compared to other communities, and their literacy rate is below the national average.

According to the census of 2011, Muslims in India are the largest religious minority in the country at 14.23 per cent of the total population. Also, India has the third largest Muslim population of any country in the world, next to Indonesia and Pakistan. The population of Muslims is almost 70 per cent of the total religious minority population in India. Although some government programmes are targeted specifically towards the Muslim community, most developmental interventions are directed towards all minority communities, conceptualised in terms of religious minorities.

Schemes for religious minorities are largely designed and funded by the Government of India, and implemented by state governments. There are many welfare schemes which the Government of India has launched and that are implemented at various levels by the concerned ministries, with the primary aim of countering poverty, deprivation and exclusion among minority communities. For instance, the Multi-Sectoral Development Programme (MSDP), pre-matric and post-matric scholarship schemes, matric-cum-means-based scholarships, the Maulana Azad National Fellowship, Naya Savera, Nai Udaan, Padho Pardesh, schemes for leadership development among

Table 4.4 *Status of Fund Allocation and Utilisation under Ministry of Minority Affairs (in ₹Crore)*

Year	Allocation		Expenditure	Utilisation* (in %)
	BE	RE		
2007–08	500	350	196.7	39.3
2008–09	1,000	650	619.1	61.9
2009–10	1,740	1,740	1,709.4	98.2
2010–11	2,600	2,500	2,080.9	77.3
2011–12	2,850	2,750	2,292.3	80.4
2012–13	3,155	2,218	2,157.9	60.4
2013–14	3,531	3,131	3,026	86

Source: CBGA (2016).
* Utilisation has been reported taking into account BE figures.

minority women, Nai Manzil and skill development initiatives for minorities are schemes directed particularly towards the betterment of religious minority communities. Table 4.4 reflects the trends in budgetary allocations, expenditure and utilisation of funds given to the Ministry of Minority Affairs (MoMA) from financial year 2007–08 to 2013–14.

When on the one hand, the BE reveals the seriousness and intention of the government to spend on a particular programme, the utilisation pattern tells us about the efficiency of the government in spending the funds for the advancement of the communities for which they were earmarked. If we look at Table 4.4, we find that the utilisation pattern since 2007–08 has been consistently disappointing, despite the inadequate budgetary allocation to MoMA—the ministry which is responsible for the development of nearly 20 per cent of our population. According to MoMA, poor utilisation in 2012–13 was primarily due to a delayed start in the implementation of major schemes such as pre-matric scholarships and MSDP for select minority-concentrated districts. Table 4.5 presents the scheme-wise allocation in the 12th Plan and also the expenditure details in the plan corresponding to each scheme.

Table 4.5 *Scheme-wise Plan Allocation and Expenditure by the Ministry of Minority Affairs in 12th Five Year Plan (in ₹Crore)*

Scheme	12th Plan Proposed Allocation	Total Allocation and Expenditure in 12th Plan	Total Allocation/ Expenditure as Percentage of Proposed Allocation for 12th Five Year Plan
Maulana Azad Education Foundation	500	499	99.8
Free Coaching and Allied Scheme	120	159.07	132.5
Merit-Cum-Means	1,580	1,472.46	93
Pre-Matric Scholarship	5,000	4,798.97	95.9
Post-Matric Scholarship	2,850	2,393.42	83.9
Maulana Azad National Fellowship	430	258.33	60
National Minorities Development & Finance Corporation	600	377.64	62.9
MSDP	5,650	4,499.33	79.6

Source: CBGA (2016).

Table 4.5 shows the expenditure percentage for the 12th Plan in each scheme that comes under MoMA. It can be seen that the allocation was 100 per cent of the proposed allocation in none of these schemes, except for free coaching and allied services. The Maulana Azad National Fellowship had the lowest allocation compared to the amount proposed in the 12th Plan. Similarly, for the National Minorities Development & Finance Corporation and MSDP, the percentage allocation was much lower than the proposed allocation in the 12th Plan under these schemes.

The MSDP is a programme which aims to improve the condition of education, health, drinking water, sanitation and access to basic public services in minority-concentrated districts. Only 80 per cent of the proposed amount was allocated in the five years of the 12th Plan period. The allocated amount under all the above-mentioned schemes was less than the actual requirement of minority communities, given the significant size of their population relative to the total population of the country.

A study conducted by the Centre for Equity Studies in 2011 revealed that programmes directed towards the betterment of disadvantaged socio-religious groups are not being implemented properly, and the benefits are not reaching the intended Muslim communities. The study found that a substantial part of the MSDP and the Prime Minister's 15-Point Programmes are not reaching settlements of Muslim communities. For instance, if industrial training institutes or anganwadi centres are to be constructed, the lack of data and absence of a robust system create doubt that these will be built in the Muslim-populated regions. Apart from this, the underutilisation of funds allocated under these schemes is another point of serious concern. In 2010–11, merely 42.5 per cent of the total allocated amount under MSDP was utilised.

It is understood that the social discrimination Muslims face in India cannot be corrected merely by increasing the budgetary allocation for them. However, improvement in their economic well-being through efficient distribution of wealth to these communities can prepare them to confidently tackle the issues of social discrimination and exclusion that they face on a daily basis. Considering the fact that around 88 per cent of Muslims are employed in casualised work, we cannot think of lasting improvement without questioning the regime of informalisation in the realm of employment. Therefore, it is crucial for the government to come up with more and more programmes and schemes targeted at Muslim communities, who constitute 70 per cent of the minorities in India. At present, the budget for minorities is distributed across communities, shifting attention away from Muslims, who are the most disadvantaged of the minority communities in India.

Women

The word 'gender' in 'gender budgeting', directed mainly towards women's empowerment, is a reflection of the binary understanding of gender and its acceptance among decision makers. It denies that gender is a complex idea, and continues to uphold the traditional belief system in which the idea of gender remains rooted in the binary of 'male' and 'female'. However, despite the skewed understanding of gender, in initiatives such as gender empowerment and gender budgeting, it is highly crucial to understand the priorities of government vis-à-vis the issues that concern women in society. Gender budgeting is one of the tools to explore the budgetary provisions by the government directed specially towards the development and empowerment of girls and women. It also tells us if the government is responding adequately to the needs of women.

According to the *Human Development Report 2015*, India falls in group five of the gender development index, which means that it is among the countries with low equality in human development index achievements between women and men. The female literacy rate in India is 65.46, which is lower than the male literacy rate of 82.14. The female literacy rate is even lower in the case of women from the SC and ST communities. Other findings from the *Human Development Report* are presented in Table 4.6.

The promise of feminisation of the workforce that the growth regime offered has been called into question, as evidenced by the data

Table 4.6 *Gender Inequality Index,* Human Development Report 2015

Gender inequality index (rank)	130
Maternal mortality rate (deaths per 100,000 live births)	190
Adolescent birth rate (births per 1,000 women aged 15–19)	32.8
Population with at least some secondary education (% ages 25 or older)—female	27% for females and 56.6% for males
Labour force participation ratio	27% for females and 79.9% for males

Source: Human Development Report 2015 (UNDP 2015).

Table 4.7 India's Rank in Gender Inequality, 2013

Indicator	Rank
Economic participation and opportunity	124
Educational attainment	120
Health and survival	135
Political empowerment	9

Source: CBGA (2014).

analysed in the preceding chapters which shows the contrary trend of a widening gender gap. That apart, a recent report by Factly (Rao 2016) reveals that India ranks 103rd out of 140 countries in terms of representation of women in Parliament, with merely a 12 per cent representation as against the global average of 22.4 per cent—India is behind Nepal, China, Pakistan and even Bangladesh. The country ranked 13th out of 18 Asian nations, 5th out of 8 SAARC countries and 4th among BRICS nations in women's representation in the Parliament. Table 4.7 reflects India's rank in different indicators of gender inequality.

Amidst the stark social, economic and political inequality between the sexes in India, the Government of India introduced the Gender Budget Statement (GBS) for the first time in 2005–06. It is aimed at highlighting the proportion of the union budget which is earmarked for women. Figure 4.19 examines the trends over 2011–16 in the gender budget in India. The information is collected from the GBS (Statement 20) published by the union government every year. There are two parts to the statement—the schemes with 100 per cent funds earmarked for girls and women are reported in Part A, whereas programmes with at least 30 per cent earmarked for girls and women are reported in Part B. Here we present only the changes in allocation during 2011–16 in Part A schemes of the GBS.

The figure reveals that the amount earmarked in the union budget for programmes that are directed 100 per cent towards girls or women has been constantly declining since 2011–12. It has been brought down from 1.55 per cent of total union budget in the year 2011–12 (RE)

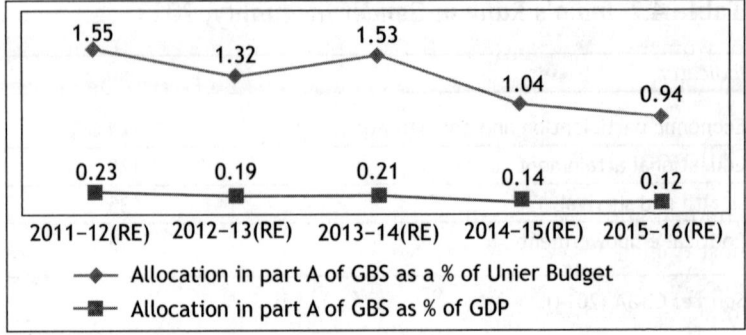

Figure 4.19 *Changes in Allocation in Part A Schemes of the Gender Budget Statement*
Source: CBGA (2015: 27).

to 0.94 per cent 2015–16 (BE). Also, the amount allocated in Part A of the GBS has remained almost constant as a percentage of GDP.

An analysis undertaken by the Centre for Budget and Governance Accountability raises serious doubts about the way schemes are reported in Part B of the GBS:

> For schemes reported in Part B, no rationale is provided for why certain proportions of the schemes' total allocations are being reported in the GBS by concerned departments/ministries. Though some schemes have clear guidelines for ensuring benefits to women (such as MGNREGA and *Nehru Yuva Kendra Sangathan*), based on which reporting is done under GBS, a number of schemes report a blanket 30–50 per cent of their total allocations in Part B. These schemes do not provide clear guidelines to justify their inclusion or any information on beneficiaries/programme objectives to substantiate such proportions (such as *Sarva Shiksha Abhiyan*, Integrated Child Protection Scheme). (CBGA 2015: 28)

Moreover, the Nirbhaya fund, which was introduced in 2013–14 and had a total corpus of ₹3,000 crore, remained unutilised in the first two years. This indeed reflects the lack of seriousness of the government in making a sensitive effort to address the issue of crimes against women. However, in the RE of 2015–16, ₹150 crore was allocated in the budget of the Ministry of Home Affairs for schemes meant for women's safety; and the BE of 2016–17 allocated ₹500 crore for schemes under the Ministry of Women and Child Development.

Children

Children are the most vulnerable of all social groups, and also the most excluded section in terms of representation in the democratic processes of the country. Children below the age of 18 constitute 39 per cent of the population. India is one of the signatories of the United Nations Child Rights Agreement, 1989. Also, the country adopted a multisectoral and multidimensional approach to securing the rights of children by releasing a National Policy for Children in 2013. The policy identified four priority areas for focused attention: (*a*) survival; (*b*) health and nutrition; (*c*) education and development; and (*d*) protection and participation. Incidents of child labour, child trafficking and physical and sexual violence against children are prevalent in India.

The HUNGaMA (Hunger and Malnutrition) Report 2011, published by the Naandhi Foundation, reveals that every third malnourished child in the world is an Indian (see Sinha 2012). Also, according to NFHS-3 data, about 48 per cent of all children under 5 are stunted. Against the backdrop of prevalent child abuse and abysmal health and child protection indicators, it is essential to pay sufficient attention—both at the policy and at the social level—to providing a dignified and respectable life to every child.

In order to tackle issues related to children, the government has initiated many targeted interventions in different sectors such as education, health and nutrition, child protection, and so on. Figure 4.20 reflects the total budgetary allocation to the welfare of children as a percentage of GDP. The figure presents the changes in the total allocations for schemes focused on children between 2012–13 and 2016–17.

It can be observed from the figure that the total expenditure on child-focused schemes as a percentage of the union budget has declined since 2012–13. Also, the allocation as a percentage of GDP has remained constant during this period. If we look at the change in

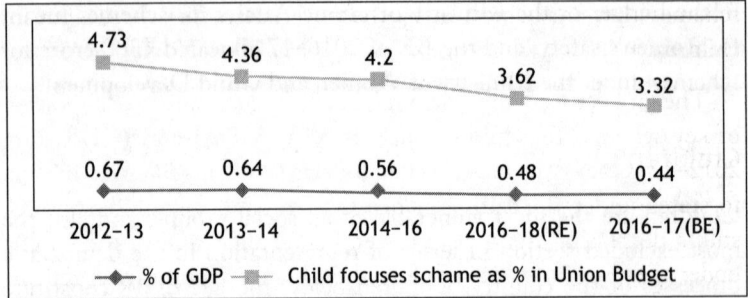

Figure 4.20 Total Budgetary Spending on Child-Focused Schemes (Per Cent of GDP)
Source: CBGA (2016).

the expenditure data for individual schemes earmarked for children between 2012–13 and 2016–17, we find that almost all the important schemes have seen cuts in their respective allocations. Table 4.8 gives the scheme-wise details of changes in budgetary allocations under

Table 4.8 Budgetary Allocation under Select Schemes for the Welfare of Children (in ₹Crore)

Sector	Schemes	2012–13 RE	2013–14 RE	2014–15 RE	2015–16 RE	2016–17 BE
Education	SSA	25,555	26,608	24,330	22,015	22,500
	MDM	11,500	12,189	11,051	9,236	9,700
Development	ICDS	15,850	16,312	16,562	15,584	14,863
	National Nutrition Mission	83	200	20	65	360
Protection	National Commission for Protection of Child Rights	11	13	14	11	19
	Integrated Child Protection Scheme	273	270	450	402	397

Source: CBGA (2016).

schemes that are being run by the government for the welfare of children.

The table reflects that there has been a reduction in the allocation of key schemes for children such as SSA, MDM and ICDS since 2012–13. One of the reasons cited for this is the increased devolution to states under the 14th Finance Commission recommendations; still, a decreasing trend can be seen in the allocation of the budget under these schemes even before the Finance Commission recommendation was brought into the picture. It is important to make sure that the states do not continue to keep the allocation at this level and that they maintain it at an adequate level by earmarking sufficient funds for 39 per cent of India's population.

Changes in India's Fiscal Architecture and States' Fiscal Autonomy

Given India's federal composition, different states have different policy and institutional structures catering to the needs of diverse populations within their boundaries. However, since 2014, when the BJP government led by Narendra Modi acquired power, India's federal fiscal architecture has witnessed significant changes, from the replacement of the Planning Commission with the NITI Aayog, to the recommendations of the 14th Finance Commission on resource sharing between the centre and state governments, and the recent rollout of the 'one country, one tax, one market' initiative in the form of the Goods and Services Tax (GST)—one indirect tax for the whole country, which is intended to make India one unified common market.

This section highlights the range of debates around the changes in the fiscal architecture to assess its impact on federal autonomy. The 2014–15 *Economic Survey* quotes the prime minister Narendra Modi: 'We want to promote co-operative federalism in the country. At the same time, we want a competitive element among the states. I call this new form of federalism Co-operative and Competitive Federalism' (Ministry of Finance 2015: 129).

Some of the major recommendations of the Finance Commission are: enhancing the share of the states in the central divisible pool from the current 32 per cent to 42 per cent; establishing a new institutional arrangement with the overarching objective of strengthening cooperative federalism; and a total grant of approximately 2.87 lakh crore for the period 2015–20 to rural and urban local bodies. The report also claims that all states are going to gain from the transfer in absolute terms. Das et al. (2017) argue that the government objective of ensuring adequate budgetary resources for the social sector and development programmes for vulnerable sections of the population by taking into account the collective share of the union and state budget outlays under the social sector may get compromised in the coming years in some states which have relatively poor fiscal health. They argue that the reason behind the insufficient budgetary allocations in certain states can be attributed to the inability of poor states to expand their fiscal space with own revenue collection, and the fact that they also face more acute shortages of funds for other sectors such as general administration, law and order, and infrastructure. Therefore, the issue of regional disparity will be aggravated in the longer run as the competition for budgetary resources could be more intense in these states, and the social sectors may not be given priority for the resources that are needed.

Also, the union government accepted the major recommendations of the Sub-Groups of Chief Ministers, set up on 8 February 2015, on the rationalisation of centrally sponsored schemes (CSS), and reduced the number of CSS to 30 after examining about 60 schemes. It also changed the funding pattern of CSS and divided them into core and optional schemes. Core schemes are those in which the 'focus of CSSs is on schemes that comprise the National Development Agenda where the Centre and States will work together in the spirit of Team India' (NITI Aayog 2015: v–vi), and optional schemes are those where 'States would be free to choose the ones they wish to implement'. Funds for these schemes would be allocated to states by the Ministry of Finance as a lump sum. The changed funding pattern between union and the state governments is as follows—90:10 for core schemes for eight North-East and three Himalayan states (Jammu and Kashmir, Himachal Pradesh and Uttarakhand), and 80:20 for optional schemes; for all other (general category) states, the ratio is 60:40 for core schemes and 50:50 for optional schemes; and for union territories it is 100 per cent for both core and optional schemes. The analysis by Das et al. (2017) highlights that after the Finance Commission recommendations, the resources available with the states will increase, and this will give them some further space to spend in priority sectors like health, education, water and sanitation, and nutrition, among others. However, since the union government has reduced the central assistance for state plans and its outlays for central schemes in the social sector, there has not been a significant increase in the states' resources.

Another decision that instilled a sense of fear among states about losing their autonomy over the levy of taxes has been the GST. The intention behind the GST is to replace all indirect taxes with a single tax system, which is based on a common base and a uniform rate across states. The operating framework of the GST suggests that the centre will levy and collect the central GST, whereas states will collect the state GST on supply of goods and services within their boundaries. The centre will also levy the integrated GST on inter-state supply of goods and services. The act also requires Parliament to compensate states for any revenue lost because of the implementation of the GST Act. Prime Minister Narendra Modi in his speech at the 18th meeting of the GST Council said that the GST would end harassment at the hands of tax officials, besides being a transparent and fair system that would end generations of black money and corruption. He also said:

> Tonight, at midnight, we will together move the nation forward. In a little while, the country will move in a new direction. 125 crore people will benefit from this. I don't agree that GST benefits are limited to just the economy. This path we have chosen is not one party or one government's. It is the result of our combined efforts. (*Hindu* 2017)

Though the act was hailed as a unifier of the indirect tax regime, with the slogan 'one nation one tax' introducing GST across India, it also allows states to levy certain taxes under the GST regime. However, under the GST regime the states are not empowered to decide the tax rate on any particular commodity or services themselves, as the rates are to be decided centrally by the GST Council. This would turn states into tax collecting agents for their own taxes, who will get a commission depending on the size of their respective tax bases (Das et al. 2017). Also, as GST is an indirect tax, any attempt to increase the tax–GDP ratio through GST would lead to higher inequality in a country like India, where the introduction of GST will only result in changes in the structure of indirect tax (ibid.). India's dependency on indirect taxes is as high as 67 per cent, and GST will lead to changes in the structure of indirect tax only; there will not be any change in the structure of direct tax collection, which is just one-third of our total tax revenue.

Therefore, the recent changes in fiscal architecture raise vital questions about the future of federal autonomy in India.

CHAPTER 5

Beyond the Neoliberal Smokescreen
Pathways for Equity and Growth

In the preceding chapters, we have reflected on the opportunities and the challenges posed by the demographic transition under way in India; undertaken an assessment of the current model of economic growth; and provided a closer examination of state investments in social development, agriculture, and directly for vulnerable groups. In this chapter, we will present a discussion of some ideas that we believe are crucial if we are to meet the challenges described in earlier chapters. We discuss these ideas in the light of the manifest failures of the existing neoliberal model of economic growth to generate assured and decent work for millions, as well as to convert the demographic opportunities into a demographic dividend. We underline the central role of the state and public policy in ensuring decent work and reaping the demographic advantage.

The chapter consists of three sections. The first section deals with questions of ideology and its effects. In particular, the focus here is on explaining that it is part of the working of the system that alternatives are made to seem absurd. From this discussion we move to the second section, which forms the bulk of the chapter. The focus here is on discussing alternatives to the currently reigning orthodoxy. We discuss proposals that we think are essential if we are to meet the challenges posed by the ongoing demographic transition. Of course, this section is not exhaustive of all the measures that would find a place in a comprehensive programme of socio-economic transformation. The effort is to highlight some of the measures that we deem indispensable. This is followed by a short concluding section that brings the focus back on the animating concerns in light of the preceding discussions.

The bulk of this chapter consists of a discussion of alternative policy pathways. We believe that we must begin by acknowledging that the failure of economic reforms to ensure decent work opportunities for the majority constitutes an enormous, looming global crisis, as millions who are joining the workforce have little to look forward to in terms of a better life based on just and secure work conditions. This also means that the opportunity to reap the potential created by India's demographic transition is being squandered. We are convinced that this acknowledgement must lead us to interrogate the dominant common sense across the world that freeing global markets alone can yield high and sustained growth; that the state's primary duty is to facilitate private business and secure private investment and growth; and that there is a necessary trade-off between growth and equity. We do not have the full answers to these questions, but of this we are certain, that neoliberal growth has failed to fulfil its promises of a better life for millions through providing them assured access to decent work; and that states are and must be responsible first and foremost to peoples disadvantaged by class, gender, caste, religious identity, disability, geography, education and a range of other factors. And that it is only through greater equity that meaningful economic growth can be sustained.

We end the book with a few, admittedly fragmented, discussions of pathways that we feel India and the world must explore to secure greater justice to millions of oppressed peoples, and achieve not just equity but sustain a just growth. Here we argue that there is a need to reframe the agenda of development, moving away from seeing economic growth as a good in itself, and instead indexing growth to metrics of human and social development. This is theoretically captured as a move from an economic system based on the logic of accumulation to one based on the logic of need accompanied by an ethic of solidarity, informed by a conception of rights.

We discuss the case of agriculture, prioritising the need to secure the interests of those who constitute the majority of cultivators who are currently being subjected to the squeezing effect we described in Chapter 3. Further, we discuss the case of 'low-skilled' workers and micro entrepreneurs, arguing for greater protection of workers' rights and a legalisation of their activity, and capacity augmentation of micro entrepreneurs. These workers form the productive backbone of the informal sector that props up the formal economy. It is our suggestion that these agents be made stakeholders in the way plans for economic development are conceived of and operationalised. This is followed by a proposal for a substantial increase in state expenditure on the provisioning of essential services. This, we believe, must happen in tandem with the de-commodification of these services. We make the case that expanding investments in people in this manner is a prudent strategy as it strengthens the economic base of the country, which is what should be the driver of economic growth in the long run. Further, given the grotesque state of affairs where the worst forms of human suffering exist alongside historically unprecedented achievements in living standards for a minority of the population, we argue that this is the only ethically viable direction to head in if we want to maintain our claim of being a democratic republic.

Confronting Neoliberal Ideology: A Political Project

Before we move on to a discussion of all of the above, it is important to confront head on the likely charge of impracticality that seems to attach itself to any such ideas. We believe it is important to take seriously the charge of being unrealistic that routinely gets levelled at critics and dissenters of the existing economic model, even as the latter produces and reproduces a manifest range of economic, social and ethical paradoxes, miscarriages, betrayals and failures. By taking this potential evaluation (and resultant dismissal) seriously, we recognise the association with impracticality as an ideological manoeuvre of neoliberal orthodoxy that seeks to repel any attempt at conceiving of another reality or alternative. The infamous 'There Is No Alternative' (TINA) thesis comes to life in the subconscious of the subject as she tries to make sense of the reality around her. We argue that this effect is as real as the material constraints resulting from free-market prescriptions that are more commonly associated with neoliberalism. Neoliberalism needs to be understood, beyond an economic doctrine, also as the governing rationality of the current historical phase of capitalist development, which legitimises the status quo by rendering opposition to it as either destructive, infantile, unrealistic or otherwise undesirable. Its specific characteristics in particular are the naturalising of the economy as a sphere separate from and standing over the social and political domains of reality, as well as the spread of an economistic logic to spheres of life that until recently had other registers of valuation, and a conversion of the erstwhile 'social' to the domain of the market (free exchange between rational individuals). This results in an ordering of normative behaviour that is measured against a scheme of rewards and benefits best understood through a regime of disciplining. By recognising the ideological manoeuvrings of neoliberalism, the attempt is to make a conceptual break from the limitations imposed by it, in order to reclaim the project of conceiving of another reality.

According to the neoliberal credo, individuals are rational actors who engage in voluntary exchange to further their private interests. Free exchange is mutually beneficial, for no one would enter into an exchange freely if it was damaging to their interests. Any imbalance will be taken care of if perfect competition (that is, zero intervention) is allowed to play out, leading to an efficient allocation of resources and consumption. The individual's freedom to choose is what makes this possible, and freedom of choice is the quintessential human characteristic. Through the spontaneous dynamic of freedom of choice and perfect competition, it is possible to achieve (a metaphysical) order.

Giving credence to the set of statements listed above is a social theory of what we are calling 'neoliberalism'. It relies heavily on the precepts of liberal political economy that can be traced back to Adam

Smith (Clarke 2005). It takes root in a very different context than faced by Smith, who encountered a mercantilist state dominated by vested trading interests. Neoliberalism develops in the 20th century as a response to the dominance and eventual crisis of Keynesianism in the West. Its advocacy of opening up the economy (by the state) to the free play of market forces is a markedly different prescription, given the developments since Smith's mercantilist state.

The 20th-century arguments for the rollback of the state build on these arguments of the past, but in changed circumstances, and through subtle calibrations to the theoretical schema. '[T]here is no such thing as society. There are individual men and women and there are families. And no government can do anything except through people, and people must look after themselves first' (Thatcher 1987). This infamous quote by Margaret Thatcher is a distillation of Friedrich Hayek's position, which is that

> social science should never start from the assumption that there is such a thing as a social 'whole'.... To do so, [Hayek] argues, is to give 'social mind', and with this rationality and power, to collective properties or entities such as government and the state that subsequently become unaccountable to the concerns and interests of individuals. For this reason, Hayek argues that all forms of methodological collectivism are essentially authoritarian, and on this basis he dismisses the term 'social'.... What he proposes instead is a method that centres on spontaneous processes of ordering that emerge from the actions of individuals and which find concrete expression through acts of exchange and competition in markets. (Gane 2014: 11)

As a social theory, neoliberalism conceives of subjects in and through the image of the free market. Nicholas Gane provides an account of the intellectual manoeuvring that led Hayek to formulate such a theory. He states,

> Hayek ... advances a neo-Kantian argument for the unknowability of the noumenal realm by insisting that the empirical world is so infinitely complex that human knowledge is always, by definition, imperfect. Because of this, truth, if there can be any such thing, is

seen not to come from that which is human or social but from the economic, or more precisely from the pricing system of the market: *that 'marvel' that is said to coordinate the lay knowledge of all actors into 'one'.* (Gane 2014: 11; emphasis mine)

Hayek makes a break from his neoclassical and libertarian predecessors by disagreeing with the placement of a rational human actor at the centre of the economic and social order. He sees the prominence accorded to *homo oeconomicus* as being mistaken, as for him individuals are bearers only of fragments of knowledge, and it is *only* through the institution of the market that these disparate fragments can be brought into harmony—via the marvel of the free market and the ingeniousness of price as a form. Prescriptively this allows him to make moves that libertarians like Ludwig von Mises would consider blasphemous—for example, giving the state an active role in economic life. This is, however, to bring social institutions kept outside the domain of the market, within its fold. Hayek thus advocates for the government to actively intervene and make competition more efficient. This makes perfect sense for him, as the central object is not the rational individual actor per se, but the marvel that is the market.

The victory of the project of neoliberalism is not so much in having impacted the macroeconomic policy of powerful states; it is in having shaped the invisible common sense. We begin to understand this only when we move beyond considering neoliberalism as an economic doctrine, and see it as an ideology that animates the governing logic of most present-day regimes in the world. The possibility of people collectivising against the operation of market forces is rendered irrational, explained away as infantile, and in need of discipline. It thus brings into play the rules of normative behaviour. Thus there is a self-disciplining involved in accordance with the rules of normative behaviour that we learn as we get acculturated into a capitalist, neoliberal society. The use of the word 'acculturated' is deliberate. The attempt here is to emphasise that this is a creation and not a natural given. We are not destined to grow into calculative beings geared towards the accumulation and appreciation of capital. We are made to grow into it through a subtle (and at times harsh) process of learning: from the school to the workplace, from the church (institutions of organised religion) to the prison. We are made in the image of the market actor as conceived of by neoliberalism.

> [T]o argue that the neoliberal model is unrealistic is somewhat to miss the point, since the neoliberal model does not purport so much to describe the world as it is, but the world as it should be. The point for neoliberalism is not to make a model that is more adequate to the real world, but to make the real world more adequate to its model. This is not merely an intellectual fantas, it is a very real political project. (Clarke 2005: 58)

Having thus understood the ideological schema of neoliberalism, the question which arises is the following: what stands behind this conception of society and the attendant subjecthood that is being protected from getting exposed? Our contention is that it is a set of organised class interests in society. The 'free market' is an ideological cover for the legitimisation of unequal exchange benefiting the owners of capital disproportionately as compared to others.[1] The outcome of such a way of organising economic activity in society is available for all to see in the sharp increase in inequality in India, as discussed in the previous chapters, and all over the world. Neoliberalism then is a politico-ideological project of the dominant capitalist classes, a counter-revolution of the globalising elite against the Keynesian welfare state of the mid-20th century.

Having understood the material interests behind the dominant ideology of our times, its attempts at branding alternatives as irrational or impractical can be stripped of their naturalising veneer and understood as the survival tactics of a very fragile system that serves to protect the interests of a small minority. It is now time to move on to considering some thoughts about what an alternative might look like.

---

[1] The first thing to note about these organised interests in society is that they are organic and dynamic in nature. They are organic in that they change in the way they reproduce themselves. Dynamic because they change how they dominate; building alliances and/or coopting other interests that are at variance with them. The distinguishing criterion remains that they do not allow other interests to get as organised as they are.

Reimagining Economic Development: Some Ingredients

Having hopefully freed ourselves of the compulsions of thought forced upon us by the governing rationality of the times, we now turn towards the task of conceptualising what a more humane economic system would look like. What would be its priorities; how would we balance the equation between productivity and growth on the one hand, and its equitable distribution on the other? With the caveat that we do not claim omniscience, we present below some thoughts on what we consider to be the necessary ingredients of a just economic system in India. As with any systematic critique, our prescriptions are based on an understanding of the flaws that we analyse in the existing system.

Agriculture: From Unviable to Sustainable

We noted in Chapter 3 that although recent years have seen a net movement of labour out of agriculture, the proportion of overall population engaged in agriculture remains high, with roughly half the population dependent on it as their primary source of income. At the same time, the contribution of agriculture to the overall GDP has shrunk from over 50 per cent in the 1950s to below 20 per cent. Further, we saw how the movement out of agriculture, which gets seen as a positive trend in classical development thinking, is in fact more distress-ridden than is acknowledged, owing to a lack of remunerative employment outside the sector. We also know that the majority of cultivators belong to the marginal and landless category. In fact, as we discussed earlier, there has been a sharp increase in the percentage of agricultural labourers, from 28.1 per cent to 54.9 per cent (see Table 3.1), and a simultaneous decline in the number of cultivators (that is, those who own some land and derive their primary income from it) from 71.9 per cent to 45.1 per cent, since independence. The overall trend when it comes to landholdings has been one of concentration in the ranks of the marginal and landless category, which together make up 83 per cent of households engaged in agriculture while owning only 29.7 per cent of the cultivated land area. At the other end, the top 2 per cent of the distribution own 24.6 per cent of the land area (Government of India 2014b).[2] A large number of these small farms are located in areas that lack irrigation facilities, and depend on rain as the only source of irrigation, which in turn means that they can grow only one crop per year. Further, the policy paradigm continues to be productivist in its outlook, and prescribes productivity maximising techniques as the solution to the distress caused by a complex set of conditions resulting in stagnation and the steady attrition of the smallholder economy.

This paradigm is the extension of the green revolution policy package to dryland farming areas without regard for the shortcomings of the policies and their mismatch with the requirements of the areas they are applied to. This has been discussed as the 'lagged' green revolution that is being prescribed in rain-fed areas that is resulting in the aggravation of agrarian distress. As we noted earlier, these policy choices have benefited a very small minority of large farmers who corner a disproportionately high share of public investment in the form of subsidies and credit, and have also strengthened their position vis-à-vis other classes in the agrarian economy as shown by disaggregated income trends post liberalisation. The adverse conditions faced by marginal and landless cultivators get compounded due to the lack of formal support systems, such as credit, know-how (extension) and marketing. The incidence of indebtedness in the post-reform era, which saw the commercial opening up of Indian agricultural markets and the introduction of accompanying risks, is an indicator of underlying strains that the smallholder economy in particular is ridden with. The epidemic of suicides in the last 20 years is a harsh indictment of the high growth system failing those near the base of the pyramid who nonetheless continue to contribute productively to the system.

---

[2] Depending on the data source used, the numbers differ. The SECC, for instance, estimates landlessness to be far higher at 56 per cent of rural households. The National Land Reforms Policy, 2013, puts the figures at 79.9 per cent of marginal and landless households owning 22 per cent of the land area. Here we use the figures from the 70th Round of the NSS. See 'Key Indicators of Land and Livestock Holdings in India', NSS 70th Round (2013) (Government of India 2014b).

The sustained crisis in agriculture does not raise alarm bells in either the urban public sphere, animated as it is by middle-class consumerist demands, or the corridors of power populated by law and policy makers. This conspiracy of silence about the fate of the majority of the population is broken only by calamities such as drought, which, contrary to popularly held assumptions, is a result of the lack of public investments and not just poor rainfall; or by flashpoints that result in violence, such as the recent protests in Mandsaur where cultivators demanded their debts be waived off and they be given better remunerative prices.[3] Efforts on the part of farmers and agricultural labourers, in line with constitutional principles demanding rights, such as the Kisan Sansad held in November 2017,[4] get routinely ignored by the ruling dispensation. It is a striking social fact that none of the huge promises that are routinely made during election campaigns is followed up by commensurate governmental action. This is indicative of the lack of influence wielded by the mass of marginal cultivators and landless labourers who make up the majority of the working population in the agrarian economy.

The situation described above is not unknown; it is ignored by naturalising the stagnation in the agrarian economy, belying the fact that it is a result of choices that, at the end of the day, are political in nature. We believe that the existing situation, rather than being natural, is actually absurd and unjust, and its naturalisation is sought by those whose interests are served by the perpetuation of such a scenario. We present below suggestions that we consider necessary to begin to rectify the situation. From the perspective that we espouse, putting people at the centre of any strategy of economic development, there is a need to shift focus from a productivist approach to one

---

[3] On this, see the report in the *Hindustan Times* (Ranjan 2017).

[4] The Kisan Sansad, held in the month of November 2017, saw close to 100,000 farmers converge on the national capital to press their demands of debt-free farming and remunerative pricing for crops. This was preceded and followed by farmer marches and demonstrations in cities across the country. The massive turnout was matched by the deafening silence of prominent media houses that set public opinion for middle-class India. For a selection of the sparse reportage the events received, see Mani (2017), Samar (2017), Varma (2017) and Vissa (2017).

that prioritises the needs of the majority of the working population in the agrarian sector, that is, the small and marginal cultivators and landless workers.

Redistribution: The Case for Land Reforms

Land reforms were a central aspect of the agrarian strategy post independence. This was so for both reasons of economic planning as well as socio-political reasons. From the economic planning perspective, redistribution of land was supposed to lead to a rise in productivity with the abolition of absentee landlords and the subsequent investment in land that owner-cultivators would make. Socio-politically, land reform was a result of the anti-colonial legacy that mobilised the peasantry against the British-appointed zamindars. With the Second Five Year Plan, as India went in for a policy of import-substituting industrialisation, the overhaul of agriculture was the understated complementing factor that would be required for the success of the plan.[5] Although at the level of the central government, consensus was achieved in favour of redistribution, the landed elite smothered the reforms at the state level.[6] This blocking of land reforms at the state level[7] by the landed elite prevented the structural change required for successful import substitution: the creation of a domestic market. With the change in track to a productivist paradigm in agricultural policy making with the green revolution era, the programme for land reforms took a back seat as a class of rich farmers began to consolidate

[5] See Bandopadhyay (1988) for an analysis of this. This is to suggest that the planners did not adequately account for the significance of how agrarian transformation was to be achieved as they did, for instance, in the case of industry. Agriculture was treated more as a bargain sector where output could increase without high levels of investment (Chakravarty 1993). This lack on the part of the planning elite would contribute to the plan strategy coming under heavy strain as time passed.

[6] Land is a state subject according to the Constitution. For more on the blocking of land reforms by the landed elite, see Joshi (1974a, 1974b, 1976), Herring (1983) among others.

[7] The exceptions to this were the communist-ruled states of Kerala and later West Bengal, as well as the state of Jammu and Kashmir.

in different parts of the country's agrarian landscape. By the 1990s, the landholding pattern was highly skewed and smallholder cultivation, as we discussed earlier, started becoming increasingly unviable. With the move towards land liberalisation, through which 'low-productivity' agricultural land is brought into circuits of capitalist accumulation where it can be utilised for high-value use such as the creation of export processing zones, or high-end real estate, land reform has effectively been erased from the agenda of the state.[8] This is evident if one looks at the trend in the surplus land available for transfer over the years as reported by the state.

However, if we are interested in development from a people-centric perspective, it is with redistribution of land that we must start. Figure 5.1 shows the highly unequal distribution of land in the rural

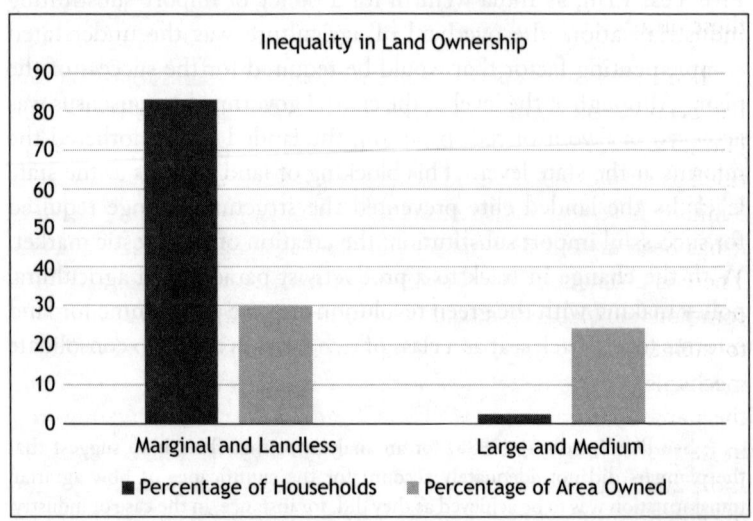

Figure 5.1 *Skewed Landholding Pattern*

Source: *Key Indicators of Land and Livestock Holdings in India*, NSS 70th Round (2013) (Government of India 2014b).

---

[8] Despite the policy shift, land reform continues to find mention in the election manifestos of parties as they appeal for votes to the mass of the rural poor.

economy in 2013, where marginal and landless cultivators own less than 30 per cent of agricultural land while constituting more than 80 per cent of those engaged in agriculture, while a miniscule minority of large and medium farmers own roughly the same amount of agricultural land. The case for land reform is necessary because that is where the majority of the population is concentrated in an extremely low-equilibrium state as a result of an adverse economic environment for them. A sound policy of transfer of legal titles to those who work the land, whether such transfer is from private owners (landlords) or the state (so-called wasteland) will go a long way in providing a modicum of security to the most vulnerable sections of the population. Further, it will help consolidate a significant number of unremunerative micro holdings. These efforts will have to be matched by a range of other policy changes to augment the capacity of smallholders to meaningfully contribute to society in a dignified way. We will discuss these other changes as we move further.

The Indian state's performance with regard to land redistribution has been dismal, with the exception of West Bengal, Kerala, and Jammu and Kashmir. Overall, close to 7 million acres have been identified as surplus (as per land ceiling rules) land, of which only about 5 million have been redistributed to 5.7 million beneficiaries.[9] Further, it has been argued that not enough land is available to redistribute. There is a sleight of hand involved in making such a claim, as it is common knowledge that landowners have exploited various loopholes to maintain large (beyond ceiling limits) landholdings. A common mechanism of doing so is *benami*, that is, transferring ownership in the name of someone else. The Committee on Agrarian Reforms in its report *The Unfinished Task in Land Reforms* (Government of India 2009) suggested, among other measures, the downward revision of ceiling limits with a cap at 10 acres for irrigated land and 15 acres for unirrigated land. Disregarding these suggestions, the figure of 2.78 million hectares has been declared as ceiling-surplus land.[10] This is a

---

[9] For this section see Government of India (2014b, 2014c), Action Aid (2016), Chaturvedi (2016).

[10] Various state governments have rejected the recommendations for land reforms by adjusting ceiling levels, cracking down on *benami* holdings, and so on. This shows the active backing of landed interests across state governments.

miniscule amount when compared to the total area under cultivation.[11] Estimated as per the guidelines of the committee report, the available surplus land has been considered to be close to 19.5 million hectares (see Action Aid 2016). That is about as much as the whole land area of Senegal! This demonstrates that the potential for land redistribution exists, and it is a political choice to not tap it for a people-centric model of development.

Such redistributive measures would also be particularly beneficial for the marginalised sections of society. The incidence of landlessness is seen to increase as one moves from the upper castes down the caste hierarchy. Bold land reforms would also contribute to enhancing the nutritional security of households. There is a causal linkage between landownership and access to adequate nutrition, as landholding households are not dependent entirely on external sources for the supply of food. These measures must be coupled with the legalisation of tenancy subject to ceiling limits, and provision of security of tenure to the cultivator. Providing workable pieces of land to households, members of which anyway contribute to the production of food crops as workers, would go a long way in ensuring the eradication of hunger, which as we saw in Chapter 1 still mars the lives of millions in the country. The importance of adequate nutrition in the early years cannot be stated enough, as it has a direct relation with the development of the mental and physical capacities of the child. If we are interested in addressing the demographic transition in a way that enables dignified lives in the future, then we have to invest in nutritional security as our foremost priority.[12] The next section discusses how.

---

[11] According to the NSS, the area under cultivation came down to 95 million hectares in 2012–13, whereas the figure stands at close to 160 million hectares if one looks at the agricultural census of 2010–11. The disparity is cause for concern and points in the direction of the necessity of better land records data, but in either case, the declared surplus land is a small fraction of the area under cultivation—2.9 per cent as per NSS data, and 1.75 per cent if we consider the agricultural census data.

[12] While food security is the availability of or access to food for people, nutritional security goes a step further and is understood as the capacity for intake of a range of food items that provide the necessary nutrients.

Nutritional Security and Economic Progress: A Holistic Approach

Contrary to the criticism of land reforms for being a populist measure, or at best serving the interest of social justice by sacrificing economic wisdom, it is possible to conceive of and operationalise a programme of economic progress that thrives on the virtues of an egalitarian structure of landownership. If our aim is to enable economic advancement and nutritional security among those disadvantaged in the current regime of 'growth', then it is important that we think of a notion of decentralised development. The current model of growth requires concentration of productive capital and private appropriation of surpluses which are then supposed to trickle down to the disadvantaged sections in society. As against this top-heavy configuration, one can imagine a system characterised by a comparatively low-equilibrium stability, based on a robust convergence of activities of producers through a cooperative arrangement.

At present our PDS is governed by the hegemony of the green revolution crops—wheat and rice—to the detriment of what are called coarse grains. The latter include a variety of millets, such as jawar and bajra, that are resilient and nutritious cereals grown in vast sections of rain-fed farmland. The state incentivises the production of wheat and rice by providing remunerative support prices and input subsidies for their cultivation. Further, given the dominance of these crops in the PDS, the government procures a large proportion of the same, thereby providing marketing support as well. This has led to a situation where the PDS is supplied by produce from farms using the input-intensive green revolution techniques. As discussed in Chapter 3, the green revolution model favours the better-off farmers over the marginal and small cultivators. Thus, we have a situation where the interests of large, rich farmers are secured through their linkage with a centralised PDS that is dominated by wheat, rice and sugar. Not only is the PDS lacking in nutritive content, but also its configuration ends up perpetuating the inequalities of the agrarian structure. The centralised PDS is infamous for wastage on account of lack of proper storage facilities and the arduous task of timely transportation of grains across the country, as a majority of procurement happens from select regions such as the green revolution belt of north-western India, comprising Punjab and Haryana. The shortcomings of the PDS identified above and its latent contribution to the perpetuation of inequalities in the agrarian structure can be addressed by changing its design to make it localised in terms of procurement and distribution.

In a country as varied as India, the PDS does not have to be centralised. It can work on the principle of localised procurement, storage and distribution, thereby giving a much-needed boost to regional economic development. Rather than bank on wheat and rice only, locally grown millets must be included in the PDS. This would improve the incomes of those engaged in dryland farming of these crops. Further, this would enhance the nutritive quotient of the supply from the PDS, while eliminating transportation losses as grain would be locally procured. Local storage facilities for these grains would need to be constructed, preferably at the village cluster level. This can be done as works undertaken through NREGA, which would allow the residents of the area to decide where the structures would come up while providing them with productive employment at the same time. The NREGA programme should also be used systematically for watershed management works to enhance the availability of water in rain-fed regions, and for drought-proofing of villages. Such an approach has the added benefit of being ecologically sustainable—something the green revolution strategy decidedly is not. Wherever possible, the cooperative mode of organising production must be deployed to minimise risks and ensure the optimal sharing of revenues.[13]

In this manner, a decentralised PDS can be based on the virtues of an egalitarian resource ownership. Further, it can make the smallholder economy viable in rain-fed areas by incorporating their produce as part of the PDS at remunerative prices, while NREGA can be used to create infrastructure facilities for the same.[14] The productive synergy between land redistribution and decentralised development must be

---

[13] The point about cooperatives is not limited to the creation of a decentralised PDS, and the mode should be encouraged otherwise as well.

[14] See Banerjee (2011) for an elaboration of this.

harnessed in order to achieve the aim of nutritional security, which is the material foundation upon which the equitable and dignified participation of all can take shape.

This would require an increase in public investment in agriculture in a structured way. The four key areas requiring greater investment are: price support, expansion of formal credit, extension services and greater allocation under NREGA. We elaborate briefly on these:

1. To ensure remunerative prices to cultivators, the implementation of the recommendations of the Swaminathan Committee report is long overdue. Its recommendation of cost price + one half was an election promise to the farming community and should be followed upon. As discussed earlier, it is important to provide price support for millets as well as for pulses and oilseeds. This needs to be complemented with protection afforded to cultivators against cheaper imports of the same.

2. The expansion of formal credit is a must, given the increase in indebtedness and the connection of this to farmer suicides. The increase in the reliance of cultivators on non-institutional sources of borrowing has been seen to have led to people getting caught in the debt trap. For the changes discussed previously to be successful, the expansion of formal credit is a prerequisite.

3. There is an urgent need for greater investment in extension and knowledge sharing. The agrarian extension system is all but broken, which has resulted in the private input dealer doubling as knowledge provider. The obvious conflict of interest this generates can be avoided through investments in increasing the scope of extension services. With better technical and economic know-how, the cultivator will be better placed to make informed decisions rather than being at the mercy of market fluctuations and the vagaries of the monsoon, as is presently the case.

4. The NREGA programme is a tool for building local capacities to enable sustainable economic development. There needs to be greater allocation under the scheme to enable the construction of infrastructural facilities such as grain storages and seed banks. Provision of work under the act must be increased to 365 days a

year, with priority accorded to districts with larger concentrations of SC and ST populations. Simultaneously, more attention needs to be paid to the creation of durable assets under the act. Since the scheme is demand-driven, the scope of underutilisation is low.

A combination of these initiatives can overhaul a stagnating system. To be sure, the widely lauded success of the green revolution model in increasing production was based upon the fourfold support of the state in the areas of price, credit, input subsidy and marketing.[15] There is then no reason to not consider the kind of investment discussed above to rejuvenate the distress-ridden rural economy and provide people the opportunities to lead better, more meaningful lives.

Informal Economy: Countering Precarity

Thus far we have focused on the revival of the agrarian economy in a way that puts people's needs at the forefront. We now turn our attention towards the non-agrarian economy. Here our focus will first and foremost be on the informal economy, where an overwhelming majority of people find employment and create value. Further on, we will address the employment-intensive sectors of construction and textiles.

It is imperative that we start with the need to change the mindset with which the question of the informal sector is approached. It is often the case that from a policy perspective, the informal sector is seen as a messy space that creates problems of measurement and legibility, and therefore control. This has the consequence of the sector being regarded as one that defies the strictures of law and as a challenge for regulation and taxing. The conduct of activity within the sector can then easily be thought of as illegal, if not criminal, instead of seeing it for what it often really is—people making do with whatever resources are available to them due to the lack of secure job opportunities.

The idea here is not to present an idyllic picture of the informal sector. Indeed, it is often here that the most gross violations of human and workers' rights take place. The purpose of arguing for a shift in

[15] See Ramakumar (2010) on this point.

the imaginary is to be able to recognise and invest in the creative and productive potential of the people engaged in such works by making them stakeholders in the way economic development is imagined. There is a need to recognise that the informal sector creates not just nominal value,[16] but structurally props up the formal economy that has seen such high growth in recent years. Once we recognise this linkage, it is then incumbent on us to ensure that workers in this sector get dignified employment opportunities, and are invested in as creative agents rather than being seen as a burden on the urban infrastructure.

The aim of a policy framework for the informal sector must be to ensure the creation of adequate opportunities for decent work.[17] This has several implications for policy around labour reforms.[18] We discuss a few of them below.

A National Living Wage

The central government should mandate the creation of a living wage floor that allows a worker to obtain not just the basic essentials of living—food, clothing and shelter—but also allows access to education for children, protection against disease, insurance and other social needs. This can be calculated differently depending on the cost of goods and services in different states, but a decently high central floor must be set below which no state should fall.

Rights at the Workplace

Issues such as minimum safety and health standards and maximum hours of work need to be legislated at the national level. The legislation or policy framework must recognise the process of collective bargaining

---

[16] It is estimated that the informal sector's contribution accounts for almost half of the national GDP. For an international comparison, see ILO (2013).

[17] The ILO defines decent work as characterised by dignity, equality, a fair income and safe working conditions. See ILO, https://www.ilo.org/global/topics/decent-work/lang--en/index.htm (accessed 12 June 2018).

[18] See the recommendations of the National Commission for Enterprises in the Unorganised Sector (NCEUS 2009).

as the legitimate way of addressing needs beyond minimum standards
and of resolving disputes between employer and employees.

Contract Workers

Work that is perennial in nature is routinely contracted out. This needs
to be recognised and addressed such that workers are not driven into
precarious employment. Further, workers employed by contractors
need to be provided the same legal cover on counts of social security
and conditions of work as those directly employed. Health and provision of gratuity/provident fund benefits, as well as the application
of standards of safety and time-bound payment of wages, must be
explicitly ensured for this set of workers as they are more prone to
being vulnerable.

Skill Development

The existing model of Skill India seems to be more about producing
numbers than jobs, as evidenced by the dismal placement levels of
trainees under the programme.[19] It is necessary to have private industry
play its part (and bear the costs) in skilling the workforce it requires to
remain profitable. The state must ensure access of members from the
marginalised sections of the population to initiatives of skilling and
vocational training, and ensure regulatory compliance by the private
sector. It is the state's responsibility to discipline capital such that it
invests in avenues that are socially relevant.

Ensuring Portability of Rights of Migrant Workers

Tens of millions of people leave their homes in search of employment opportunities, stay and work in our cities living all the while in
inhuman conditions. Not being from the area, they are denied their
rights to various welfare benefits. It is an obligation of the state to

---

[19] A year after its launch, Skill India placement records show a 5 per cent
placement rate for trainees under the scheme as reported by *Hindustan Times*.
See the report by J. P. Sharma (2016).

ensure that denial of welfare benefits does not take place to compound the hardships of seasonal migrant workers. There is a pressing requirement for a robust policy framework to ensure the portability of rights for migrant workers and their families. Not only would this alleviate some of the hardships faced by this highly vulnerable group of people, by ensuring better nutrition and health services, it would contribute to their being able to live and work better.

Social Housing

While the real estate boom has made many rich people richer in recent years, India's urbanisation is a patently unjust phenomenon, where those who build houses for others have no place to call home. Housing in cities is unaffordable for most of the working poor, and where it is available, it is usually of extremely inferior quality. It is time for the state to recognise this gap and commit to a nationwide programme of social housing. This should include the creation of urban workers' hostels, efforts to curb predatory rentiers from exploiting migrants, as well as improvement of living standards in low-income housing colonies.

Urban Employment Programmes

Like NREGA in rural areas, a guarantee of work should be extended in urban areas as well. Adults in urban areas should be provided work guarantees to the tune of 100/150 days of work, at the minimum daily wage (by category according to state). As in rural areas, this can provide a much-needed base for real wages in the urban informal economy. A programme of this kind will require much consideration to be given to the nature of public works to be generated, with provision of work at different levels of skill, and greater integration with the provision of public services. For example, the employment programme could include provision of tuition to schoolchildren, care for the elderly and disabled, promotion of skills and training in traditional crafts, and so on. Thus, such an employment programme needs to dovetail with the provisioning of public services in order to achieve the twin results of: (*a*) tackling unemployment and underemployment by providing a work guarantee and a base for real wages in urban areas; and (*b*) meeting the extant demand for basic services by vast sections of the population.

Cluster-Based Growth Poles and Cooperative Management

In order to tackle the challenge of job creation, it is imperative to focus on cluster-based economic growth and cooperative forms of management of firms. The idea of cluster-based growth poles is not new. It was recommended by the National Commission for Enterprises in the Unorganised Sector (NCEUS 2009: 350–56, 373–74), and, over time, several others have also advocated the same. India has approximately 6,000 cluster towns, which should be developed by being made the focus of urban infrastructure missions and dedicated policy packages. The policy framework should provide incentives to small firms to develop and grow, thus addressing the question of 'the missing middle' in Indian manufacturing. Such an approach will also make India's urbanisation experience less frenzied. Rather than having unsustainable, burgeoning metropoles that attract millions who have been driven out of farms, it would be far better from the perspective of regional planning to have decently-provided-for mid-level towns and cities that serve as hubs of decent work opportunities for labour that is seeking non-agricultural work. To this must be added the component of cooperative management ensuring equitable distribution of surplus generated. India has witnessed great success in cooperative initiatives, be it in the dairy, farming or other sectors. Globally as well, there are shining examples of sustainable cooperatives that have been able to curb excessive inequality and generate a culture of participatory workplace democracy. The example of Mondragon[20] is highly relevant, despite criticisms of the project. Yet, the idea of cooperatives is met with a sense of casual dismissal in business and economic policy circles, where it is regarded as impractical. It is time to move past such non-engagement into a world where those who produce can claim a seat at the table when it comes to making decisions about what, when and

[20] See Whyte and Whyte (1991) for a detailed analysis of Mondragon. See Richard Wolff's advocacy of Mondragon (Wolff 2012a), and his book (Wolff 2012b) on economic democracy in the 21st century.

how to produce. Genuine workplace democracy would be the mark of a mature democratic culture and of the substantial realisation of the constitutional promise of equality.

Construction: The Need for Entitlements

The construction sector has seen the sharpest rise in employment in the last two decades, accounting for roughly 50 million jobs, surpassing textiles as the second largest employer after agriculture. While the number of jobs created has been impressive, there are grave concerns regarding the quality of employment available. Most construction sector jobs are precarious in nature. By precarious we mean both in terms of job security as well as being hazardous. There is scant regulation of the multitude of construction sites that dot the peripheries of large cities in particular. The rapid urbanisation that we are witness to has involved a spurt in infrastructure building as well as a real estate boom. The construction industry is reported to have registered an awesome 80 per cent growth rate over the last four years, jumping from $78 billion in 2013 to $140 billion in 2017 (see Jain and Matharu 2017). At the heart of these lucrative activities is the labour of millions of people who toil at times in exceptionally harsh conditions. With low formal skill requirements, most of these people come from the marginalised sections of our population and are very often migrant labourers—those squeezed out of a distress-ridden agrarian economy.

A couple of basic questions raise serious doubts over the nature of growth in the sector and its ability to contribute towards social development. The first concerns the wage situation in the sector. The distribution of gains within the industry is highly skewed in favour of capital owners and intermediaries who arrange the supply of labour. Findings from a survey (Srivastava and Sutradhar 2016) of construction workers in the Delhi National Capital Region show that 79 per cent of workers get employed through contractors, and that most workers see the contractor as their employer. It also shows that remuneration remains below minimum wage standards and depends on the mode of recruitment, with the bulk of workers who come through intermediaries getting a poor deal. The survey findings show abysmal wage rates in the National Capital Region, with the range for monthly earnings for unskilled workers being only ₹4,956 to ₹5,522. The case of skilled workers is not much better, with the reported monthly range for them being ₹5,945 to ₹7,925.

The role of the intermediary is of importance, as he allows the company management (who is undertaking the work) to 'side-step responsibility that comes with direct recruitment of workers' (Srivastava and Sutradhar 2016: 21). Most of the workforce in the industry is informalised and often casualised; survey findings report that 94.66 per cent of workers are in casual employment with no written contract (ibid.). This results in an absence of the possibility of collective bargaining. In the absence of labour's bargaining power, what we have is a booming industry marred by abysmal wage rates and hazardous conditions of work.

With a lack of regulation, there is hardly any investigation into working conditions in an industry that employs so many people. Anecdotal evidence suggests a very high incidence of injuries and even fatalities. A couple of journalists recently unearthed the huge discrepancy between officially reported deaths of construction workers and actual fatalities over the period 2013–16. As against the official number of 77 deaths at construction sites during the period, they found cases of at least 1,092 deaths (Jain and Matharu 2017). The real numbers are expected to be much higher, as the investigation was limited to construction worker deaths in major cities. Yet this is a telling figure that highlights the highly hazardous working conditions in which workers toil. With the available evidence, it can be said that about 50 million people work in a sector characterised by widespread criminal negligence.

Given that the labour market in the construction industry is highly informal and segmented, there is a need to create mechanisms through which labour supply can be judiciously synchronised with demand. This should result in the elimination of intermediaries who manage labour supply and discipline the workforce, and the assumption of greater responsibility by the principal employers. This should be done in a manner that allows for the safeguarding of rights and provision of welfare services to those engaged in work in the industry. Arrangements of housing and healthcare services, as well as access to education for accompanying minors, must be ensured if there is any chance of work in this industry to approximate decent work standards.

Further, given that the workforce in this sector is almost entirely composed of migrants, with a high representation of marginalised communities,[21] it is imperative that we investigate ways of ensuring portable entitlements for such a vast population. Given the lack of local identification, migrant workers across industries suffer handicaps in accessing their legal entitlements as citizens. The suggestions regarding rejuvenation of the agrarian economy would help stem the tide of distress migrants to urban centres, but labour migration will continue to be a phenomenon we must be prepared to address. The following section provides suggestions regarding the social sector, which could address some of the concerns raised here.

Radical Welfarism: Increased Investment and Universal Access

In this last section, we consider the case of provision of essential services in India. Keeping in mind the context described in the first chapter of the book, it is evident that if the human development index of the population is to rise, then a lot depends on how access to essential services such as health, education, housing and transport is made available. There are competing schools of thought on this issue that provide opposed ways of addressing the concern.

First we consider the case put forward by the market-led approach to economic development. From this position, one would contend that for the provision of quality services, it is imperative to privatise the public services. This would lead to competition among service providers, which would result in the best-quality outputs being delivered at the most competitive rates. This would benefit both consumers, who would gain from the high quality of service, as well as producers who would have to constantly innovate owing to market pressures.

---

[21] This was an important finding of Srivastava and Sutradhar's (2016) study.

The state in this view must sit out, its only role being to ensure a uniform playing field for the various competing private actors. Any interference from the state, let alone state provisioning of services, would lead to distortions in the market and hamper efficiency. It would also create incentives for political capture of state agencies by competing interests in the society, which would result in exclusion on the basis of social fault lines. Thus, for the optimal provisioning (both in terms of quality and price) of public services, the free play of market forces should be enabled. The discussion in Chapter 4 has shown that increasingly Indian policy makers are heeding this view by cutting social sector expenditure.

While such a view may seem to champion the creative potential of individual actors and extol the virtues of competition for the larger society, it obfuscates the reality of market-based competition. This is particularly relevant when we consider the case of essential public services, to which all members of society need access to have the opportunity to develop their potential. The mechanism of service delivery is based on effective demand, and in a market-oriented setup, this demand is indexed to the purchasing power of the subject. The demand for essential public services in reality is universal, but a market-based approach can only address a subset of it that is backed by adequate purchasing power. Further, the inevitable claim by market proponents of any interference by the state disrupting the system reveals the logic of accumulation that runs contrary to the concern of universal provisioning. Following from such a claim, we would arrive at the conclusion that although the market mechanism can only provide for a subset of the demand, it must necessarily be allowed to function even if it denies access to services for a section of the population. The others must wait till they *make it* before accessing essential services delivered through the market mechanism. This inversion of logic (achieving the necessary level of purchasing power requires access to essential services to begin with) is commonplace in what is often called 'market fundamentalism'.

The question that confronts us then is the following: if our aim is to ensure access to essential services or public goods for all, then is the market mechanism the best way of achieving this? The answer from the competing school of thought is a resolute 'No'. This is so not just because the market necessarily excludes a set of people, but also because it often builds on existing fault lines within society and ends up exacerbating inequality. Moreover, there is a way of ensuring universal access to quality public services. This requires an approach that does not see public goods as commodities to be bought and sold in the open market, but as common resources to which everyone is entitled. We need to think in terms of de-commodification of essential services and socialised provisioning of the same, in order to ensure universal access to them.

With close to 40 per cent of our population under the age of 18, it is crucial that structural changes be made to the schooling system. The state should invest in a quality, publicly funded common schooling system that can cater to the needs of the teeming numbers of young Indians. The importance of investing in the future cannot be overstated. This is not so just for economic reasons—the creation of a better-equipped workforce—but also because of the societal consequences. The aim should be to create thinking individuals through a wholesome educational experience, who learn through the experience of diversity. At present, our schooling system is intensely hierarchical with private schools catering to the requirement of the middle and upper strata, while most students suffer through an inadequately provisioned public schooling system. It is true that there are high-quality public schools as well, but it is well known that those are the exception rather than the rule. While enrolment in schools has been increasing, it has not resulted in a rise in capability.[22] The schooling system needs a systemic overhaul, and a common schooling framework is needed to address the extent of the problem confronting us.

---

[22] The latest *Annual Status of Education Report* (ASER Centre 2018), focusing on the 14–18-year bracket, tells us that 86 per cent of 14–18-year-olds are in formal schooling. This age bracket accounts for 100 million Indians, and school enrolment has risen significantly over the last decade. Yet the same cannot be said for actual learning, as 57 per cent of this group could not do basic division, 25 per cent could not read in their own language, and about half could not read in English.

India ranks among the worst examples of healthcare provisioning when compared with similar countries globally. Public expenditure on healthcare has been abysmally low over the years. The country ranks among the highest in terms of out-of-pocket expenditure, with over 60 per cent of all expenditure on healthcare being out-of-pocket. With this being the major characteristic of healthcare financing, it is revealing that the most prevalent ailments are actually common communicable diseases. Investments in a system of universal healthcare, with particular attention to primary healthcare services, are the need of the hour. Not only is preventing avoidable misery and death an ethical obligation of the state, it is economically prudent to invest in the working capacity of individuals.

Conceiving of such a project has consequences. Primary among them is the question of expenditure. A system of socialised universal public services would require much greater investment than is currently afforded owing to the strictures of fiscal prudence and maintenance of a 'favourable business environment'.[23] An economic system that prioritises people's needs over the logic of accumulation would demand increased investment in essential services. The provision of quality health and education would in the long run increase the capacity of the overall system while improving the life chances of the millions who are disempowered by the current regime of growth.

Financing for an Equitable Future: The Case for Progressive Taxation

It is sometimes argued that India cannot afford the public spending required to ensure universal quality education, healthcare and social protection, and the strengthening of Indian agriculture, which are the principal recommendations of this chapter. However, this ignores that the amount of public resources available for public investment is not

---

[23] These conditions are the impositions of a global economic order that seeks to preserve the dominance of international finance capital by demanding from countries that they provide for the free movement of capital as well as favourable terms for its operation.

simply a given, but is the result of conscious public choices. As pointed out by Malhotra and Kundu (2016: 141),

> The magnitude of tax revenue and the manner of its mobilisation, in terms of its composition and incidence on different segments of the population, is of a direct consequence to the development process and human wellbeing in a society.... [A] high tax–GDP ratio with moderate tax rates (and a broad tax base) could spur growth through improved scope for provisioning of public goods in the economy. It could also support State capacity to create a social protection floor and, if required, specific entitlements, especially for the poor and the vulnerable of a society to help create more equal outcomes in the society. Similarly, a progressive tax system, where taxes levied take into account the ability of an individual to pay, is a potent redistributive tool, which could potentially support a more inclusive and an equitable development process.

'In India's case', the authors point out,

> unlike some other emerging economies, neither is the tax–GDP ratio adequately favourable to create the required fiscal space for augmenting the supply and quality of public goods and essential social services (primarily on account of narrow tax base and weaknesses in tax administration), nor is the tax system progressive enough, particularly at the state level, to address equity and inclusion in the development process. Furthermore, since there is inadequate production of public goods, inefficient delivery and uneven access of the poor and the marginalised to those goods, the development process is resulting in rising inequalities in social outcomes and exclusion of significant segments of people from the economic and social mainstream in the country. (Ibid.)

What is important is not just how much tax is raised, but who is taxed. The *India Exclusion Report* explains:

> Direct taxes in India are more or less progressive in their impact. However, that is not true of indirect taxes, which, by definition, are regressive in nature as they do not distinguish potential tax payers on the basis of their ability to pay or, in other words, on the

basis of their incomes. At the aggregate level (centre and states together), India collects only one-third of its total tax revenue from direct taxes, most of the developed countries and a few developing countries (like South Africa and Indonesia) depend on direct taxes to a much higher extent. (Malhotra and Kundu 2016: 141)

The report makes a cross-country analysis of public finances that shows that India mobilises comparatively less revenue with respect to its GDP. In 2013, India's total revenue (tax and non-tax) was 20 per cent of its GDP, and its tax revenue was around 16 per cent of GDP. A much smaller economy like Kenya (with about half of India's per capita income both in USD and purchasing power parity) also raised about the same magnitude of revenues. Figure 5.2 shows the revenue and total expenditure as a proportion of national GDP for India and a few developing and developed countries. France generates revenue equal to 53 per cent of its GDP compared to the US's 31 per cent (2014 figure). Accordingly, government expenditure in France and the US is 57 per cent and 37 per cent of the GDP respectively.

Figure 5.3 reflects the contribution of direct and indirect taxes in the overall revenue of the government. We may observe from the figure that there has not been a significant increase in either the direct or the indirect tax as a percentage of GDP. Government however is

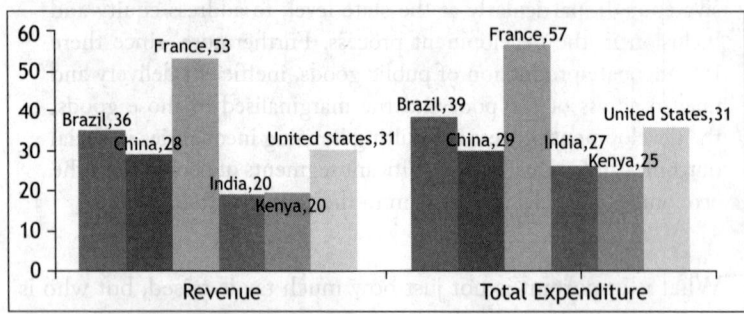

Figure 5.2 *Government Revenue and Expenditure as a Proportion of GDP in 2013*

Source: IMF World Economic Outlook Database, 2015.

Note: Revenue consists of taxes, social contributions, grants receivable and other revenue.

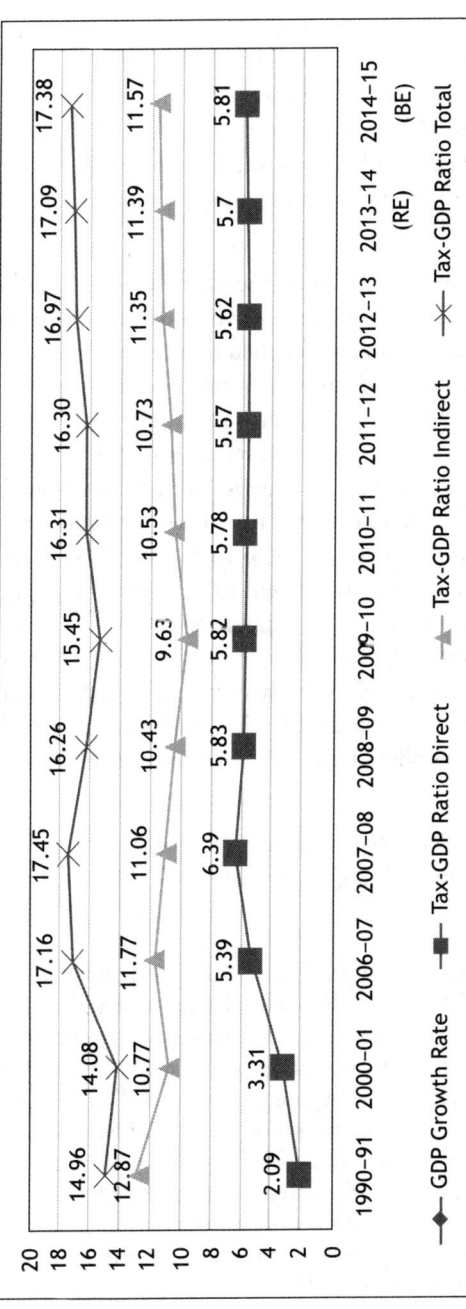

Figure 5.3 *India's Tax-GDP Ratio (Percentage of GDP)*

Source: Compiled by the author from Indian Public Finance Statistics 2014–15.

trying to increase its indirect tax base through a number of tax reforms whose primary purpose is to bring stability in tax laws, as demanded by private investors, rather than a conscious effort towards stepping up the country's tax–GDP ratio. It is important to note that the increase in indirect taxes is certainly going to affect the most vulnerable and disadvantaged communities of our country, as it applies equally across all the sections of the society—rich or poor.

It is evident from Figure 5.3 that the overall tax–GDP ratio of India has not increased much in the past 25 years. Although the economic reforms of 1991 claimed to have opened tremendous employment and business opportunities, the same is not reflected in the share of direct taxes. Also, since 2006–07, the direct tax share and overall tax–GDP ratio have remained constant. However, during this period there has been an increase in the share of indirect taxes in the overall revenue of the government. Despite such a poor tax–GDP ratio, the finance minister in his budget speech of 2015–16 proposed a reduction in the rate of corporate tax from 30 per cent to 25 per cent over a period of time—this despite the amount of tax revenue forgone due to many exemptions given to corporates. However, the finance minister stated in his budget speech the following year that: 'The reduction in corporate tax rate will be calibrated with additional revenue expected from the incentives being phased out.' The outcome of this decision is yet to be examined.

The report by Malhotra and Kundu (2016: 144–45) notes that there is no significant change in India's tax–GDP ratio in the high growth years:

> It has varied, for most of the last decade-and-half between 10 to 12 per cent of GDP for the central government and between 14 to 16 per cent for the central and state government combined. This is despite a spurt in GDP growth rate averaging about 8.5 per cent per annum in the first decade of this millennium, a steady growth of the tax base in the service sector, which now accounts for nearly 58 per cent of India's GDP, considerable improvements in tax administration, particularly in the ease of filing tax returns, interface with the tax authorities and the overall reforms in tax policy. In other words, there is little, if any, growth in tax revenues in response to growth in GDP.

Malhotra and Kundu (2016) demonstrate that there are fewer persons filing income tax returns than desirable, and that the income tax revenues of the government could be a multiple of the realised amounts. There is significant underreporting of incomes when it comes to filing income tax returns in India. In the process, the study provides some quantitative evidence to support the popular perception regarding the tax avoidance behaviour of Indians. Besides the fact that indirect taxes are regressive in their impact, as they do not distinguish a poor person from a non-poor tax-paying person, the study provides evidence to suggest that significant proportions of persons, both in the better-off and the backward states, are being pushed into poverty (that is, into household consumption expenditure levels below the official poverty line) on account of the indirect tax burden they face on their consumption expenditure.

Therefore, we conclude that given the extant direct tax policy regime, India is certainly not collecting tax revenues from those who can and should pay taxes, in keeping with the size of its economy and the growth in average per capita incomes that it has witnessed in recent decades. It does have the potential resources, if it summons the social and political will, to revive its dying agriculture, to ensure decent work conditions for all, and to invest in universal education, healthcare and social protection, to end the continuing tragedy of highly unequal life chances for people based only on the accident of their birth.

The financing of this investment can be arranged by increasing compliance with taxation norms as well as by introducing a substantive progressive taxation policy. Further, a look at the value of bad loans, or non-performing assets, on the balance sheets of public sector banks paints a striking picture of where our priorities lie at the moment. Since the former governor of the Reserve Bank of India, Raghuram Rajan, instituted assets quality norms, about ₹600,000 crore of bad loans have been recognised (*Hindu* 2016). The public sector banks share a much greater burden of these debts, with the non-performing assets of the top 20 public sector banks amounting to ₹154,000 crore. This makes India one of the worst performers globally in terms of bad loans as a percentage of total advances, standing at 9.9 per cent, and places the country among the top five major economies of the world with high levels of non-performing assets (*Times of India* 2017). This is not including restructured loans, accounting for which would raise the stressed assets percentage up to 16 per cent (T. Bandopadhyay 2017).

Indicative of our priorities is the fact that the biggest defaulters on public money are big businesses. The *Financial Stability Report*, 2016, shows that as of March 2016, 'large borrowers had taken 58 per cent of the loans but were responsible for 86.4 per cent of the non-performing assets' (Jain 2016). Further, there are indications that the repayment of corporate debt might not be smooth sailing for public sector creditors, further stressing public finances. These facts represent the extent of avoidable waste if the private sector is disciplined to institute a modicum of financial prudence in its workings. Recovery of even half the public debt could make available a very substantial amount for investments in essential services that benefit all citizens and not just a handful of companies and their shareholders. An increase in tax rates for the top decile in income distribution, along with a reduction in the tax exemptions provided to the private sector, coupled with efforts to increase compliance would generate substantial resources to invest adequately in avenues such as health and education. A doubling of the tax to GDP ratio should be the minimum target, which would make a fifth of the value of total output available for investment in people's capacities.

Ensuring access for millions of underprivileged members of society to quality essential services, particularly health, education and housing, is not only imperative from the vantage point of ethics, but also makes sound economic sense as one is investing in the long-run productive capacities of a great many people, who would then be able to contribute more efficiently to economic activity.

Summing Up: Towards a People-centric Model of Economic Development

In this chapter, we have attempted to outline the basic course correction that needs to take place in order for economic development to have a substantively positive impact on the lives of the majority of people in the country. The idea has been to take a step back from the obsession around growth as an end in itself—which we understand as one of the hallmarks of neoliberal orthodoxy in the current phase of capitalist development—and to frame the problematic of economic development in terms of people's needs. Implicitly, the discussions in this chapter have been concerned with the question: why is economic development important? Depending on how one answers this question, the pathways to development or growth can accordingly be spoken about meaningfully. We answer this question by drawing a relation between economic development and the possibility of people realising their potentials as human beings. Economic growth or development is meaningful in so far as it creates possibilities for people in society to realise their potential and express the same.

Judging by such a metric, the current situation as it obtains in India leaves a lot to be desired. As we noted in earlier chapters, the current model of economic growth, rather than fostering people's self-realisation, is often the reason for the brutalisation of their lives. We therefore have to think of creative ways of transcending such a scenario. The first step in doing so is to denaturalise the claims of the neoliberal orthodoxy, which contends that any attempt to interfere with the workings of 'market forces' will result in imbalances in the economy, the cost of dealing with which will always be higher than whatever value the intervention can deliver. This naturalisation of particular modes of organising economic activity in society, as we discussed in the first section of this chapter, is an ideological manoeuvre to protect the interests served by the status quo. The effort in this chapter has been to overcome this manoeuvre and to imagine the possibilities we are capable of as a collective. This reimagination of economic development is a task much greater than we had set ourselves in this book, and requires the creative coming together of myriad participants. However, we think that there are some basic ingredients that any such reimagination must include. We end our discussion by summarising these ingredients, and call for further research and action towards understanding the kind of economic development that would be desirable given the needs of our society, and towards realising the same.

The preceding discussion has brought to the fore some suggestions that we think are necessary if we are to move away from an economic system that thrives on the creation of inequality, inhibiting people from realising their potentials. Here we sum up the long-term vision of economic development from a people-centric perspective.

Support of and investment in the agrarian economy, particularly the productive sustenance of the smallholder economy, by engaging it in the task of ensuring nutritional security for all would stem the tide of distress migration and allow people to engage productively in the rural/agrarian economy. Over time, this would result in increased demand from those engaged in the sector. Development of small and medium agro cooperatives adding value to farm produce and engaged in marketing the same would go a long way in ensuring a fair price to the producers, as well as absorbing a large segment of young workers seeking non-agricultural work.

Protection of workers in the unorganised sector against excessive exploitation while providing them with basic entitlements would result in a better distribution of value created in the sector. This would enable the working population to increase its consumption and would lead to enhancement of the human capital stock of the country.

Initiatives in these two broad areas (the agrarian economy and the unorganised sector) need to be complemented with increase in expenditure on the provisioning of public services, the delivery of which needs to be socialised. This would result in the comprehensive increment of effective demand from the vast majority of the population. This broad-based demand would form the engine of long-term economic development. It would also create a large number of jobs in the essential services category. There is a pressing need to recognise that these are much-needed jobs that must be created.[24]

[24] With a growing economy and increasing working population, it is imperative that the state sector expands. This was the case in the historical development of the so-called developed countries as well. The 19th and early 20th centuries saw a massive expansion of state jobs and governmental provision of basic services in these countries. The reason for this is very simple—it is only the state which can be tasked with the provision of these basic services. Thus, even from a thoroughly capitalist point of view, to reap the benefits of a young workforce in the long run, it is important to have the state ensure the provision of necessary healthcare, nutrition, education and housing.

This is a simplified version of what is an extremely complicated project. The purpose of discussing it here was to highlight some principles and necessary features of what a model of economic growth that prioritises people's needs over the logic of accumulation might look like. In the context of the debate around the demographic dividend, it is imperative to reimagine economic development along such lines if we are to avoid a catastrophe and to equip ourselves to create a sustainable and peaceful community in the future.

Appendix

A.1 Demographic Transition in India

The age–sex pyramid captures the demographic development in illuminating ways. The age pyramid of developing countries today is peculiar, with a wide base and a bulge in the middle and a shrinking top. However, the shape has changed over a period of time.

As seen in Figure A.1, in 1975 the pyramid was wide at the bottom with the maximum percentage of the population belonging to age group 0–4, with shrinking sides and a pointed top. However, by 2000, there was a fall in the population in age groups 0–14, more so among the 0–4 group due to reductions in fertility, with the bulge moving upwards. By 2025, the bulge is expected to be at its peak with heavy population in the middle age group (15–64), a narrower base and an increase at the top. However by 2050, India will experience an odd-shaped age pyramid, with a narrower base and a wider top with a shrinking middle signalling the closing of the opportunity to secure a demographic dividend from then on. But it can still continue to reap a demographic dividend as long as the percentage of the working age population is higher than child and old age dependency combined.

A.2 Inter-group Variations in the Demographic Transition in India

The demographic transition has been unfolding for both SCs and STs during 2001–11, with a fall in the child population and increase in the 'working age' population (15–24 and 25–59 years), and a marginal increase in the older population (see Figures A.2 and A.3).

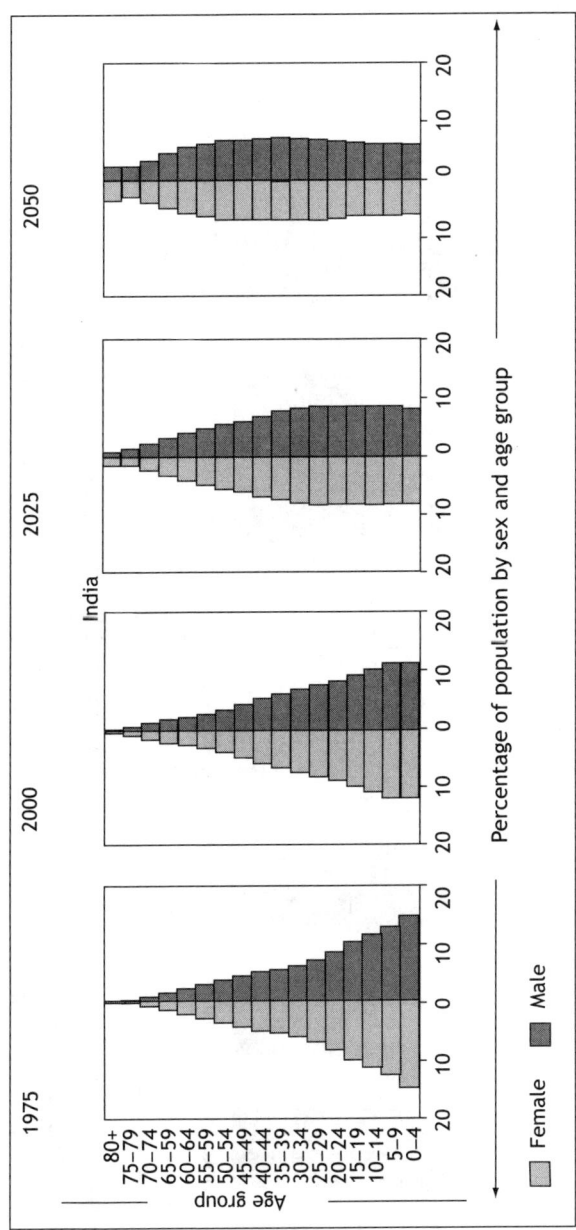

Figure A.1 *Changing Age Pyramids in India, 1975–2050*
Source: Drawn from WHO (2008: 38).

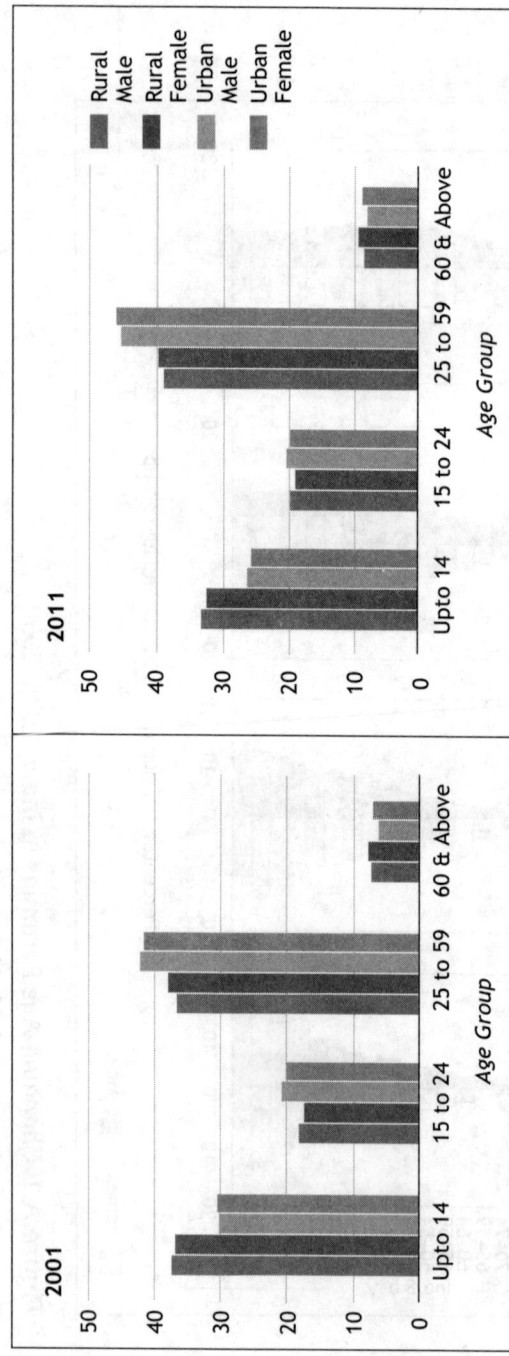

Figure A.2 Percentage Population Distribution of SCs by Residence and Gender, 2001–11
Source: Census 2001 and 2011.

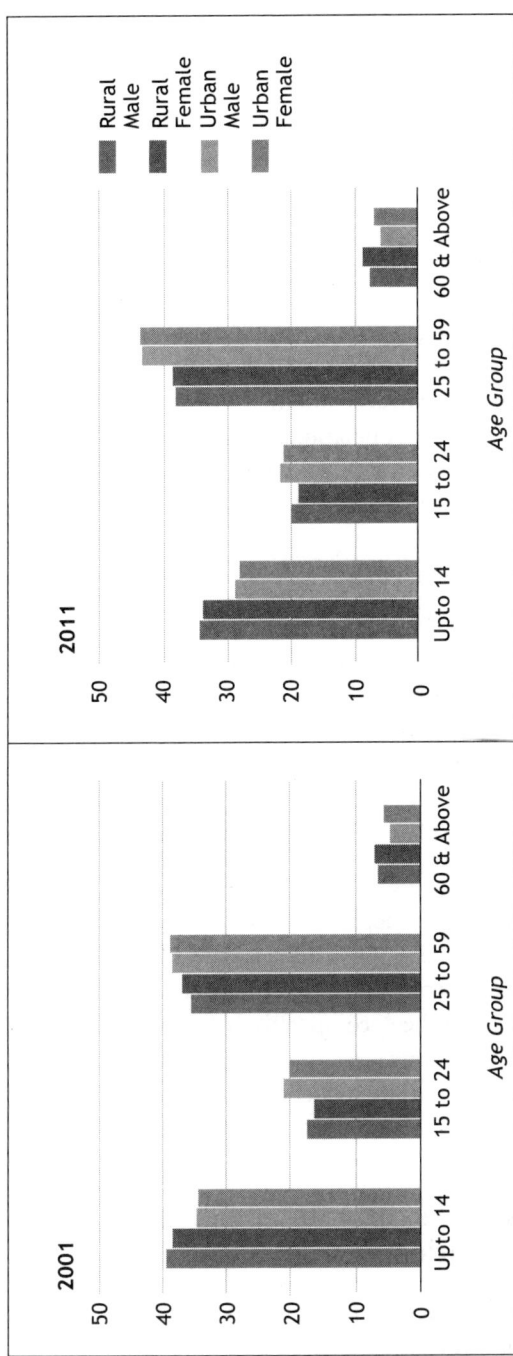

Figure A.3 *Percentage Population Distribution of STs by Residence and Gender, 2001–11*

Source: Census 2001 and 2011.

There exist rural–urban differentials in population distribution for both SCs and STs, with the population aged 0–14 and 60 and above concentrated more in rural areas, whereas the population belonging to the working age group (15–24 and 25–59 combined) is more concentrated in urban areas. This indicates that there exists an increasing opportunity to secure a demographic advantage for both SCs and STs in rural areas from transitions in age structure by providing them equal life chances in health, nutrition, education and employment, as they are yet to reach their maximum working age population. Such opportunities are however nullified by facts that speak to the contrary. The SC and ST populations rank highest in IMR (NFHS 2005–06) and MMR (RCH-2 2002–04) respectively. Also, STs have the highest U5MR (NFHS 2005–06) and illiteracy. In such a context, these historically marginalised people are also overrepresented in rural indebtedness, seasonal migration and casualised workforce with near-absent social security.

The transition in the age structure of the Muslim population is presented in Figure A.4. During 2001–11, the Muslim population in the working age group increased but not as much as in India overall. The demographic transition has been slower for Muslims in rural areas, as a large proportion of the population still belonged to the age group 0–14 in both 2001 and 2011. However, the transition has been better for Muslims in urban areas.

A comparison of the demographic transition across SCs, STs and Muslims shows that the pace of transition is slower for Muslims as compared to SCs and STs, because of high fertility. However, the transition among SCs and STs has been comparatively fast, with the population moving towards the 'working age' group. The demographic bonus that depends on the pace of fertility reduction has still a long way to go for Muslims in India, and more so for those who live in rural areas.

A.3 Changes in Fertility Rates across Different Categories

Fertility transition has been occurring across all states and all sections of the population, but some are ahead and have lower fertility than

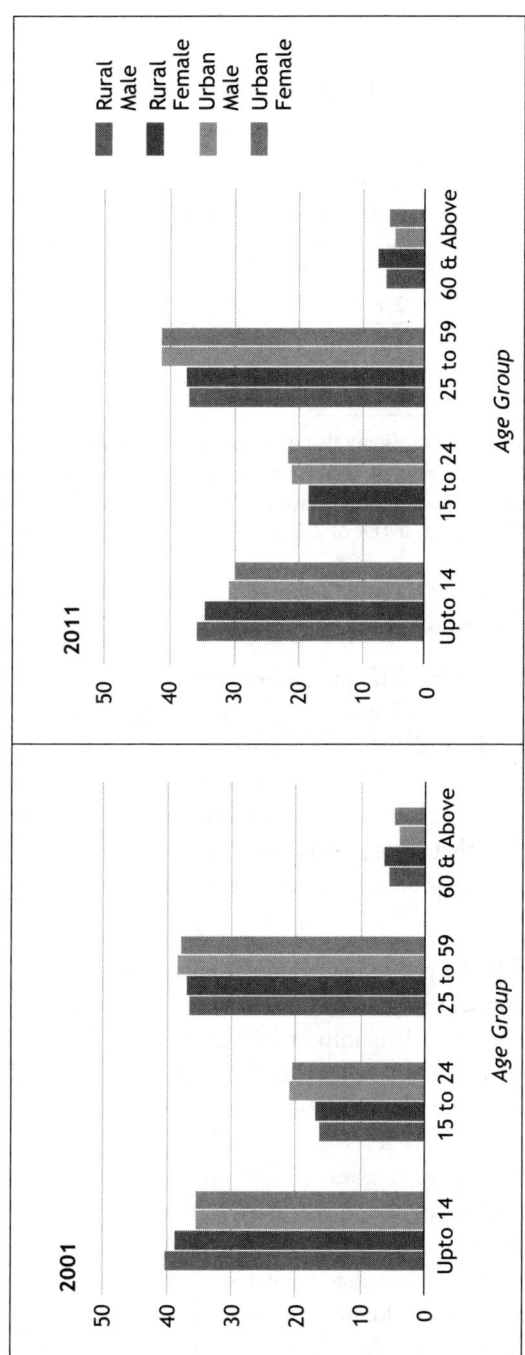

Figure A.4 *Percentage Population Distribution of Muslims by Residence and Gender, 2001–11*

Source: Census 2001 and 2011.

Table A.1 Total Fertility Rate per Woman as per Census 2001 and 2011

	Scheduled Castes		Scheduled Tribes		Muslim		All India	
	2001	2011	2001	2011	2001	2011	2001	2011
Total	2.9	2.3	3.2	2.6	3.1	2.7	2.5	2.4
Rural	3.1	2.5	3.2	2.7	3.5	3.0	2.8	2.7
Urban	2.1	1.8	2.2	1.8	2.3	2.2	1.8	1.9

Source: Office of the Registrar General and Census Commissioner, 2001 and 2011.
Note: TFR is defined as the average number of children that would be born per woman during her entire reproductive period. With a nearly equal chance of male and female births, a TFR of 2.0 is considered a replacement level.

average, while some are lagging. Table A.1 shows changes in the TFR among SCs, STs and Muslims vis-à-vis all-India during 2001–11.

It can be seen that the differentials between caste and tribe exist but are not very wide. Fertility levels among STs are higher than SCs, more so in rural areas than urban areas. However, the TFR for Muslims (2.7) is high compared to SCs (2.3), STs (2.6) and the all-India level (2.4) as per census 2011. The rate of decline in total fertility among STs is greater than that among Muslims. A rural–urban comparison of TFRs across all categories reflects that the gap has narrowed between 2001 and 2011.

The high TFR of 3 per woman among rural Muslims in 2011 compared to the national level and to other socially disadvantaged groups needs a deeper analysis. It is important here to state that comparing fertility rates between Muslims and Hindus as though these are homogeneous categories is not appropriate and can be misleading. This is because Muslims face high levels of economic deprivation compared to Hindus as a whole. Large families are not a result of Muslim culture and norms, but rather the result of low education levels, poverty and social exclusion, resulting in unequal life chances for the community. There is increasing evidence that suggests that socio-economic characteristics rather than religion actually explain fertility differentials in India (Iyer 2002). Hindus and Muslims of comparable economic and educational status have comparable fertility levels. For instance, TFR among Muslims in Kerala is 1.6, which is the same as the TFR in the state overall. However, in northern states where TFR is high, the difference between the fertility levels of Hindus and Muslims is high. Increased age at marriage, improved women's education levels, improved child survival due to adequate healthcare provision and increased adoption of contraception are key factors that lead to fertility decline.

A.4 Life Expectancy

An analysis of life expectancy levels in India reveals that longevity increased substantially during the 1970s and 1980s, and slowed down during the 1990s and 2000s. Figure A.5 shows the trends in life expectancy at birth during 1970–2013, demonstrating a continuous rise in longevity which primarily reflects improvements in infant and child mortality rates. However, it is noteworthy that female life expectancy at birth was lower than male life expectancy up until the 1980s, and that it was only after the 1990s that it became higher than male life expectancy. This is observed to be due to lower mortality rates among females than males.

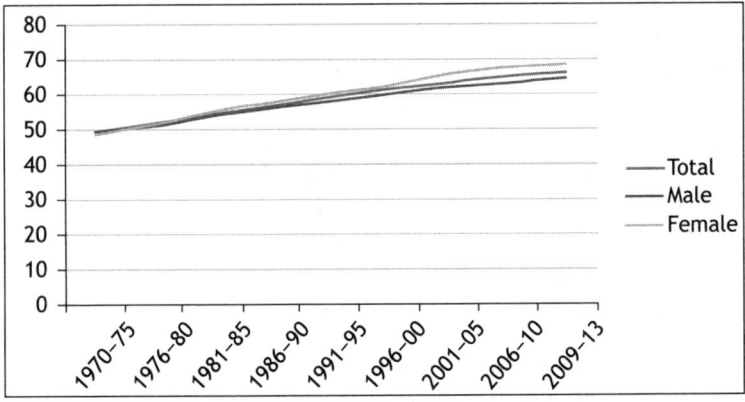

Figure A.5 *Trends in Life Expectancy at Birth by Sex, 1970–75 to 2009–13*

Source: Sample Registration System, Compendium of India's Fertility and Mortality Indicators, 2007–13.

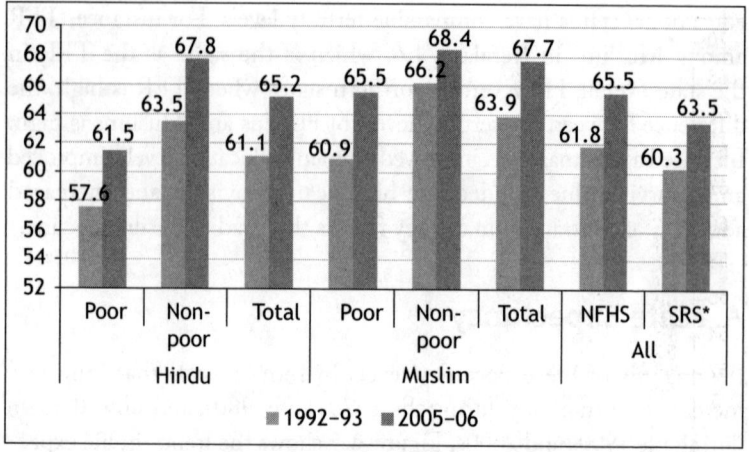

Figure A.6 *Trends in Life Expectancy at Birth (in Years) by Poverty Level and Religion, 1992–93 to 2005–06*
Source: Analysis based on tables drawn from Mohanty and Ram (2010).

There are variations in life expectancy levels among caste and tribe groups, poverty level and religions. Figure A.6 shows the trends in life expectancy by poverty level and religion using estimates from NFHS-1 (1992–93) and NFHS-3 (2005–06). During 1992–2006, the life expectancy at birth for Muslims increased from 64 to 68 years, while for Hindus it increased from 61 to 65 years. This is because Muslims are more urban based, and there are better health facilities in urban areas. As per the census of 2011, about 40 per cent Muslims live in urban areas compared to 30 per cent Hindus. Life expectancy differentials exist among the poor and non-poor for both Hindus and Muslims. In the case of Muslims, life expectancy rose from 61 to 66 years among poor economic groups, compared with a rise from 66 to 68 years among non-poor economic groups.

Economic class continues to affect life expectancy outcomes across religious groups, although there is an interesting interplay between caste and class when it comes to life expectancy. Figure A.7 shows the trends in life expectancy by poverty level and caste group using estimates from NFHS-2 (1998–99) and NFHS-3 (2005–06). The difference in life expectancy between the poor belonging to SCs and STs

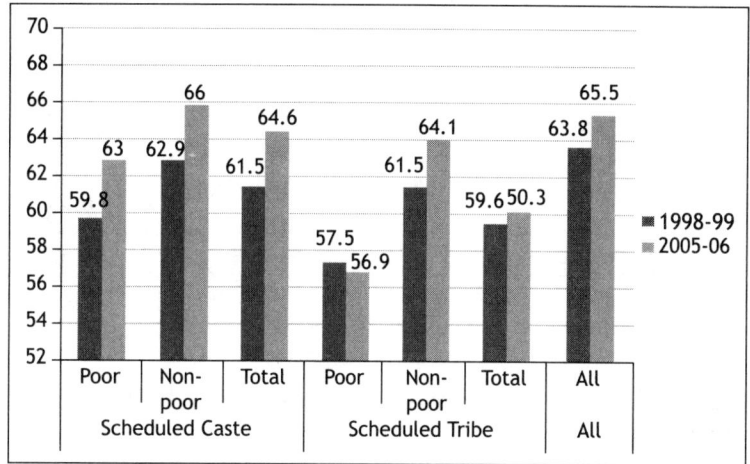

Figure A.7 *Trends in Life Expectancy at Birth (in Years) by Poverty Level and Caste Groups, 1998–99 to 2005–06*

Source: Analysis based on tables drawn from Mohanty and Ram (2010).

and people from the non-poor category belonging to SCs and STs is not high, but the levels of life expectancy for STs are lower than for SCs.

A.5 Infant Mortality Rate and Under-5 Mortality Rate

The levels of child mortality are determined by a multiplicity of factors. There are maternal factors (mother's education, mother's nutritional status, spacing between childbirths and age of mother), social and economic factors (caste group of the child, standard of living and sex of the child), household and community factors (water, sanitation and housing facilities) and proximate factors (medical care at birth and during the antenatal and postnatal periods). The U5MR declined from 126 in 1990 to 91 in 2000 and to 48 in 2015, with an annual rate of reduction of 3.9 per cent during 1990–2015. The IMR (deaths per 1,000 live births) also declined from 88 in 1990 to 38 in 2015.

There has been a consistent decline in the IMR and U5MR over the years. The trends in IMR in rural and urban areas are shown in Figure A.8. The rural–urban gap in IMRs during 1991–2013 narrowed

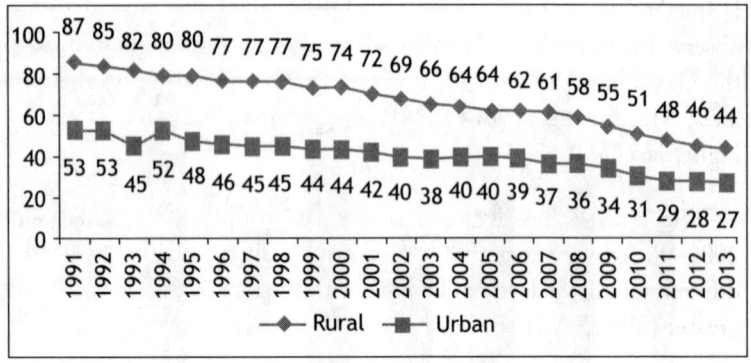

Figure A.8 *Trends in Infant Mortality Rates by Residence,*
1991–2013
Source: Sample Registration System.

from 34 to 17. In 1991, the IMR in rural areas stood at 87 per 1,000
live births, compared to 53 per 1,000 live births in urban areas. The
IMR declined to 44 per 1,000 live births in rural areas, and to 27 per
1,000 live births in urban areas.

It is, however, important to highlight the level of inter-group disparities in IMR across SCs, STs and Muslims in India (Figure A.9).

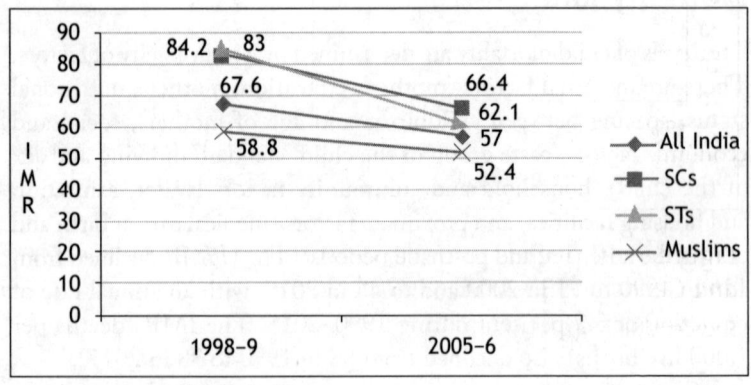

Figure A.9 *Trends in Infant Mortality Rates by SCs, STs and
Muslims, 1998–99 to 2005–06*
Source: Government of India (2011).

Using NFHS-2 (1998–99) and NFHS-3 (2005–06) estimates, it is observed that IMR declined for all groups during this period, with the maximum fall occurring among STs. Compared to the all-India level, Muslims had a lower IMR level whereas SCs and STs had a higher level.

The U5MR has declined across all groups from 1992–93 to 2005–06. It is evident that a rural–urban differential and a gender differential exist in levels of U5MR, with the former differential being greater (Figure A.10).

Trends in under-5 mortality across SCs and STs (see Figure A.11) indicate that the rates were higher for SCs in 1992–93, after which STs showed higher rates both in 1998–99 and in 2005–06. Though there has been a decline in mortality for both SCs and STs, the decline is higher for SCs.

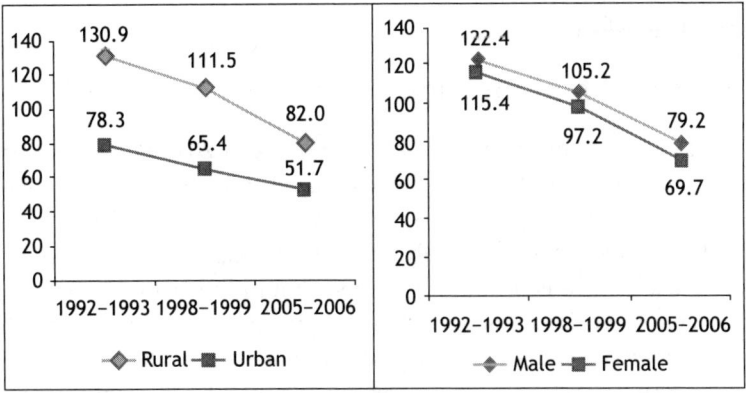

Figure A.10 *Trends in Under-5 Mortality Rates by Residence and Gender, 1992–1993 to 2005–06*
Source: UNICEF (2011).

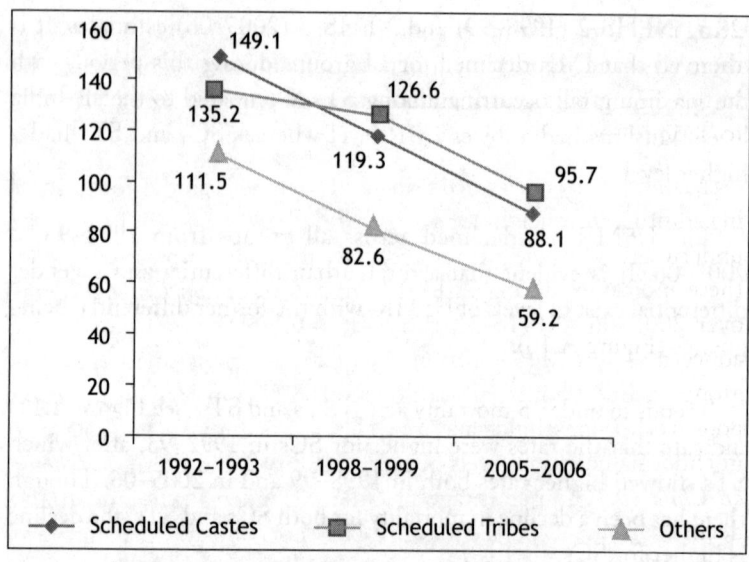

Figure A.11 *Trends in Under-5 Mortality Rates by Caste Group, 1992–1993 to 2005–06*
Source: UNICEF (2011).

A.6 Child Malnutrition

India's ranking on the Global Hunger Index in 2016 was 97 out of 118 countries, which is very low compared to its neighbours' rankings, especially China which is way ahead (at 29), but also Nepal (72) and Bangladesh (90). It is only a few steps ahead of Pakistan (107). The Global Hunger Index presents a multidimensional measure of national, regional and global hunger, including the proportion of undernourished as a percentage of the population, the prevalence of underweight children under the age of 5 and the mortality rate of children under the age of 5 (calculated average, in percentages). India's Global Hunger Index ranking fell from a low 83 in 2000 to 97 in 2016, but with an improvement in index value[1] from 36.2 to

---

[1] According to the International Food Policy Research Institute, an index value in the range 10–19.9 indicates moderate hunger situation, 20–34.9 serious, 35–49.9 alarming, ≥50 extremely alarming and ≤9.9 a low hunger situation.

28.5, indicating that other countries have outstripped India though there was some improvement in nutrition outcomes. This means that in the high growth years, India's standing has risen from 'alarming' to 'serious' levels.

Malnutrition is measured using anthropometric indicators, including stunting (low height for age), wasting (low weight for height) and underweight (low weight for age). Despite some impressive gains in these indicators during 2013–14 (*Rapid Survey on Children* data[2]) over 2005–06 (NFHS-3), the high absolute levels are of serious concern. There are significant inequalities across socio-economic groups in India, with malnutrition levels higher in rural areas, among poor wealth households and SCs. There is significant improvement in child malnutrition levels between NFHS-3 and the *Rapid Survey on Children*. The percentage of children under 5 who are stunted declined from 48 per cent to 39 per cent, and the percentage of wasted declined from 20 per cent to 15 per cent; the percentage of underweight declined from 43 per cent to 29 per cent between 2005–06 and 2013–14. The incidence of malnutrition is high both among STs and SCs compared with overall malnutrition levels in India (Figure A.12).

Across most malnutrition indicators, the situation of Muslims is worse than that of Hindus and in India overall. Figure A.13 shows the changes in child malnutrition levels for Muslims relative to Hindus. During 2005–06, 50 per cent of under-5 children from Muslim households were stunted compared with 48 per cent from Hindu households. Though there was some improvement during 2013–14, it has been greater in the case of Hindus (39 per cent) than Muslims (42 per cent). The Muslims performed better than Hindus with respect to the prevalence of wasting in both 2005–06 and 2013–14.

---

[2] The nationwide *Rapid Survey on Children* was conducted by the Ministry of Women and Child Development and the United Nations Children's Fund in 2013–14 (see Government of India 2014a). This was the first nationwide survey on child nutrition conducted in almost a decade after NFHS-3 in 2005. The NFHS-3 and the *Rapid Survey on Children* use different population sets and different methodologies, therefore they are not entirely comparable. But in the absence of any recent data on malnutrition, these sources have been used.

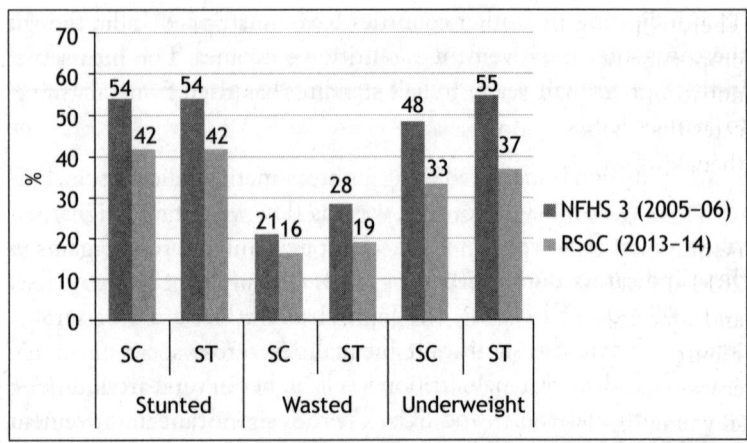

Figure A.12 *Changes in Stunting, Wasting and Underweight among Children under 5 Years by SC/ST, 2005–06 and 2013–14*

Source: NFHS-3, 2005–06; and *Rapid Survey on Children 2013–14* (Government of India 2014a).

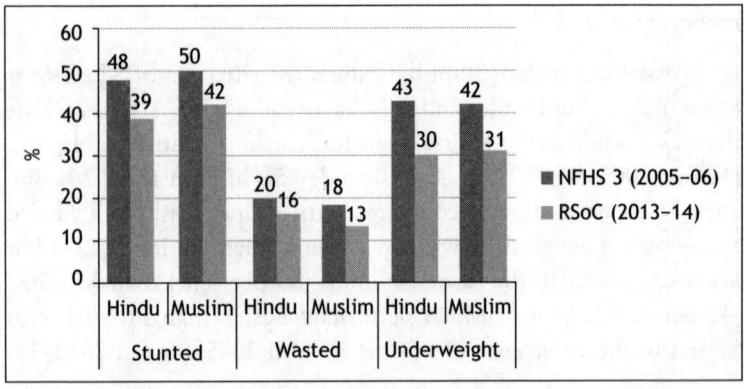

Figure A.13 *Changes in Stunting, Wasting and Underweight among Children under 5 Years among Hindu and Muslim Populations, 2005–06 and 2013–14*

Source: NFHS-3, 2005–06; and *Rapid Survey on Children 2013–14* (Government of India 2014a).

There is not much of a gap between Hindus and Muslims in the proportion of under-5 children being underweight. A comparison of nutrition outcomes across caste and tribe groups and Muslims indicates that malnutrition levels are worse for STs followed by SCs and then Muslims.

There were improvements in the habits of defecating in the open, institutional deliveries, and provision of vitamin A supplements in 2013–14 over 2005–06; but these were not sufficient in rural areas, and among SCs and STs, Muslims and the poorest households. Figure A.14 shows that the number of people who practise open defecation has come down from 55 per cent to 45 per cent. Malnutrition in young children is strongly related to adverse toilet facilities. Also, institutional deliveries have increased from 41 per cent to 79 per cent, and provision of vitamin A from 30 per cent to 46 per cent during this period. As already mentioned, these indicators have not improved much in the case of vulnerable sections, indicating skewed public health efforts.

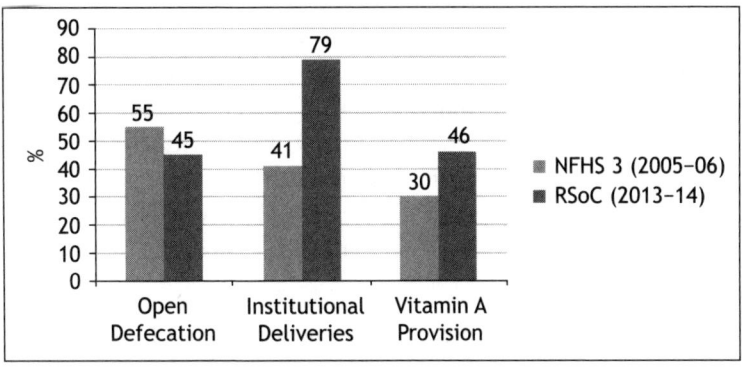

Figure A.14 *Changes in Open Defecation Practices, Institutional Deliveries and Vitamin A Provision among Children under 5 Years, 2005–06 and 2013–14*

Source: NFHS-3, 2005–06; and *Rapid Survey on Children 2013–14* (Government of India 2014a).

A.7 Sex Ratio

Trends in the sex ratio at birth reveal that in rural areas and in India as a whole, the sex ratio declined from 1999 to 2004, after which it improved but only slowly. This is attributed to the fertility decline experienced by most states, which contributed to a change in total population. Except Punjab, Haryana, Himachal Pradesh, Gujarat and Maharashtra, there is less discrimination against girls in other states (Unisa 2009). Compared to 1999–2004, when the sex ratio dropped from 898 to 880, the period 2004–12 saw an increase from 892 to 909. However, in urban areas, the sex ratio declined till 2002, after which it rose. It is interesting to note that low sex ratio at birth is more an urban phenomenon than rural. During 2012, the sex ratio at birth stood at 910 in rural areas compared with 906 in urban areas. However, the sex ratio varies widely by place of residence, caste group and religion. Figure A.15 shows that sex ratio at birth for Muslims has worsened more than in any other group, from 931 in 2001 to 918 in 2011. However, it is striking to note that the sex ratio among marginalised sections such as SCs, STs and Muslims is better than the sex ratio of the overall population.

Figure A.16 shows that the overall sex ratio increased from 933 in 2001 to 940 in 2011. There was a significant improvement in the sex ratio in urban areas from 900 to 943, in contrast with rural areas where sex ratio declined from 946 to 929. This indicates an increase in the gender gap in rural areas. Inter-group comparisons reveal that STs have the highest sex ratios (990 in 2011 over 978 in 2001) followed by Muslims (951 in 2011 over 940 in 2001) and SCs (946 in 2011 over 936 in 2001).

Child sex ratio denotes the number of females per 1,000 males in the age group 0–6 years. It dropped to its lowest level of 918 in 2011 from 927 in 2001, the lowest since independence. Though the child sex ratio is better in rural areas than urban areas, the gap has narrowed from 28 to 18 percentage points during 2001–11 (Figure A.17). Child sex ratio patterns across SC and ST groups and Muslims also showed considerable change during this period. Among other categories, STs had the highest child sex ratio both during 2001 (957) and 2011 (951),

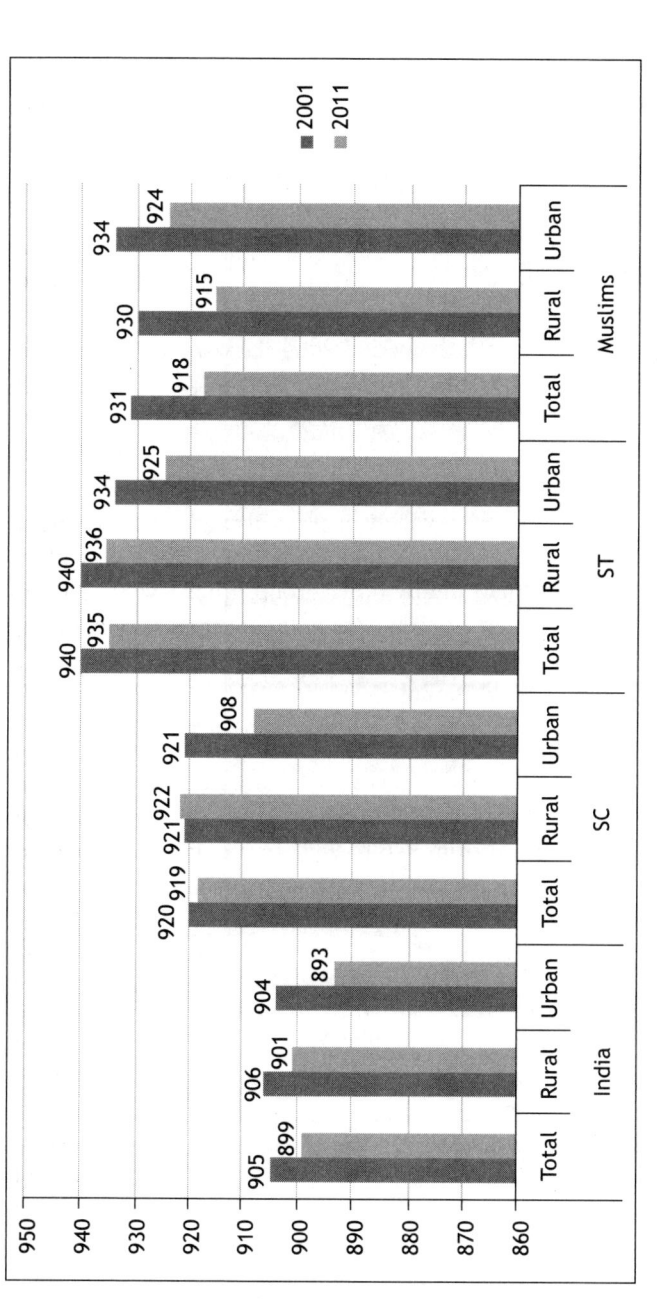

Figure A.15 *Sex Ratio at Birth by SC, ST, Religion and Residence, 2001 and 2011*

Source: Primary Census Abstract, Census of India 2001 and 2011.

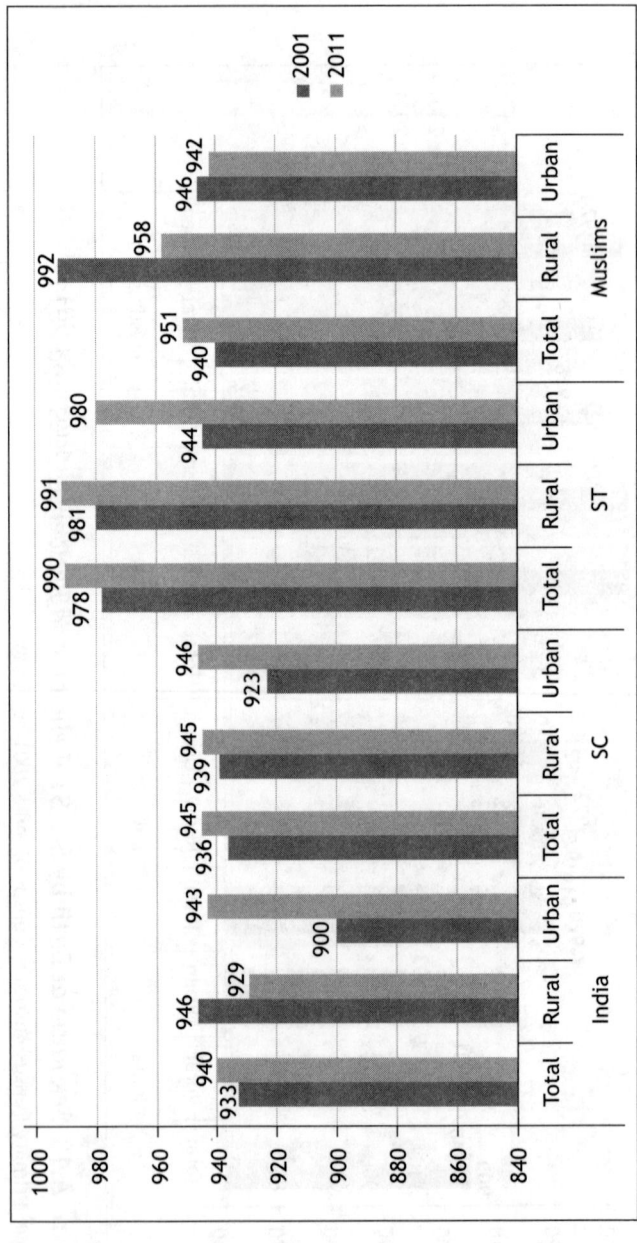

Figure A.16 *Overall Sex Ratio by SC, ST, Religion and Residence, 2001 and 2011*

Source: Primary Census Abstract, Census of India 2001 and 2011.

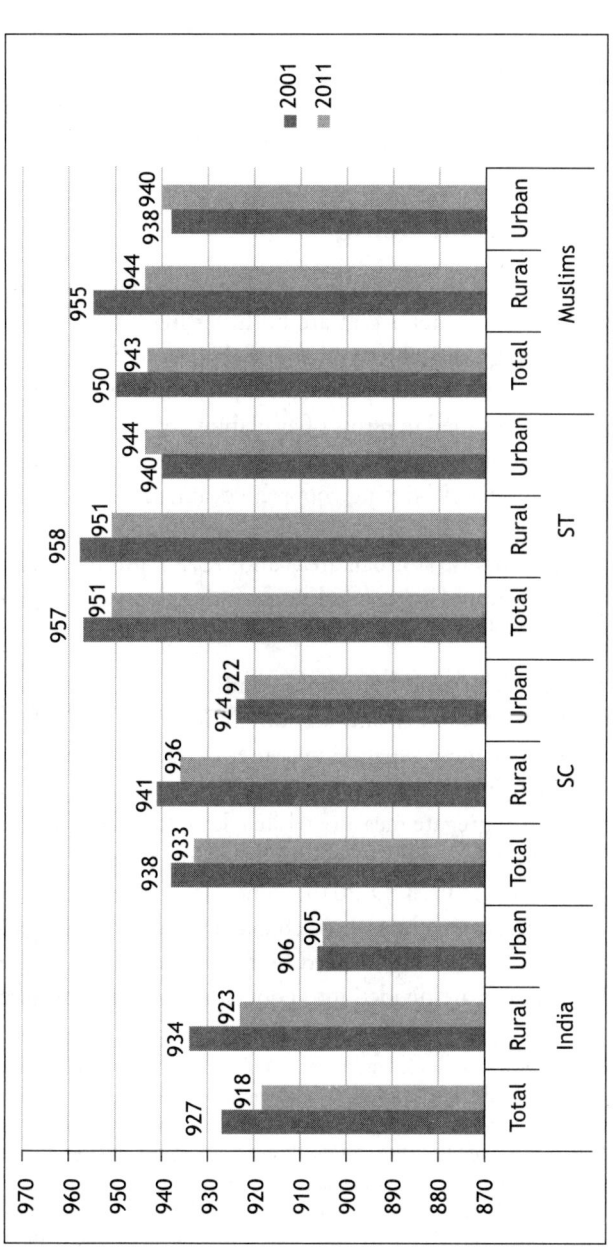

Figure A.17 *Child Sex Ratio (0–6) by SC, ST, Religion and Residence, 2001 and 2011*
Source: Primary Census Abstract, Census of India 2001 and 2011.

followed by Muslims (950 in 2001 and 943 in 2011) and SCs (938 in 2001 and 933 in 2011). The child sex ratio is worsening faster for Muslims and then for STs as compared to the general population.

A.8 Economic Well-Being

In order to understand the true human cost of economic and demographic changes using criteria that are both pertinent to evaluating economic well-being, and objectively verifiable, with fewer pitfalls than those that income, consumption and expenditure carry, changes in well-being are examined in terms of availability of housing amenities and ownership of household assets. The Census of India brings out a detailed dataset on housing, household amenities and assets. Using the censuses of 2001 and 2011, a disaggregated analysis has been conducted across rural/urban areas and SC/ST groups to show the unequal economic and living conditions among them as compared to the overall population (Table A.2).

An analysis of changes in household conditions and assets holds importance for the credibility and accountability of public policies. Despite the fact that these separate measures determine the level of well-being of each individual, the assessment of well-being in the society requires an aggregate measure while taking into consideration both population averages and inequalities based on their preferences and value judgements (OECD 2013). The NFHS constructs the wealth index[3] by combining household characteristics and assets using the principle of factor loading derived by factor analysis in its construction. Households are divided into poorest and richest across the

---

[3] The NFHS-3 wealth index is based on the following 33 assets and housing characteristics: household electrification; type of windows; drinking water source; type of toilet facility; type of flooring; material of exterior walls; type of roofing; cooking fuel; house ownership; number of household members per sleeping room; ownership of a bank or post office account; and ownership of a mattress, a pressure cooker, a chair, a cot/bed, a table, an electric fan, a radio/transistor, a black and white television, a colour television, a sewing machine, a mobile telephone, any other telephone, a computer, a refrigerator, a watch or clock, a bicycle, a motorcycle or scooter, an animal-drawn cart, a car, a water pump, a thresher and a tractor.

Table A.2 Household Facilities and Household Assets, 2001 and 2011 (Percentage of Households)

	Rural		Urban		SCs		STs		India	
	2001	2011	2001	2011	2001	2011	2001	2011	2001	2011
Household Facilities										
Electricity	43.5	55.3	87.5	92.7	44.3	59.0	36.5	51.7	55.9	67.3
Latrine facilities within premises	21.9	30.7	73.7	81.4	23.6	33.9	17.0	22.6	36.4	46.9
Household Assets										
Telephone	3.8*	54.3	23*	82.0	3.4*	53.1	2.5*	34.8	9.1*	63.2
Television	18.9	33.4	64.3	76.7	21.2	39.1	12.0	21.9	31.6	47.2
Scooter/ motorcycle/moped	6.7	14.3	24.7	35.2	5.3	12.0	4.1	9.0	11.7	21.0
Car/jeep/van	1.3	2.3	5.6	9.7	1.0	1.8	0.8	1.6	2.5	4.7
None of these assets	40.5	22.9	19.0	7.0	42.6	22.6	54.0	37.3	34.5	17.8

Source: Census 2001 and 2011.

* Data only for landline; data on household assets and amenities are not available for religious groups.

wealth quintiles from lowest to highest. Table A.3 shows inter-group disparities in the percentage distribution of households by residence, caste group and Muslims using NFHS-3 (2005–06) and *Rapid Survey on Children 2013–14* (Government of India 2014a).[4] During 2005–06, half of the population of STs belonged to the poorest wealth quintile followed by 28 per cent of SCs and 19 per cent of Muslims. The economic status improved during 2013–14, but only significantly for STs with a fall of 10 percentage points in the number of poorest households.

There has been improvement in the level of well-being among Muslims too. During 2005–06, 19 per cent belonged to the lowest quintile and 17 per cent to the highest quintile, whereas during 2013–14, 17 per cent belonged to the lowest quintile and 21 per cent to the highest quintile. Thus, levels of economic well-being among Muslims are low, but they are still better off than SC and ST groups, indicating that SCs and STs are even more economically marginalised.

A.9 Educational Attainment

The level of educational attainment seems to be a key component explaining the demographic dividend, rather than just changes in the age structure. Though enrolments in primary schools have increased substantially in recent years, poor retention and substandard educational quality reflects the weakness of the education system. Lower completion of middle, secondary and higher education levels makes it difficult to sustain continued economic development and reap the potential benefits of demographic transition, which requires a dependable supply of highly educated and skilled human capital. The more serious concern is even lower educational attainment levels across disadvantaged groups for whom factors like poverty/low economic well-being, lack of access to health and nutrition facilities and absence

---

[4] *Rapid Survey on Children 2013–14* is used for comparison as it also follows a DHS pattern like NFHS 2005–06, while the wealth index is based on 39 assets and household characteristics.

Table A.3 Change in Percentage Distribution of Household Population by Wealth Quintile by Residence, Caste Group and for Muslims, 2005–06 and 2013–14

	Lowest		Second		Middle		Fourth		Highest	
	2005–06	2013–14	2005–06	2013–14	2005–06	2013–14	2005–06	2013–14	2005–06	2013–14
Rural	27.7	25.8	26.1	25.5	22.8	21.7	16	16.3	7.4	10.7
Urban	3	3.8	6.4	8.3	13.8	16.2	28.9	28.4	47.9	43.3
SC	27.9	25.6	24.6	25.5	20.8	21.1	16.6	16.3	10.2	11.5
ST	49.9	39.5	23.6	23	13.4	17.3	8	12.6	5.2	7.5
Muslim	18.9	17	19.7	20.8	20.6	20	23.6	21.3	17.2	20.9

Source: NFHS-3, 2005–06; and *Rapid Survey on Children 2013–14* (Government of India 2014a).

of assured employment after schooling come in the way of their access to education and performance.

A comparison of educational attainment levels[5] in India between 2004–05 and 2011–12 shows that the proportion of population having completed/attained primary education remains at 14 per cent, whereas the proportion of population having completed middle, secondary and higher education has seen some increase (Figure A.18). This indicates that though a lower percentage of the population has attained secondary and higher secondary education, there has been some improvement. But it is to be noted that 32 per cent of the population was still not literate in 2011–12 compared to 40 per cent in 2004–05, and there is no change in the percentage of the population which is literate but below primary level. In 2011–12, the percentage of the population which was illiterate or literate but below primary level made up altogether 50 per cent of the total population. This means that if they have a share in India's growth story, it can only be by adding to the already mammoth reserve army of cheap and footloose labour.

Educational attainment, however, varies and is more unequal across SCs, STs and Muslims as compared to India overall. Table A.4 reflects the educational attainment across different social groups such as SCs, STs, upper Muslims and lower Muslims. The upper Muslims include the entire Muslim (general category) population except those reporting their social group as OBCs, SCs and STs. On the other hand, the lower Muslims include all Muslims reporting their social group as OBCs, SCs and STs.

---

[5] According to the NSS, only a person who has successfully passed the final year of a given level is considered to have attained that level of education. Educational attainment levels are classified into the following categories. Not literate: if the person cannot read and write a simple message in at least one language with understanding. Literate but below primary consists of all those who are literate without formal schooling (EGS/NFEC/AEC/TLC and others) and literate with formal schooling but below primary. Primary education level covers all those who have completed Classes I–V, middle level covers Classes VI–VIII and secondary level covers Classes IX–X (lower secondary level) and Classes XI–XII (higher secondary level). The category 'higher secondary and above' consists of all those who have completed diploma/certificate courses, graduation and post-graduation, and higher.

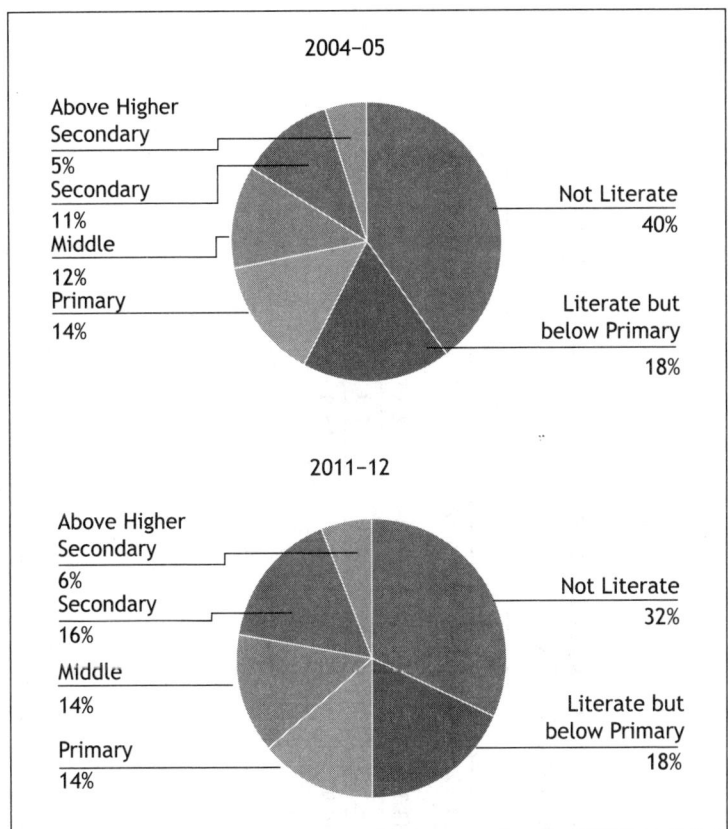

Figure A.18 *Distribution of Population by Completed Level of Education, 2004–05 and 2011–12*

Source: Estimates based on NSS 61st Round (2004–05) and NSS 68th Round (2011–12), *Employment and Unemployment Survey.*

The 2015 *Education for All* report by UNESCO (2015) revealed the progress made in the goals since 2000, and found that India was leading in bringing down the number of children who were out of school. Also, the gender disparity in enrolment at the primary, upper primary and secondary levels had been steadily coming down since 2010–11. The report also found that though India would achieve gender parity at primary level by 2015, the goal of gender parity

Table A.4 Changes in the Percentage Distribution of Population Belonging to Different Social Groups by Completed Level of Education, 2004–05 and 2011–12

Education Level	SCs		STs		Upper Muslim		Lower Muslim	
	2004–05	2011–12	2004–05	2011–12	2004–05	2011–12	2004–05	2011–12
Not Literate	49	38.2	53.6	41	42.1	33.4	47	39.1
Literate but below Primary	18.6	19.1	19.6	20.3	21.5	21.9	20.8	20.2
Primary	13.3	14.9	12	14.8	15.8	16.5	13.3	14.3
Middle	10.5	13.2	8.6	12.2	10.7	12.4	10.9	12.8
Secondary	6.7	11.6	4.8	9.3	7.4	12.2	6.3	11
Above Higher Secondary	1.9	3.1	1.4	2.4	2.5	3.7	1.8	2.6

Source: Estimates based on NSS 61st Round (2004–05) and NSS 68th Round (2011–12), Employment and Unemployment Survey.

in secondary level education remained still far. The gender gap in educational attainment between 2004–05 and 2011–12 came down, with greater narrowing in middle and secondary level education (Figure A.19). The gender gap in primary education remained at 2 percentage points in both 2004–05 and 2011–12. There has been a fall in the percentage of non-literates among both males and females, but the fall has been greater in the case of females, from 49 per cent in 2004–05 to 39 per cent in 2011–12. The gender gap among non-literates reduced from 17 per cent points to 14 per cent points. With respect to educational attainment above higher secondary level, 8 per cent of the male population has attained this level compared with 5 per cent of the female population. However, national-level inequalities between genders hide the glaring inequalities that exist across different caste, tribe and religious groups.

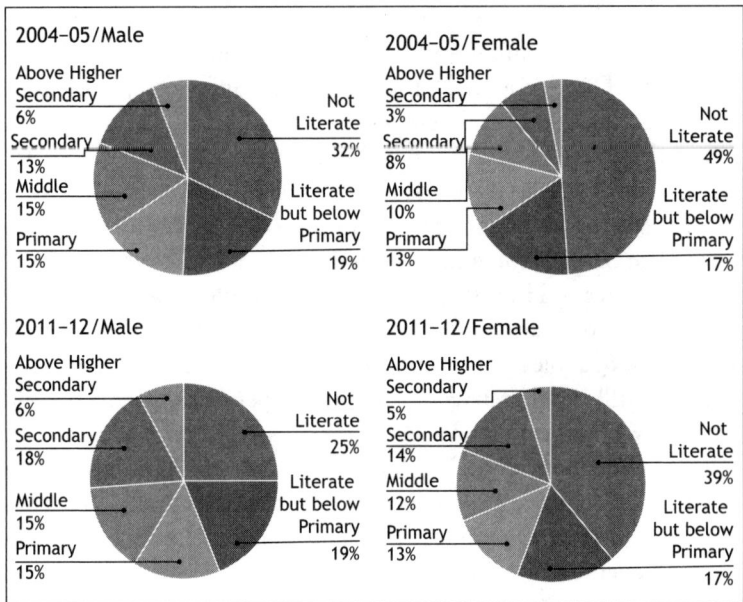

Figure A.19 *Changes in the Percentage Distribution of the Male and Female Population by Completed Level of Education, 2004–05 and 2011–12*

Source: Estimates based on NSS 61st Round (2004–05) and NSS 68th Round (2011–12), *Employment and Unemployment Survey.*

As shown in Table A.5, the gender gap in educational attainment across vulnerable categories came down for all levels except secondary level and above between 2004–05 and 2011–12, indicating slow improvements in female education beyond the middle level.

The level of educational attainment increases sharply with increase in the wealth status of the household. Though a gender gap exists at both lower and higher income levels, the gap is more pronounced at lower income levels. A comparison of the educational attainment levels of SCs, STs and Muslims across the lowest and highest income groups reveals a disturbing picture, as shown in Figure A.20.

A.10 Age-Specific Educational Attainment

Educational attainment across different age groups is analysed so as to capture the true extent of inequity. The significance of understanding education levels of children aged 0–14 is the intergenerational impact on poverty. There exist rural–urban and gender differentials in the educational attainment of children aged 0–14, with levels higher in urban areas and for males. The educational attainment across adolescents also improved from 2004–05 to 2011–12 with a fall in non-literates from 13 per cent to 5 per cent, increase in primary education attainment from 31 to 32 per cent, and in secondary education attainment from 13 to 21 per cent. However, adolescents from vulnerable groups have lower educational attainment levels compared to India overall, with 14 per cent of adolescents from lower castes, 8 per cent STs and 7 per cent SCs still not literate compared with 5 per cent in India overall. Also, only 14 per cent adolescents from STs, 17 per cent SCs and 16 per cent from lower-caste Muslims had completed secondary education in 2011–12 compared with 21 per cent in India overall. This has implications for their productivity, thus making it difficult to reap growth benefits.

Educational attainment of young men aged 15–24 improved more than women in this age group between 2004–05 and 2011–12. The percentage of illiterates came down from 13 per cent to 7 per cent in the case of young males and from 27 per cent to 14 per cent in the case of young females (Table A.6). There is not much difference between

Table A.5 Gender Differentials in Educational Attainment across Various Categories

		Not Literate		Literate but below Primary		Primary		Middle		Secondary		Above Higher Secondary	
		2004–05	2011–12	2004–05	2011–12	2004–05	2011–12	2004–05	2011–12	2004–05	2011–12	2004–05	2011–12
SCs	Male	39.4	29.8	20.3	20.5	15.7	16.5	13.3	15.1	8.8	14	2.6	4.1
	Female	59.1	47	16.8	17.6	10.8	13.2	7.6	11.1	4.5	9	1.2	2.1
STs	Male	44.7	33	22.1	21.5	14.4	16.6	10.7	14	6.2	11.5	1.9	3.3
	Female	63	49.4	16.9	19.1	9.5	12.9	6.4	10.3	3.3	7	0.9	1.4
Lower Muslim	Male	40.6	33.3	22.9	20.4	14.7	15.6	12.3	15	7.1	12.6	2.3	3.2
	Female	53.5	45	18.7	19.9	11.8	13.1	9.4	10.6	5.4	9.5	1.2	2
Upper Muslim	Male	35.7	28.3	22.7	23	16.8	17.3	12.3	12.7	9.1	13.9	3.3	4.7
	Female	48.9	38.8	20.2	20.6	14.7	15.7	9	12.1	5.6	10.3	1.6	2.5

Source: Estimates based on NSS 61st Round (2004–05) and NSS 68th Round (2011–12), *Employment and Unemployment Survey.*

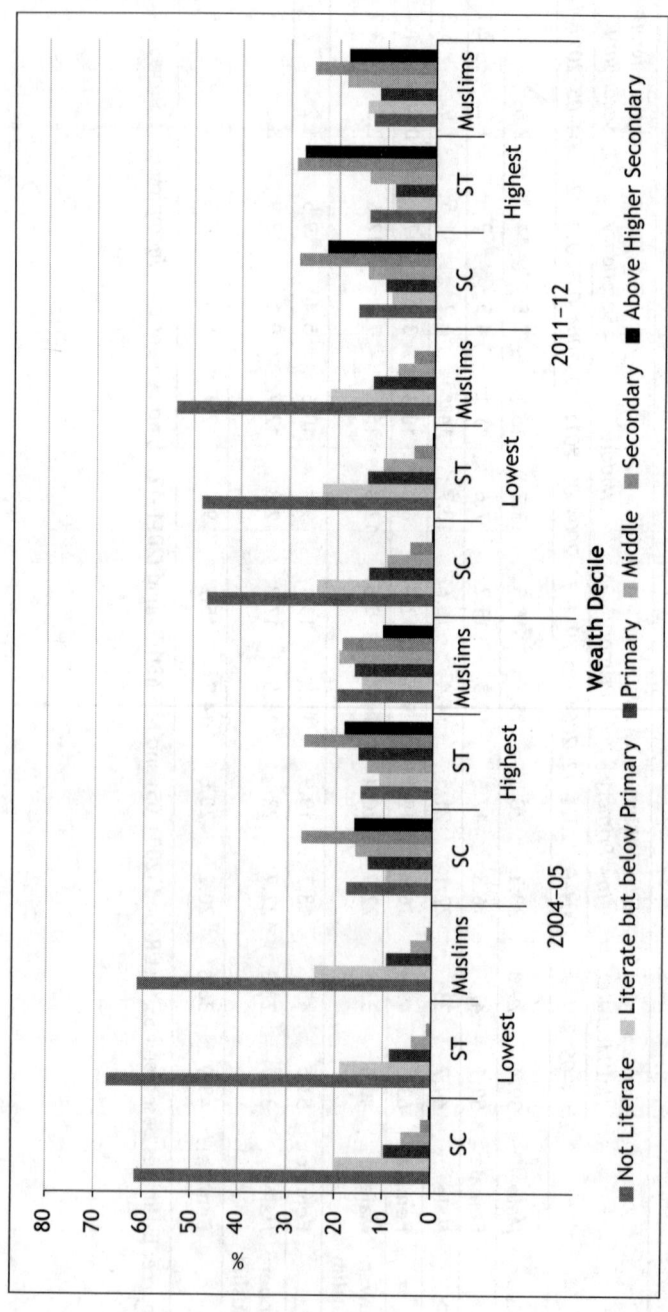

Figure A.20 Educational Attainment among SCs, STs and Muslims across Lowest and Highest Wealth Decile, 2004–05 and 2011–12

Source: Estimates based on NSS 61st Round (2004–05) and NSS 68th Round (2011–12), Employment and Unemployment Survey.

Table A.6 Educational Attainment in Age Group 15–24, 2004–05 and 2011–12

Education Level	Male		Female	
	2004–05	2011–12	2004–05	2011–12
Not literate	12.6	6.6	27.4	13.9
Literate but below primary	8.9	6.2	8.7	6.7
Primary	16.2	11.8	14.1	11.9
Middle	28.4	25.3	22.1	23.3
Secondary	28.5	42.2	23.0	36.8
Above higher secondary	5.4	8.0	4.6	7.3

Source: Estimates based on NSS 61st Round (2004–05) and NSS 68th Round (2011–12), *Employment and Unemployment Survey.*

males and females in the percentage of young population that completed just primary and middle level education.

Women's education is the most important variable, explaining fertility differences across the country and over time. Educational attainment levels of women from the reproductive age group 15–49 are analysed in Table A.7. Though there was improvement in educational attainment levels across all categories between 2004–05 and 2011–12, the proportion of the population having attained higher than secondary education was still low. This indicates that besides urban areas with 32 per cent of women having completed secondary education, all the other socially disadvantaged groups have fewer women with secondary education vis-à-vis all of India. Low educational attainment among women from these sections has severe implications in terms of low age at marriage, increased maternal deaths, child malnutrition and low-end employment.

Table A.7 Educational Attainment of Women in the Reproductive Age Group 15–49, across Various Categories, 2004–05 and 2011–12

Categories/Education Level		Not Literate	Literate but below Primary	Primary	Middle	Secondary	Above Higher Secondary
Rural	2004–05	51.3	9.8	12.4	13.8	10.5	2.1
	2011–12	38.1	10.3	13.1	16.9	18.2	3.5
Urban	2004–05	22.4	6.8	12.2	18.5	25.4	14.7
	2011–12	16.6	6.2	9.7	16.4	32.4	18.7
SCs	2004–05	57	8.9	11.6	11.9	8.4	2.3
	2011–12	41.7	9.2	12.9	16.3	16.1	3.7
STs	2004–05	63.7	9.4	9.3	10	6.1	1.6
	2011–12	45	12.2	12.9	15.2	12.3	2.4
Upper Muslim	2004–05	44.9	12.6	15.5	14	10.1	2.9
	2011–12	33.3	12.2	15.4	17.1	17.8	4.1
Lower Muslim	2004–05	48.9	11.5	11.8	15	10.6	2.2
	2011–12	38.2	10.7	14.3	15.9	17.4	3.6
Overall India	2004–05	43.5	9	12.3	15.1	14.5	5.5
	2011–12	31.6	9.1	12	16.7	22.4	8.1

Source: Estimates based on NSS 61st Round (2004–05) and NSS 68th Round (2011–12), Employment and Unemployment Survey.

Bibliography

Abraham, V., and S. K. Sasikumar. 2017. 'Declining Wage Share in India's Organized Manufacturing Sector: Trends, Patterns and Determinants'. ILO Asia-Pacific Working Paper Series, Decent Work Technical Support Team for South Asia and Country Office for India, International Labour Organization.

Acharya, S. S. 2010. 'Caste and Patterns of Discrimination in Rural Public Health Care Services', in Sukhdeo Thorat and Katherine S. Newman (eds), *Blocked by Caste: Economic Discrimination in India*, pp. 208–29. New Delhi: Oxford University Press.

Action Aid. 2016. *Land to the Tiller: Revisiting the Unfinished Land Reforms Agenda* (ed. P. K. Trivedi). New Delhi: Land and Livelihood Knowledge Activist Hub.

Agnihotri, Indu. 2011. 'Gender and Migration in India'. National Workshop on 'Internal Migration and Human Development in India', Indian Council of Social Science Research, New Delhi, 6–7 December. Workshop Compendium, vol. 2: Workshop Papers.

Aloysius, G. 1997. *Nationalism without a Nation in India*. New Delhi: Oxford University Press.

Alvaredo, F., L. Chancel, T. Piketty, E. Saez and G. Zucman. 2018. *World Inequality Report*. Cambridge, MA: Harvard University Press.

ASER Centre. 2015. *Annual Status of Education Report (Rural)*. http://img. asercentre.org/docs/Publications/ASER%20Reports/ASER%202014/ fullaser2014mainreport_1.pdf (accessed 27 March 2019).

———. 2018. *Annual Status of Education Report 2017: 'Beyond Basics'*. New Delhi: ASER Centre.

Bandopadhyay, T. 2017. 'Why India's Bad Loan Problem Is Really Bad'. *Livemint*, 12 June. http://www.livemint.com/Opinion/o883yxDtd5D4 OAVHGMWXTK/Why-Indias-bad-loan-problem-is-really-bad.html (accessed 26 December 2017).

Banerjee, K. 2011. 'Decentralised Procurement and Universalised PDS'. *Economic and Political Weekly*, 46(52): 19–22.

Banik, Somdev. 2012. 'Marginalisation of the "Tribal": An Evolutionary Overview'. *TJELLS: Journal for English Language & Literary Studies*.

Bhaduri, A. 2007. 'Economic Growth: A Meaningless Obsession?' *Seminar*, 569: 50.

———. 2008. 'Predatory Growth'. *Economic and Political Weekly*, 43(16): 10–14.

Bhagwati, Jagdish, and Arvind Panagariya. 2012. *Why Growth Matters: How Economic Growth in India Reduced Poverty and the Lessons for Other Developing Countries*. New York: Public Affairs.

Bhan, G. 2014. 'Call Them Destitution Lines'. *Indian Express*, 23 July. https://indianexpress.com/article/opinion/columns/call-them-destitution-lines/ (accessed 12 January 2018).

Bhat, P. N. Mari. 2002. 'Maternal Mortality in India: An Update'. *Studies in Family Planning*, 33(3): 227–36.

Bhowmick, N. 2017. 'As India's Muslims Are Lynched, Modi Keeps Silent'. *Washington Post*, 28 June. https://www.washingtonpost.com/news/global-opinions/wp/2017/06/28/as-indias-muslims-are-killed-modi-keeps-silent/?noredirect=on&utm_term=.7c0d6563c1df (accessed 19 February 2018).

Breman, Jan. 1994. *Wage Hunters and Gatherers: Search for Work in the Urban and Rural Economy of South Gujarat*. New Delhi: Oxford University Press.

———. 1996. *Footloose Labour: Working in India's Informal Economy*, vol. 2. Cambridge: Cambridge University Press.

CBGA (Centre for Budget and Governance Accountability). 2014. *Major Dimensions of Inequality in India: Gender*. New Delhi: CBGA.

———. 2015. *Of Bold Strokes and Fine Prints: Analysis of Union Budget 2015–16*. New Delhi: CBGA.

———. 2016. *Connecting the Dots: An Analysis of Union Budget 2016–17*. New Delhi: CBGA.

CBGA (Centre for Budget and Governance Accountability), Dalit Arthik Adhikar Andolan and National Campaign on Dalit and Human Rights. 2011. *Implementation of the Scheduled Caste Sub Plan & Tribal Sub Plan in the Union and State Budgets of India*. New Delhi: United Nations Development Programme.

CES (Centre for Equity Studies). 2016. *The Extent and Nature of Individual Tribal Land Alienation in Fifth Schedule States in India*. http://centreforequitystudies.defindia.org/wp-content/uploads/2018/03/TribalLandAlienation.pdf (accessed 31 January 2019).

Chandrasekhar, C. P., and J. Ghosh. 2012. 'Factor Shares in the Indian Economy'. *Hindu Business Line*, 16 April. https://www.thehindubusinessline.com/opinion/columns/c-p-chandrasekhar/Factor-shares-in-the-Indian-economy/article20422306.ece (accessed 12 December 2017).

Chaturvedi, S. 2016. 'Land Reforms Fail, 5% of India's Farmers Control 32% Land'. *IndiaSpend*, 4 May. http://www.indiaspend.com/cover-story/land-reforms-fail-5-of-indias-farmers-control-32-land-31897 (accessed 17 December 2017).

Chopra, Surabhi, and Prita Jha. 2014. *On Their Watch: Mass Violence and State Apathy in India—Examining the Record*. Gurgaon: Three Essays Collective.

Clarke, S. 2005. 'The Neoliberal Theory of Society', in A. Saad-Filho and D. Johnston (eds), *Neoliberalism: A Critical Reader*, pp. 50–59. London: Pluto Press.

Credit Suisse. 2015. *Global Wealth Databook 2015*. Credit Suisse Research Institute.

———. 2017. *Global Wealth Databook 2017*. https://www.credit-suisse.com/corporate/en/research/research-institute/publications.html (accessed November 2017).

Das, Subrat, et al. 2017. 'Recent Changes in India's Fiscal Architecture: Implications for Public Provisioning in Social Sectors', in *India Exclusion Report 2016*. New Delhi: Yoda Press.

Das Gupta, Moushumi. 2018. 'In Struggle for Education, Girls of Odisha Tribal Community Break Barriers'. *Hindustan Times*, 27 January. https://www.hindustantimes.com/india-news/in-struggle-for-education-girls-of-odisha-tribal-community-break-barriers/story-NbnYaeqYTVqavdziAOjUdJ.html (accessed 24 March 2019).

Deshingkar, P., P. Sharma, S. Kumar, S. Akter and J. Farrington. 2008. 'Circular Migration in Madhya Pradesh: Changing Patterns and Social Protection Needs'. *European Journal of Development Research*, 20(4): 612–28.

Deshpande, Satish. 2006. 'Exclusive Inequalities: Merit, Caste and Discrimination in Indian Higher Education Today'. *Economic and Political Weekly*, 41(24): 2438–44.

———. 2015. 'Reservations Are Not Just about Quotas'. *Hindu*, 27 March. http://www.thehindu.com/opinion/lead/reservations-are-not-just-about-quotas/article7036459.ece (accessed 22 December 2017).

Drèze, Jean. 2014. 'On the Mythology of Social Policy'. *Hindu*, 8 July. https://www.thehindu.com/opinion/lead/on-the-mythology-of-social-policy/article6186895.ece (accessed March 2018).

Economic Times. 2018. 'India's Richest 1% Corner 73% of Wealth Generation: Survey', 23 January. https://economictimes.indiatimes.com/news/politics-and-nation/indias-richest-1-corner-73-of-wealth-generation-survey/articleshow/62598759.cms (accessed March 2018).

Elliott, Larry. 2014. 'Climate Change Will "Lead to Battles for Food", Says Head of World Bank'. *Guardian*, 4 April. https://www.theguardian.com/environment/2014/apr/03/climate-change-battle-food-head-world-bank (accessed 23 January 2019).

FAO (Food and Agriculture Organization). 2015. *FAO Statistical Pocketbook 2015*. Rome: FAO.

Gandhi, Divya. 2015. 'Displacement Cuts Life Expectancy among Tribal People'. *Hindu*, 18 February. https://www.thehindu.com/sci-tech/science/displacement-cuts-life-expectancy-among-tribal-people/article6909409.ece (accessed 31 January 2019).

Gane, N. 2014. 'Sociology and Neoliberalism: A Missing History'. *Sociology*, 48(6): 1–15.

Ghose, A. K. 2016. *India Employment Report 2016*. New Delhi: Oxford University Press.

Ghoshal, S. 2016. 'A Decade since the Chilling Khairlanji Massacre, Little Let-Up in Crimes against Dalits'. *Huffington Post*, 29 September.

https://www.huffingtonpost.in/2016/09/29/a-decade-since-the-khairlanji-massacre-theres-been-no-let-up-i_a_21483135/ (accessed 28 March 2018).

Government of India. 2006a. *Population Projections for India and States 2001–2026*. Report of the Technical Group on Population Projections Constituted by the National Commission on Population. New Delhi: Office of the Registrar General and Census Commissioner, India.

———. 2006b. *Employment and Unemployment Situation in India, NSS 61st Round: July 2004–June 2005*. National Sample Survey Office, Ministry of Statistics and Programme Implementation. New Delhi: Government of India.

———. 2008. *Development Challenges in Extremist Affected Areas: Report of an Expert Group to Planning Commission*. New Delhi: Government of India.

———. 2009. *Report of the Committee on State Agrarian Relations and the Unfinished Task of Land Reforms*. New Delhi: Ministry of Rural Development.

———. 2010. *Rural Labour Enquiry Report on Indebtedness among Rural Labour Households 2009–10*. New Delhi: Ministry of Labour and Employment.

———. 2011. *India Human Development Report 2011: Towards Social Inclusion*. Institute of Applied Manpower Research, Planning Commission of India. http://www.im4change.org/docs/340IHDR_Summary.pdf (accessed October 2016).

———. 2012. *Employment & Unemployment and Migration Survey, NSS 64th Round: July 2007–June 2008*. National Sample Survey Office, Ministry of Statistics and Programme Implementation. New Delhi: Government of India.

———. 2013. *Employment and Unemployment Survey, NSS 68th Round: July 2011–June 2012*. National Sample Survey Organisation, Ministry of Statistics and Programme Implementation. New Delhi: Government of India.

———. 2014a. *Rapid Survey on Children 2013–14*. New Delhi: Ministry of Women and Child Development.

———. 2014b. *Key Indicators of Land and Livestock Holdings in India*. National Sample Survey Office, Ministry of Statistics and Programme Implementation. New Delhi: Government of India.

———. 2014c. *Agricultural Census 2010–11*. Agriculture Census Division, Department of Agriculture and Cooperation. New Delhi: Ministry of Agriculture.

———. 2017. *Agricultural Statistics at a Glance 2016*. New Delhi: Ministry of Agriculture and Farmers' Welfare.

———. 2018. *Agricultural Statistics at a Glance 2017*. Ministry of Agriculture and Farmers' Welfare, Department of Agriculture, Cooperation and Farmers' Welfare, Directorate of Economics and Statistics. New Delhi: Government of India.

Gurukkal, Rajan. 2018. 'Death of Democracy: An Inevitable Possibility under Capitalism'. *Economic and Political Weekly*, 53(34): 104–11.

Haq, Mehboob Ul. 1995. 'The Human Development Paradigm', *Reflections on Human Development*. New York: Oxford University Press.

Herring, R. 1983. *Land to the Tiller: The Political Economy of Agrarian Reform in South Asia.* New Delhi: Oxford University Press.

Hindu. 2016. 'Details of NPA Figures of Public, Private Sector Banks'. *Hindu,* 1 November. http://www.thehindu.com/data/Details-of-NPA-figures-of-public-private-sector-banks/article16670548.ece (accessed 12 November 2017).

———. 2017. 'Goods and Services Tax Formally Launched in Parliament by Prime Minister Narendra Modi and President Pranab Mukherjee', 30 June. https://www.thehindu.com/business/Economy/live-goods-and-services-tax-launch/article19185917.ece (accessed 25 March 2019).

Hindu Business Line. 2014. 'Income Inequality Increasing Globally: Lagarde', 4 February. https://www.thehindubusinessline.com/news/world/income-inequality-increasing-globally-lagarde/article22991835.ece (accessed 23 January 2019).

Husain, Z. 2015. 'Rajasthan: Dalits Killed, Thrashed in Violence over Land Dispute'. *Hindustan Times,* 17 May. https://www.hindustantimes.com/india/rajasthan-dalits-killed-thrashed-in-violence-over-land-dispute/story-w5UXl7euB7BZtXI4zFNGCM.html (accessed 28 March 2018).

IIPS (International Institute for Population Sciences). 2006. *District Level Household Survey (DLHS-2), 2002–04: India.* Mumbai: IIPS.

IIPS (International Institute for Population Sciences) and Macro International. 2007. *National Family Health Survey (NFHS-3), 2005–06: India,* vol. I. Mumbai: IIPS.

ILO (International Labour Organization). 2013. *Women and Men in the Informal Economy: A Statistical Picture.* Women in Informal Employment Globalizing and Organizing. Geneva: ILO.

———. 2014. *World Social Protection Report 2014/15: Building Economic Recovery, Inclusive Development and Social Justice.* Geneva: ILO. https://ilo.org/global/research/global-reports/world-social-security-report/2014/WCMS_245201/lang--en/index.htm (accessed 25 January 2019).

Iyer, S. 2002. 'Understanding Religion and the Economics of Fertility in India'. Occasional Paper 2, Centre of South Asia Studies, Cambridge.

Jaffrelot, C., and A. Kalaiyarasan. 2018. 'The Myth of Appeasement'. *Indian Express,* 20 April. https://indianexpress.com/article/opinion/columns/muslims-socio-economic-development-5144318/ (accessed 18 July 2018).

Jain, M. 2016. 'India Inc Is Sunk in Bad Debt—and Unlikely to Pay Up'. *Scroll.in,* 5 July. https://scroll.in/article/810998/india-inc-is-sunk-in-bed-debt-and-unlikely-to-pay-up (accessed 27 December 2017).

Jain, S., and S. Matharu. 2017. 'Fatal Heights: The Untold Deaths of India's Construction Workers'. NDTV, 5 August. https://www.ndtv.com/india-news/fatal-heights-the-untold-deaths-of-indias-construction-workers-1733974 (accessed 5 February 2018).

Jodhka, Surinder S., and K. S. Newman. 2010. 'In the Name of Globalization: Meritocracy, Productivity and the Hidden Language of Caste', in Sukhdeo

Thorat and Katherine S. Newman (eds), *Blocked by Caste: Economic Discrimination in India*, pp. 52–87. New Delhi: Oxford University Press.

Joshi, P. C. 1974a. 'Land Reform and Agrarian Change in India and Pakistan since 1947: I'. *Journal of Peasant Studies*, 1(2): 164–85.

———. 1974b. 'Land Reform and Agrarian Change in India and Pakistan since 1947: II'. *Journal of Peasant Studies*, 1(3): 326–62.

———. 1976. *Land Reforms in India: Trends and Perspectives*. New Delhi: Allied.

Karthikeyan, D. 2011. 'Suicide by Dalit Students in 4 Years'. *Hindu*, 5 December. http://www.thehindu.com/news/cities/Madurai/suicide-by-dalit-students-in-4-years/article2425965.ece (accessed 27 March 2018).

Karunakaran, N. 2015. 'Muslims Constitute 14% of India, but Just 3% of India Inc'. *Economic Times*, 7 September. https://economictimes.indiatimes.com/news/politics-and-nation/muslims-constitute-14-of-india-but-just-3-of-india-inc/articleshow/48849266.cms (accessed 17 July 2018).

Kompier, Coen. 2014. 'Labour Markets: Exclusion from Decent Work', in *India Exclusion Report 2013–14*. Bengaluru: Books for Change.

Kompier, C., A. Prasad, S. Hassan, S. Premchander et al. 2014. 'Labour Markets: Exclusion from Decent Work', in Harsh Mander (ed.), *India Exclusion Report 2013–14*, pp. 109–39. New Delhi: Books for Change.

Kumar, John. 2013. *SCP in Tamil Nadu: Lopsided Growth and Development*. New Delhi: Centre for Budget and Governance Accountability.

Kumar, V. 2005. 'Situating Dalits in Indian Sociology'. *Indian Sociological Society*, 54(3): 514–32.

Kundu, A. 2009. 'Exclusionary Urbanisation in Asia: A Macro Overview'. *Economic and Political Weekly*, 44(48): 48–58.

———. 2014. *Post Sachar Evaluation Committee Report*. New Delhi: Ministry of Minority Affairs, Government of India.

Lagarde, C. 2014. 'A New Multilateralism for the 21st Century'. Richard Dimbleby Lecture, 3 February. https://www.imf.org/en/News/Articles/2015/09/28/04/53/sp020314 (accessed 22 November 2017).

Levien, Michael. 2015. 'From Primitive Accumulation to Regimes of Dispossession: Six Theses on India's Land Question'. *Economic and Political Weekly*, 50(22): 146–47.

Mahapatra, B. 2016. 'Malkangiri Child Deaths: Disease or Malnourishment—or Both?' *Wire*, 25 December. https://thewire.in/health/malkangiri-child-deaths-disease-malnourishment-both (accessed 24 March 2019).

Malhotra, Rajeev, and Sridhar Kundu. 2016. 'Towards a Tax System for Inclusive Development: Some Aspects of Tax Incidence and Tax Mobilisation in India', in *India Exclusion Report 2015*, pp. 141–61. New Delhi: Yoda Press.

Mallapur, C. 2015. 'Sexual Assault, Rape Top Crimes against Scheduled Castes'. *IndiaSpend*, 26 October. http://www.indiaspend.com/cover-story/sexual-assault-rape-top-crimes-against-scheduled-castes-34410 (accessed 28 March 2018).

Mander, Harsh. 2014. 'Formal Industry, Informal Work'. *Livemint*, 26 January. https://www.livemint.com/Opinion/38tuZShjftafBaQtvlf5nI/Harsh-Mander--Formal-industry-informal-work.html (accessed 27 March 2019).

———. 2015. *Looking Away: Inequality, Prejudice and Indifference in New India*. New Delhi: Speaking Tiger.

———. 2016. *Fatal Accidents of Birth: Stories of Suffering, Oppression and Resistance*. New Delhi: Speaking Tiger.

———. 2018. '25 Years of Economic Reforms: A Blotted Balance Sheet'. *Perspectives*, 43(1): 1–13.

Mani, R. 2017. 'Kisan Mukti Sansad to Converge at Parliament Street in Allahabad'. *Times of India*, 17 November. https://timesofindia.indiatimes.com/city/allahabad/kisan-mukti-sansad-to-converge-at-parliament-street-in-allahabad/articleshow/61691154.cms (accessed 28 December 2017).

Mehrotra, S., J. Parida, S. Sinha and A. Gandhi. 2014. 'Explaining Employment Trends in the Indian Economy: 1993–94 to 2011–12'. *Economic and Political Weekly*, 49(32): 49–57.

MHRD (Ministry of Human Resource Development). 2016. *All India Survey on Higher Education 2014–15*. Department of Higher Education, Government of India, New Delhi. http://aishe.nic.in/aishe/viewDocument.action?documentId=206 (accessed 24 March 2019).

———. 2017. *All India Survey on Higher Education*. Department of Higher Education, Government of India, New Delhi. aishe.nic.in/aishe/view Document.action?documentId=239 (accessed 24 March 2019).

Ministry of Finance. 2015. 'The Fourteenth Finance Commission (FFC): Implications for Fiscal Federalism in India?' in *Economic Survey 2014–15*, vol. 1, ch. 10. New Delhi: Government of India.

Mishra, S. 2006. 'Suicide Mortality Rates across States of India, 1975–2001'. *Economic and Political Weekly*, 41(16): 1566–69.

Mishra, V., and A. Bhattacharya. 2017. 'GDP Grows but Job Security Falls: Only 16% Indians Earn Regular Wage'. *IndiaSpend*, 25 March. http://archive.indiaspend.com/special-reports/gdp-grows-but-job-security-falls-only-16-indians-earn-regular-wage-99612 (accessed 12 December 2017).

Mohanty, S., and F. Ram. 2010. 'Life Expectancy at Birth among Social and Economic Groups in India'. Research Brief for the International Institute for Population Sciences. http://iipsindia.org/pdf/RB-13%20file%20for%20uploading.pdf (accessed 29 January 2019).

Mosse, D., S. Gupta and V. Shah. 2005. 'On the Margins in the City: Adivasi Seasonal Labour Migration in Western India'. *Economic and Political Weekly*, 40(28): 3025–38.

MSPI (Ministry of Statistics and Programme Implementation). 2014. *Key Indicators of Land and Livestock Holdings in India*. New Delhi: National Sample Survey Office, Government of India.

Munshi, I. 2012. *The Adivasi Question: Issues of Land, Forest and Livelihood*. New Delhi: Orient BlackSwan.

Munshi, S. 2017. 'Shambulal Regar, New Face of Hindu Far Right in Poll-Bound Rajasthan'. News18, 26 December. https://www.news18.com/news/india/meet-shambulal-regar-new-face-of-hindu-far-right-in-poll-bound-rajasthan-1614327.html (accessed 19 February 2018).

Nair, P. V. 2012. 'Enrolment of Women in Higher Education Increases'. *Times of India*, 12 September. https://timesofindia.indiatimes.com/home/education/news/Enrolment-of-women-in-higher-education-increases/articleshow/16244028.cms (accessed 16 December 2017).

Nair, S. 2018. 'Rising Pendency, Falling Convictions: What Data on SC/ST Act Trials Show'. *Indian Express*, 3 April. http://indianexpress.com/article/explained/rising-pendency-falling-convictions-what-data-on-sc-st-act-trials-show-prevention-of-atrocities-act-5113689/ (accessed 23 March 2018).

Nambissan, G. B. 2010. 'Exclusion and Discrimination in Schools: Experiences of Dalit Children', in Sukhdeo Thorat and Katherine S. Newman (eds), *Blocked by Caste: Economic Discrimination in India*, pp. 253–86. New Delhi: Oxford University Press.

Natti, S. 2017. 'India's Half-a-Billion Jobs Conundrum'. *New Indian Express*, 31 December. http://www.newindianexpress.com/nation/2017/dec/31/indias-half-a-billion-jobs-conundrum-1741132.html (accessed 12 January 2018).

NCEUS (National Commission for Enterprises in the Unorganised Sector). 2009. *The Challenge of Employment in India*. New Delhi: Government of India.

NITI Aayog. 2015. *Report of the Sub-Group of Chief Ministers on Rationalisation of Centrally Sponsored Schemes*. New Delhi: NITI Aayog.

OECD (Organisation for Economic Co-operation and Development). 2013. *Measuring Well Being and Progress*. Brochure, OECD Statistics Directorate.

Omvedt, G. 2005. 'Capitalism and Globalisation, Dalits and Adivasis'. *Economic and Political Weekly*, 40(47): 4881–85.

Outlook Web Bureau. 2017. 'In Support of Shambu Lal Regar, Hindu Groups Unfurl Saffron Flag on Udaipur Court Premises, Attack Police'. *Outlook India*, 15 December. https://www.outlookindia.com/website/story/hindu-groups-attack-police-unfurl-saffron-flag-on-udaipur-court-premises-in-supp/305606 (accessed 19 February 2018).

Oxfam. 2014. *Even It Up: Time to End Extreme Inequality*. https://oxfamilibrary.openrepository.com/bitstream/handle/10546/333012/cr-even-it-up-extreme-inequality-291014-en.pdf;jsessionid=1EC15A831D366260CFD5A8DBD2860CC9?sequence=43 (accessed 1 March 2018).

———. 2016. 'The Case for a Billionaire Tax'. Oxfam Discussion Papers, December. https://www.oxfam.org/sites/www.oxfam.org/files/file_attachments/dp-case-for-billionaire-tax-100117-en.pdf (accessed March 2018).

———. 2017. *An Economy for the 99%*. Oxford: Oxfam International.

———. 2018a. *Reward Work, Not Wealth*. Oxfam Briefing Paper, January 2018. https://d1tn3vj7xz9fdh.cloudfront.net/s3fs-public/file_attachments/bp-reward-work-not-wealth-220118-en.pdf (accessed 21 January 2019).

Oxfam. 2018b. '15 Shocking Facts about Inequality in India'. https://www. oxfamindia.org/blog/15-shocking-facts-about-inequality-india (accessed March 2018).

Pandey, P. 2018. 'First Conviction in Lynching over Cow: 11 Held Guilty in Jharkhand'. *Indian Express*, 17 March. https://indianexpress.com/article/india/ jharkhand-lynching-first-conviction-in-meat-traders-killing-over-cow-11-held-guilty-5100691/ (accessed 20 July 2018).

Panitch, L. 2014. 'Europe's Left Has Seen How Capitalism Can Bite Back'. *Guardian*, 12 January. https://www.theguardian.com/commentisfree/2014/ jan/12/europe-left-capitalism-social-democrats-reforms (accessed 16 December 2017).

Patel, V. 2015. 'Universal Coverage Is the Only Cure for Health Scandals'. *Hindustan Times*, 18 December. https://www.hindustantimes.com/analysis/ universal-coverage-is-the-only-cure-for-health-scandals/story-YD3bTTJJu APP6chVOqu4kJ.html (accessed 25 March 2019).

Patnaik, Prabhat. 2015. 'Syriza's Act Is a Historic Revolt against Austerity'. Interview with Pragya Singh, *Outlook*, 20 July. https://www.outlookindia.com/ magazine/story/syriza-s-act-is-a-historic-revolt-against-austerity/294831 (accessed 31 January 2019).

Planning Commission. 2009. *Report of the Expert Group to Review the Methodology for Estimation of Poverty*. New Delhi: Government of India.

———. 2014. *Data-Book Compiled for Use of Planning Commission*. New Delhi: Government of India .

PTI (Press Trust of India). 2018. 'Horrendous Acts of Mobocracy Can't Be Allowed, Create Law against It, SC Asks Government'. *Economic Times*, 17 July. https://economictimes.indiatimes.com/news/politics-and-nation/ supreme-court-asks-government-to-create-law-against-mob-lynching/ articleshow/65019193.cms (accessed 20 July 2018).

Rajagopal, K. 2018. 'SC/ST Act Being Used for Blackmail, Says Supreme Court'. *Hindu*, 20 March. http://www.thehindu.com/news/national/scst-atrocities-act-has-become-a-means-to-blackmail-citizens-public-servants-sc/ article23303970.ece (accessed 20 March 2018).

Rajalakshmi, T. K. 2016. 'Assault on Tribal Rights'. *Frontline*, 25 November. https://frontline.thehindu.com/the-nation/assault-on-tribal-rights/article 9319983.ece (accessed 31 January 2019).

Rajan, Ravi. 1998. 'Imperial Environmentalism or Environmental Imperialism? European Forestry, Colonial Foresters and the Agendas of Forest Management in British India 1800–1900', in Richard Grove, Vinita Damodaran and Satpal Sangwan (eds), *Nature and the Orient: The Environmental History of South & Southeast Asia*. New Delhi: Oxford University Press.

Ramakumar, R. 2010. 'Continuity and Change: Notes on Agriculture in "New India"', in A. P. D'Costa (ed.), *A New India? Critical Reflections in the Long Twentieth Century*, pp. 43–70. London: Anthem Press.

Ranjan. 2017. '5 Killed in Firing during Farmers' Protest in Mandsaur, Oppn Attacks MP Govt'. *Hindustan Times*, 7 June. https://www.hindustantimes. com/india-news/1-dead-2-injured-as-farmers-agitations-turns-violent-in-mp-s-mandsaur/story-SfoJMNG4R1o25O0ftd1qMI.html (accessed 10 December 2017).

Rao, B. 2016. 'Women in Parliament: Where Does India Stand?' Factly, 6 March. https://factly.in/women-in-parliament-where-does-india-figure-among-the-rest-world/ (accessed 25 March 2019).

Rao, S. L., P. Deshingkar and J. Farrington. 2006. 'Tribal Land Alienation in Andhra Pradesh: Processes, Impacts and Policy Concerns'. *Economic and Political Weekly*, 41(52): 5401–07.

Reddy, D. N., and S. Mishra. 2012. 'Introduction', in D. N. Reddy and S. Mishra (eds), *Agrarian Crisis in India*, pp. 3–43. New Delhi: Oxford University Press.

Reserve Bank of India. 2007. *Report of the Working Group to Suggest Measures to Assist Distressed Farmers*. New Delhi: Reserve Bank of India.

Robinson, R. 2007. 'Indian Muslims: The Varied Dimensions of Marginality'. *Economic and Political Weekly*, 42(10): 839–43.

Rozindar, F. 2016. 'Woman Gives Birth outside Health Centre in Karnataka'. *Hindu*, 11 September. https://www.thehindu.com/todays-paper/tp-national/ Woman-gives-birth-outside-health-centre-in-Karnataka/article14632821.ece (accessed 25 March 2019).

Sachar Committee Report. 2006. *Social, Economic and Educational Status of the Muslim Community of India*. Prime Minister's High Level Committee. New Delhi: Government of India.

Sahu, S. 2016. 'Indian Man Carries Dead Wife's Body for 12km'. BBC News, 25 August. https://www.bbc.com/news/world-asia-india-37183011 (accessed 25 March 2019).

Sainath, P. 2015. 'The Slaughter of Suicide Data'. People's Archive of Rural India, 5 August. https://psainath.org/the-slaughter-of-suicide-data/ (accessed 17 December 2017).

Salve, Prachi. 2013. 'How India's Scheduled Castes & Tribes Are Empowering Themselves'. *IndiaSpend*, 13 December. http://www.indiaspend.com/cover-story/how-indias-scheduled-castes-tribes-are-empowering-themselves-34628 (accessed 28 March 2018).

———. 2017. 'Caste, Father's Education, Sanitation Affect Child Malnutrition: New Data'. *IndiaSpend*, 25 October. http://www.indiaspend.com/cover-story/ caste-fathers-education-sanitation-affect-child-malnutrition-new-data-36560 (accessed 28 March 2018).

———. 2018. 'Muslims Have Highest Fertility Rate, Lack Access to Healthcare'. *IndiaSpend*, 27 April. http://www.indiaspend.com/indias-great-challenge-health-sanitation/muslims-have-highest-fertility-rate-lack-access-to-healthcare-36353 (accessed 7 May 2018).

Samar. 2017. 'Protesting Farmers Hold Their Parliament, Pass Bills as the Real One Looks Away'. *Countercurrents*, 21 November. https://countercurrents.

org/2017/11/21/protesting-farmers-hold-their-parliament-pass-bills-as-the-real-one-looks-away/ (accessed 26 December 2017).

Saran, B. 2018. 'Jayant Sinha Garlands Ramgarh Lynching Convicts, Says "Honouring Law"'. *Hindustan Times*, 7 July. https://www.hindustantimes. com/india-news/hc-has-suspended-sentence-was-honouring-the-law-jayant-sinha-on-garlanding-ramgarh-lynching-convicts/story-oawPKViVZHs VcPAK84zN6N.html (accessed 12 July 2018).

Sarkar, S., S. Mishra, H. Dayal and D. Nathan. 2006. 'Development and Deprivation of Scheduled Tribes'. *Economic and Political Weekly*, 41(46): 4824–27.

Sen, Amartya. 1999. *Development as Freedom*. New Delhi: Oxford University Press.

———. 2016. *The Country of First Boys and Other Essays*. New Delhi: Oxford University Press.

Shani, Ornit. 2007. *Communalism, Caste and Hindu Nationalism: The Violence in Gujarat*. Cambridge: Cambridge University Press.

Sharma, B. 2018. 'The Uttar Pradesh Police Are Sabotaging Their Own Investigation into the Hapur Lynching, Lawyers for the Victims Say'. *Huffington Post India*, 13 July. https://www.huffingtonpost.in/2018/07/12/ the-uttar-pradesh-police-are-sabotaging-their-own-investigation-into-the-hapur-lynchings-lawyers-for-the-victims-say_a_23479920/ (accessed 14 July 2018).

Sharma, J. P. 2016. 'PM's Skill India Initiative Scores Low on Placements'. *Hindustan Times*, 1 June. https://www.hindustantimes.com/india/pm-s-skill-india-initiative-scores-low-on-placements/story-0oU24Izpqb7JHSCjpudXUJ. html (accessed 15 December 2018).

Shrivastava, S. 2014. *Scheduled Caste Sub-Plan and Tribal Sub-Plan*. New Delhi: Yojana.

Singh, A. K. 2013. 'Income and Livelihood Issues of Farmers: A Field Study in Uttar Pradesh'. *Agricultural Economics Research Review*, 26: 89–96.

Singh, Manmohan. 1991. 'Budget 1991–92: Speech of Shri Manmohan Singh, Minister of Finance, 24 July, 1991'. https://www.indiabudget.gov.in/bspeech/ bs199192.pdf (accessed March 2018).

Sinha, K. 2012. 'Malnourishment a National Shame: Manmohan Singh'. *Times of India*, 11 January. https://timesofindia.indiatimes.com/india/Malnourishment-a-national-shame-Manmohan-Singh/articleshow/11443478.cms (accessed 25 March 2019).

Skaria, Ajay. 1998. 'Timber Conservancy, Dessicationism and Scientific Forestry: The Dangs 1840s–1920s', in Richard Grove, Vinita Damodaran and Satpal Sangwan (eds), *Nature and the Orient: The Environmental History of South & Southeast Asia*, pp. 596–601. New Delhi: Oxford University Press.

Sood, A. 2016. 'Politics of Growth'. *Economic and Political Weekly*, 51(29): 56–60.

Srivastava, Ravi. 2012. 'Internal Migration in India: An Overview of Its Features, Trends and Policy Challenges'. National Workshop on Internal Migration and

Human Development in India, Indian Council of Social Science Research, New Delhi, 6–7 December. Workshop Compendium, vol. 2: Workshop Papers.

Srivastava, R., and R. Sutradhar. 2016. *Migrating Out of Poverty? A Study of Migrant Construction Sector Workers in India*. New Delhi: Institute for Human Development.

Sundar, Nandini. 1997. *Subalterns and Sovereigns: An Anthropological History of Bastar, 1854–1996*. New York: Oxford University Press.

———. 2016. *The Scheduled Tribes and Their India: Politics, Identities, Policies, and Work*. New Delhi: Oxford University Press.

Takravarty, Lalita. 1978. 'Emergence of an Industrial Labour Force in a Dual Economy: British India, 1880–1920'. *Indian Economic and Social History Review*, 15(3): 249–327.

Thatcher, Margaret. 1987. Interview by D. Keay. *Women's Own*, 23 September. https://www.margaretthatcher.org/document/106689 (accessed 28 March 2019).

Thorat, Sukhdeo. 2009. *Dalits in India: Search for a Common Destiny*. New Delhi: Sage.

Thorat, Sukhdeo, and Paul Attewell. 2010. 'The Legacy of Social Exclusion: A Correspondence Study of Job Discrimination in India's Urban Private Sector', in Sukhdeo Thorat and Katherine S. Newman (eds), *Blocked by Caste: Economic Discrimination in India*, pp. 35–51. New Delhi: Oxford University Press.

Times of India. 2017. 'Bad Loans: Only 4 Major Nations Have Higher Bad Loans Than India'. *Times of India*, 28 December. https://timesofindia.indiatimes.com/business/india-business/only-4-major-nations-have-higher-bad-loans-than-india/articleshow/62275553.cms (accessed 13 November 2018).

UNDP (United Nations Development Programme). 2013. *Human Development Report 2013: The Rise of the South—Human Progress in a Diverse World*. New York: UNDP.

———. 2015. *Human Development Report 2015: Work for Human Development*. New York: UNDP.

UNESCO (United Nations Educational, Scientific and Cultural Organization). 2015. *Education for All 2015: Achievements and Challenges*. https://unesdoc.unesco.org/ark:/48223/pf0000232205_eng (accessed 23 March 2019).

UNESCO (United Nations Educational, Scientific and Cultural Organization) and UNICEF (United Nations Children's Fund). 2012. *National Workshop on Internal Migration and Human Development in India*. New Delhi: UNESCO and UNICEF.

UNICEF (United Nations Children's Fund). 2011. *The Situation of Children in India: A Profile*. https://www.unicef.org/sitan/files/SitAn_India_May_2011.pdf (accessed 26 March 2019).

Unisa, S. 2009. 'An Investigation into Masculinization of Sex Ratio in India'. http://iussp2009.princeton.edu/papers/91884 (accessed 21 January 2019).

Vakulabharanam, Vamsi, and Sripad Motiram. 2011. 'Political Economy of Agrarian Distress in India since the 1990s', in S. Corbridge, J. Harriss and S. Ruparelia (eds), *Understanding India's New Political Economy: A Great Transformation?*, pp. 101–26. New York: Routledge.

Varma, S. 2017. 'Farmers Lost over ₹2 Lakh Crore Due to Low Prices of Crops This Year'. *NewsClick*, 15 November. https://newsclick.in/farmers-lost-over-rs2-lakh-crore-due-low-prices-crops-year (accessed 26 December 2017).

Vasavi, A. R. 1999. 'Agrarian Distress in Bidar: Market, State and Suicides'. *Economic and Political Weekly*, 34(32): 2263–68.

———. 2012. *Shadow Space: Suicides and the Predicament of Rural India*. New Delhi: Three Essays Collective.

Vera-Sanso, P. 2012. 'Gender, Poverty and Old-Age Livelihoods in Urban South India in an Era of Globalisation'. *Oxford Development Studies*, 40(3): 324–40.

Vijay, G. 2005. 'Migration, Vulnerability and Insecurity in New Industrial Labour Markets'. *Economic and Political Weekly*, 40(22–23): 2304–12.

Vissa, K. 2017. 'How Long Can India's Farmers Subsidise the Nation?' *Wire*, 20 November. https://thewire.in/198485/farmers-protests-kisan-ki-loot-msp-fair-price/ (accessed 28 December 2017).

WHO (World Health Organization). 2008. 'Demographic Trends'. *Health in Asia and the Pacific*, pp. 35–48. http://www.wpro.who.int/health_information_evidence/documents/Health_in_Asia_Pacific.pdf (accessed 26 January 2019).

Whyte, W. F., and K. K. Whyte. 1991. *Making Mondragón: The Growth and Dynamics of the Worker Cooperative Complex* (Cornell International Industrial and Labor Relations Reports). New York: Cornell University.

Wire. 2018a. 'Richest 1% Cornered 73% of Wealth Generated in India in 2017: Oxfam Survey'. https://thewire.in/economy/richest-1-cornered-73-wealth-generated-india-2017-oxfam-survey (accessed March 2018).

———. 2018b. 'BJP Lawmaker Says Will Pay Legal Bill of Lynching Accused', 15 June. https://www.thewire.in/uncategorised/bjp-lawmaker-says-will-pay-legal-bill-of-lynching-accused (accessed 22 June 2018).

Wolff, R. 2012a. 'Yes, There Is an Alternative to Capitalism: Mondragon Shows the Way'. *Guardian*, 24 June. https://www.theguardian.com/commentisfree/2012/jun/24/alternative-capitalism-mondragon (accessed 24 February 2018).

———. 2012b. *Democracy at Work: A Cure for Capitalism*. Chicago: Haymarket Books.

Index

About the Authors

Harsh Mander is a writer, human rights activist, teacher and peace worker. He works with survivors of mass violence and hunger, homeless persons and street children. He is associated with movements for communal harmony, right to food, right to information, bonded labour and the right of adivasis. He is the Director of Centre for Equity Studies, New Delhi.

Anirban Bhattacharya worked on plantation labour history in his PhD dissertation submitted in Jawaharlal Nehru University (JNU), New Delhi. He currently works as a senior researcher at the Centre for Equity Studies.

Vivek Mishra is a PhD student at the School of Public Policy and Urban Affairs, Northeastern University, Boston. Formerly, he worked at the Centre for Equity Studies and coordinated the *India Exclusion Report 2017–18*.

Astha Singla is a Research Scholar at the Centre for the Study of Regional Development, JNU. Her main research interests cover various aspects of labour economics (youth labour markets, disadvantaged groups in the labour market, school to work transition, skill development, evaluation of labour policy) and development economics.

Usman Jawed Siddiqi has an MPhil in Sociology from the University of Delhi. He works as a senior researcher at the Centre for Equity Studies and coordinates the *India Exclusion Report*. He is interested in debates about the nature of capitalist development in India and in exploring alternatives to the same.